Leviathan

Leviathan Vs. Behemoth

Leviathan vs. Behemoth

The Roman-Parthian Wars 66 BC-217 AD

CAM REA

CreateSpace, Charleston, SC

2014

Leviathan Vs. Behemoth

ISBN
ISBN-13: 978-1500424039

ISBN-10: 150042403X

Cover design provided by Vikki at http://fiverr.com/vikncharlie

Dedication

To my family

Leviathan Vs. Behemoth

Contents

List of Illustrations X

Acknowledgments XIV

INTRODUCTION 1

1. THE COMING STORM 7
   PARTHIA'S STRUGGLE 14
   ROME DECIDES THE BORDERS 23

2. CLASH OF THE TITANS 37
   ROMAN INTERVENTION 40
   BUILDUP TO WAR 44
   MANDATORY SUICIDE 51
   A DESERT FUNERAL PROCESSION 60
   THE BATTLE OF CARRHAE 63
   INTO THE DARKNESS 81
   A GREAT TRIUMPH! 89
   AFTERMATH 93

3. PARTHIAN COUNTER ATTACK 101
   ALL QUIET ON THE EASTERN FRONT 103
   THEY'VE CROSSED THE EUPHRATES 107
   REFLECTION 121

4. CALM BEFORE THE STORM 127
   ANTONY BEATS THE WAR DRUMS 139
   SHOCK AND AWE 143
   THE INVASION OF JUDEA 146
   THE INVASION OF ASIA MINOR 151
   REVERSING THE TIDE 153

BATTLE OF THE CILICIAN GATES	155
BATTLE OF AMANUS PASS	157
THE BATTLE OF MOUNT GINDARUS	158

5. ANTONY'S WAR TO AVENGE CRASSUS TO FULFILL CAESAR'S DREAM 175

ANTONY'S PARTHIAN WAR	179
ON THE ROAD TO HELL	188
ARTAVASDES MUST PAY!	202
ANTONY'S DEFEAT IS OCTAVIAN'S VICTORY	208

6. PROXY ALONG THE EUPHRATES 217

A GIFT FOR PHRAATES	219
PHRAATACES THE UNWANTED	221
HEROD, JESUS, AND THE MAGI	225
PARTHIA'S STRUGGLE	232
THE TALE OF TWO BROTHERS	237
ROME'S PROXY WAR IN ARMENIA	241
ROME'S POLITICAL PROXY WAR IN PARTHIA	250

7. THE WAR FOR ARMENIA 267

THE ROAD TO WAR	270
CORBULO	275
CORBULO'S CAMPAIGN	278
COUNTERATTACK	290
THE BATTLE OF RHANDEIA	294
THE AFTERMATH	301
A NEW FRONTIER	310

8. TRAJAN'S PARTHIAN WAR 317

TRAJAN'S PREWAR PLANNING AND PREPARATION 320

THE ARMENIAN CAMPAIGN OF 114 CE 324

THE INVASION OF MESOPOTAMIA 115 CE 331

THE CAMPAIGN OF 116 CE 333

BLOWBACK 339

AFTERMATH 342

9. FROM HADRIAN TO THE COLLAPSE OF THE PARTHIAN EMPIRE
.... 349

PARTHIAN WAR OF LUCIUS VERUS 353

COUNTERATTACK 163 CE 358

THE CAMPAIGN OF 165-166 CE 360

SEPTIMIUS SEVERUS CAMPAIGNS IN MESOPOTAMIA 367

SEPTIMIUS SEVERUS' SECOND CAMPAIGN TO MESOPOTAMIA
.... 373

THE PARTHIAN WAR OF CARACALLA 379

TROJAN HORSE DIPLOMACY 381

BATTLE OF NISIBIS 217 CE 386

FALL 391

CONCLUSION 401

BIBLIOGRAPHY 405

INDEX 419

List of Illustrations

FIGURE 1 MAP OF TIGRANES THE GREAT'S ARMENIAN EMPIRE (C. 80 BC)..29
FIGURE 2 COIN WITH TIGRANES THE GREAT PORTRAIT (ARMENIAN KING, RULED 95 BCE–55 BCE 30
FIGURE 3 PORTRAIT OF THE KING OF PONTUS MITHRIDATES VI AS HERACLES. MARBLE, ROMAN IMPERIAL PERIOD (1ST CENTURY). 31
FIGURE 4 SO-CALLED "SULLA", PROBABLY FROM THE TIME OF AUGUSTUS AFTER A PORTRAIT OF AN IMPORTANT ROMAN FROM THE 2ND CENTURY BC. 32
FIGURE 5 KING OF CAPPADOCIA ARIOBARZANES I 95-63 BC. 33
FIGURE 6 COIN OF MITHRIDATES II OF PARTHIA FROM THE MINT AT SELEUCIA ON THE TIGRIS. 34
FIGURE 7 POMPEY...35
FIGURE 8 COIN OF PHRAATES III 36
FIGURE 9 ORODES II 96
FIGURE 10 MARCUS LICINIUS CRASSUS 97
FIGURE 11 STATUE THOUGHT TO REPRESENT SURENA AT NATIONAL MUSEUM OF IRAN................................98
FIGURE 12 CRASSUS CAMPAIGN ROUTE TO CARRHAE. THE GROWTH OF ROMAN POWER IN ASIA MINOR. ...99
FIGURE 13 CRASSUS DEFEATED BY THE PARTHIANS..........100
FIGURE 14 CICERO 124
FIGURE 15 PACORUS I OF PARTHIA 125
FIGURE 16 CLASSICAL SYRIA DURING ROMAN TIMES........126
FIGURE 17 GAIUS JULIUS CAESAR (100-44 BCE) 166
FIGURE 18 ASSASSINATION OF POMPEY 167
FIGURE 19 GAIUS OCTAVIUS......................................168
FIGURE 20 MARCUS AEMILIUS LEPIDUS 169
FIGURE 21 MARK ANTONY 170
FIGURE 22 ANTIGONUS II MATTATHIAS...................171
FIGURE 23 QUINTUS LABIENUS PARTHICUS.. 172
FIGURE 24 GENERAL PUBLIUS VENTIDIUS BASSUS 173
FIGURE 25 THE PARTHIAN INVASION OF JUDEA 174

FIGURE 26 ANTONY'S PARTHIAN CAMPAIGN 214
FIGURE 27 MARK ANTONY'S TARGET. 215
FIGURE 28 KING ARTAVAZDES II. 216
FIGURE 29 PHRAATES IV 260
FIGURE 30 MAP OF CHARACENE 261
FIGURE 31 COIN OF THE PARTHIAN KING PHRAATACES AND OF MUSA 262
FIGURE 32 AUGUSTUS OF PRIMA PORTA 263
FIGURE 33 COIN OF ARTABANUS III OF PARTHIA 264
FIGURE 34 LUCIUS VITELLIUS 265
FIGURE 35 EMPEROR TIBERIUS 266
FIGURE 36 COIN OF VOLOGASES I. 312
FIGURE 37 BUST OF NERO AT THE CAPITOLINE MUSEUM, ROME 313
FIGURE 38 MAP OF THE TROOP MOVEMENTS DURING THE FIRST TWO YEARS (58 TO 60 CE) 314
FIGURE 39 MAP OF THE TROOP MOVEMENTS DURING THE LAST YEARS (61 TO 63 CE) 315
FIGURE 40 TRAJAN'S JOURNEY EAST 345
FIGURE 41 TRAJAN'S CAMPAIGN OF 114 CE. ROMAN NUMERALS = LEGION NUMBERS 346
FIGURE 42 TRAJAN'S CAMPAIGN OF 115 CE 347
FIGURE 43 TRAJAN'S CAMPAIGN OF 116 CE 348
FIGURE 44 VOLOGASES IV 393
FIGURE 45 MARCUS AURELIUS 394
FIGURE 46 MARBLE PORTRAIT OF THE CO-EMPEROR LUCIUS VERUS 395
FIGURE 47 MARCUS AURELIUS RECEIVING THE HOMAGE OF THE PARTHIANS 396
FIGURE 48 BUST OF SEPTIMIUS SEVERUS (REIGN 193–211 CE) 397
FIGURE 49 VOLOGASES V 398
FIGURE 50 CARACALLA 399
FIGURE 51 ARTABANUS V 400

Leviathan Vs. Behemoth

XIII

Acknowledgments

First, I would like to thank my wife and our two sons for their support and putting up with my odd hours. Second, I want to thank Brett Schlotterback for his advice when it comes to keeping the computer running smoothly. He's been a big help in all the books I have written. I'd also like to thank Classical Wisdom Weekly (http://classicalwisdom.com/), for their help and promotion. Next, I'd like to thank historian Rose Mary Sheldon for providing me with some much needed maps. Lastly, I want to thank Joan Griffith for her time and advice. She has been very valuable, honest, and tough when it comes to advice and editing. I've learned a lot from her and continue to learn what to do and what not to do. Her guidance is always welcomed and greatly appreciated.

INTRODUCTION

The Roman-Parthian Wars were cultural clashes between eastern and western titans. Parthia was the antithesis of Rome, not only culturally, but also on the battlefield. What started out as a diplomatic meeting in 92 BCE eventually led to a series of wars, starting with the Battle of Carrhae in 53 BCE and ending with the Battle of Nisibis in 217 CE.

The book you're about to read on the Roman-Parthian Wars is a narrative and analysis of their military and political relationship with one another and those who shared a border with the two powers.

Much of the history discussed is primarily from the Roman sources, since Parthia left us with little to nothing to discuss on their end. While sources on the topic are of great importance, many with whom I discussed the topic have made the mistake of thinking that information on the conflict between the two powers is limited. This is true and false. We have the greatly important and yet limited primary sources provided by Plutarch, Justin, Appian, Cassius Dio, Herodian, and many others that give us great insight into the conflict. There are only a handful of books written in the last 140 years that deal with Parthian history and even fewer that focus on the Roman-Parthian Wars. The works written on Parthia that have been beneficial in my research are George Rawlinson's *Parthia;* Neilson C. Debevoise's *A Political History of Parthia;* Malcolm A. R. Colledge, *The Parthians;* and Rose Mary Sheldon's *Rome's Wars in Parthia*. Besides books dealing with Parthia, there are many other books that deal indirectly with the subject, particularly biographies of Roman emperors, not to mention the plethora of articles written on the topic, which can be located at many universities and at JSTOR.

Parthia's empire was not as large as the Seleucids' was; however, they still held a considerable amount of land. Parthia, which gradually conquered the Seleucid Empire, stretched from the borders of India to the borders of Armenia, from fringes of Central Asia to the Indian Ocean. Rome, the other massive empire, stretched from Northern Europe to North Africa, from the Atlantic Ocean to the Near East, and would eventually adjoin Parthia.

As Rome continued to push militarily and diplomatically eastward during the 90's BCE, they eventually arrived near the Upper Euphrates to discover that many of the mini-kingdoms were in fact Parthian client states, especially Armenia. Once Rome officially discovered and understood the sphere of influence Parthia had over its western neighbors, Rome gradually took that model and began to court the eastern kingdoms subject to Parthian influence. However, before they can accomplish this, they must first meet their equals.

Around 92 BCE, their first diplomatic meeting took place. The relationship between both empires started peacefully. As time went on, tensions began to grow over

Introduction

the control of the Near East. While Parthia's sphere of influence dominated the region, Rome's political push at Parthia's client states slowly caused a rift between the two powers that eventually led to war when Crassus invaded Parthia and was obliterated with his Roman forces at the Battle of Carrhae in 53 BCE. After Carrhae, their relations would never be the same, as both sides would continue a tug of war with the kingdoms between their borders, at times directly engaging each other.

While Parthia's overall strategy during this long conflict was a defensive one, Rome had created a grand strategy of its own, which was to confiscate the client states and eventually turn them into Roman provinces. Men like Julius Caesar dreamed of conquering Parthia, but he was assassinated before he could set out on his grand adventure. His friend, Mark Antony, attempted the feat, only to fail. Taking Parthia on directly seemed futile. Therefore, Rome continued to place pressure on the client states. But as the decades passed, Rome's grand strategy began to stagnate. The client states, such as Armenia, were unreliable and caused problems by changing their allegiance from one side to the other.

Eventually Rome did conquer Mesopotamia under Trajan in 114-116 CE. Once Trajan died, however, his successor, Hadrian, handed Mesopotamia back to the Parthians. After Hadrian died, Roman emperors Marcus Aurelius and Lucius Verus renewed the war in 161-166 CE with Lucius leading the war effort in Mesopotamia while General Avidius Cassius did all the work. While the results were successful in capturing Mesopotamia again for a second time and sacking the Parthian capital of Ctesiphon, they did not last long. Instead of a dead emperor and an overextended Roman army causing Rome to hand over the captured regions, it was plague that weakened the Roman forces. In addition, they were overextended both in resources and men, which allowed Parthia once again to regain their lost territory. Rome would invade Mesopotamia twice more under the Emperors Septimius Severus 198 CE and Caracalla 216-217 CE. While both emperors were successful, the borders of Rome would once again recede.

While Parthia was able to beat Rome multiple times during their early relations, Parthia was far more stable at the time and could put up great resistance. However, as time passed, the Parthian nobility became increasingly hostile to the king, which led to rebellions. Because of these sporadic civil wars, Parthia became weak and open for invasion. Rome took advantage of this situation, as you will read in the later chapters, and was able to defeat them, and at times, Rome attempted to make Parthia a client state. Understand that Parthia, unlike Rome, did not have a centralized government, and because of this, they were in fact a loosely held confederacy.

The purpose of this book is not only to give new life to a subject often overlooked, but also to highlight the many reasons why Rome and Parthia battled. The primary reason is that Rome did not tolerate equals. Second, Rome had a grand strategy: wine, dine, and confiscate client

Introduction

states. Third, their grand strategy and objective in dealing with Parthia turned to raiding its coffers to satisfy their financial needs. Fourth, Rome inevitably failed in their Alexanderphile dreams due to military intelligence failures, gullibility, lack of planning, and overextending their forces and resources, only to feel the effects of blowback once they got comfortable. However, unlike Parthia, Rome continued, while Parthia fell into the dustbin of history.

Leviathan Vs. Behemoth

1

THE COMING STORM

In 92 BCE, an envoy consisting of Lucius Cornelius Sulla Felix, better known as Sulla, proconsul of Cilicia (in Anatolia), and Ariobarzanes, king of Cappadocia, approached Parthia from the west. The two men spent some time by the Euphrates River. From the east came a Parthian envoy, Orobazus, likely with an entourage. Plutarch provides no comment on how this meeting came about. However, this was the first meeting between Parthia and Rome. Once the three men met, Sulla ordered three chairs to be brought out – one for Ariobarzanes, one for Orobazus, and one for himself. Sulla sat in the middle chair and gave audience. Orobazus offered an alliance and friendship to Sulla. After the meeting had concluded, Orobazus returned to Mithridates' court, presented him with the news, and promptly was executed. Orobazus had committed the unthinkable act of allowing a foreigner (Sulla) to sit in the middle and dictate terms on Parthian territory. As for Sulla, some praised his meeting while others damned him as an ignorant fool for his actions.[1]

---

[1] Plutarch, *Sulla*, 5.3.

Plutarch provides no further details to the event, which in turn begs the question. Why were Ariobarzanes and Sulla traveling into Parthian territory?

Ariobarzanes was king of Cappadocia, elected by the citizens of that country around 95 BCE. Before Ariobarzanes ascended the throne, King Mithridates VI of Pontus had occupied Galatia and Cappadocia with the support of King Nicomedes III of Bithynia around 104 BCE. From that time on, Cappadocia experienced many regime changes.

First, Ariarathes VII was placed on the throne at a very young age. His mother Laodice, the eldest sister of the King Mithridates VI, acted as regent until the boy was of age. However, Nicomedes had other plans. In 103/02 BCE, Nicomedes invaded Cappadocia, which may have been at Laodice's request. She seems to have supported and possibly married Nicomedes for fear of what happened to her husband Ariarathes VI. Without some kind of support, Laodice feared that if her son, Ariarathes VII, were killed like her former husband and she would be irrelevant to Mithridates. However, Mithridates had other plans.

First, he expelled Nicomedes from Cappadocia, replacing him with his nephew Ariarathes VII as king. So long as Ariarathes supported Mithridates, all would remain well. Unfortunately, that did not happen. Ariarathes would be murdered about 100/99 BCE.[2]

---

[2] B. C. McGing, *The Foreign Policy of Mithridates VI Eupator, King of Pontus* (Leiden: E.J. Brill, 1986), 73-75.

The Coming Storm

With Ariarathes removed from the throne, Mithridates decided to place his son, Ariarathes IX, on the throne to keep Cappadocia stable and continue as a useful satellite. This did not last long. Once Ariarathes IX ascended the throne, he soon was replaced by the brother of Ariarathes VII, also called Ariarathes VIII. Ariarathes VIII was defeated and escaped from Cappadocia, only to die of a disease brought on by anxiety.[3]

Nicomedes grew fearful that Mithridates might invade his kingdom and retake Cappadocia for himself. Therefore, Nicodemus sent his wife to Rome to plead his case. Rome was an ally of both Pontus and Bithynia. Both kingdoms were independent and could act on their own behalf; however, certain issues, like dynastic or territorial disputes, would be taken before the Roman Senate.

Nicomedes instructed his wife to tell the Roman Senate that she had a third son with her previous husband. The issue caused such a commotion among the Roman Senate that Mithridates quickly sent an embassy to counter the claim. The Senate listened to both arguments and concluded that neither side had a legal claim.

The Senate made it clear that both Nicomedes and Mithridates were to leave Cappadocia at once. Cappadocia was free to do as they pleased, and the people decided it was best to have a king, for "their nation could not subsist without a king." The people of Cappadocia chose

---

[3] Ibid., 76.

Ariobarzanes as their king and the Roman Senate approved him around 95 BCE.

With the loss of Nicomedes as an ally, Mithridates had to look elsewhere to avoid problems with Rome. Yes, Rome was still an ally in some sense. However, Mithridates was walking on eggshells and had to be careful not to gain any negative attention that might cause Rome to intervene against him. Mithridates could not look to the west for an ally, thus he turned his attention towards the east and found the Kingdom of Armenia.[4]

Armenia was not by any standards a strong ally with a powerful army, but Mithridates saw its potential for one reason and that reason was Parthia.

Mithridates knew that Armenia was a vassal of the Parthian Empire. If Mithridates were to go to war with Rome, he needed an indirect ally that could match Rome. In other words, Mithridates needed a wild card in his deck.

Enter, Tigranes II. In 95 BCE, after King Tigranes I of Armenia died, Tigranes II was the next in line for throne, but only if the Parthians agreed to this. At the time of his father's death, Tigranes had been a hostage at the Parthian court for quite some time, possibly 20 years. When Mithridates II of Parthia invaded Armenia, he may have placed Tigranes I on the throne while taking his son Tigranes II back to Parthia as a hostage. In this way, Mithridates II kept Tigranes I loyal to Parthia. This does

---

[4] Ibid., 76-78.

not explain how Tigranes II acquired his freedom, but the historian Justin does provide a clue.[5]

> The king of Armenia, at this time, was Tigranes, who had long before been committed as a hostage to the Parthians, but had subsequently been sent back to take possession of his father's throne. This prince Mithridates was extremely desirous to engage as an ally in the war, which he had long meditated, against the Romans.[6]

The passage from Justin may imply that Mithridates VI negotiated with Mithridates II to release the heir to the Armenian throne, and why not? If Mithridates VI can acquire a mildly strong ally that is vassal to the Parthians, then war with Rome is desirable. Mithridates VI's move was strategic and political, for a war with Rome would include Armenia aiding Pontus, which potentially could bring in Parthia to defend its vassal, Armenia. To make the deal even more binding, Mithridates VI married off his daughter Cleopatra to Tigranes II. In a sense, you could say that Tigranes must honor his father-in-law's wishes.

---

[5] Marek Jan Olbrycht, "Subjects and Allies: the Black Sea Empire of Mithradates VI Eupator (120-63 BC) Reconsidered" in *PONTIKA 2008: Recent Research on the Northern and Eastern Black Sea in Ancient Times: Proceedings of the International Conference, 21st-26th April 2008*, Krakow Ewdoksia Papuci-Władyka; et al., (Oxford: Archaeopress, 2011), 275-276.

[6] Justin 38.3.1.

However, father-in-law hoped that his son-in-law's master, Parthia, would be pulled into the conflict, for an attack on Armenia would be an attack on Parthia.

Around 95/94 BCE, Gordius, a Cappadocian noble and friend of Mithridates VI, went to the court of Tigranes II and persuaded him to invade Cappadocia and remove Ariobarzanes from the throne.[7]

Gordius' mission, once in Cappadocia, is questionable. A small group supported Gordius as being the next king. However, he may have taken Cappadocia in an attempt to restore Ariarathes IX. There is no doubt that Mithridates was looking to reestablish influence over the province; but his move backfired when Sulla arrived.[8]

Sulla was praetor of the province of Cilicia when Gordius along with the forces of Tigranes invaded and disposed of the king chosen by Rome. Sulla's original mission was to fight piracy, but that mission changed to restoring Ariobarzanes to the throne. Roman armies had not intervened since 188 BCE to settle dynastic quarrels in Anatolia. Sulla's armed invasion of Cappadocia was a success for the time being. He was able to restore Ariobarzanes for a brief moment.[9]

Once Sulla reestablished Ariobarzanes on the throne, Mithridates II of Parthia sent his envoy, Orobazes, to meet with the men. This meeting took place in Cilicia along the Euphrates River. It's obvious that Sulla, along

---

[7] B. C. McGing, *The Foreign Policy of Mithridates VI Eupator, King of Pontus*, 78.
[8] Ibid, 79.
[9] Ibid.

with Ariobarzanes, arranged a meeting with the Parthians to avoid the possibility of potential conflict.[10]

Sulla learned quickly that Armenia was a vassal to the Parthians. As the story goes, Orobazes offered Rome an alliance and friendship. Sulla took the offer due to the political implications, which not only benefited Rome, but Rome's ally, Cappadocia.[11]

Sulla was safeguarding the Anatolian region from possible Parthian involvement if a war between Rome and the Kingdoms of Pontus and Armenia was to break out. He hoped that the Parthians would keep Armenia under control and out of Cappadocia. Sulla likely understood that a war with the Parthians would be too much for Rome.

Sulla saved Rome's weak ally, Cappadocia, not once, but twice, from foreign takeover. That would not last. In a few years, Mithridates VI and Tigranes II set out to secure the region. Mithridates sought to conquer Roman lands in western Asia Minor, while Tigranes II would extend his influence in the east. Thus, in 90 BCE, Mithridates VI made his advance on Roman-held territory, igniting the first of three Mithridatic Wars. Tigranes II would stay out of the first war, but supported Mithridates VI from the sideline. Tigranes' decision was based on seeing a much greater opportunity in the east.[12]

---

[10] Warwick Ball, *Rome in the East: The Transformation of an Empire* (London: Routledge, 2007), 13.
[11] Plutarch, *Sulla*, 5.3.
[12] Charles Freeman, *Egypt, Greece, and Rome: Civilizations of the Ancient Mediterranean* (Oxford: Oxford University Press, 1996), 360.

Leviathan Vs. Behemoth

PARTHIA'S STRUGGLE

When Mithridates II died around 88/87 BCE, Parthia fell into dynastic turmoil. Parthian coins indicate that before and after Mithridates death, the country fell into a dynastic power struggle between Gotarzes I and Orodes I. However, it is possible that many actors also vied for power during this altercation. The dynastic infighting caused great instability throughout Parthia, which in turn allowed Tigranes to invade, conquer, and confiscate portions of Parthia.[13] The historian Strabo mentions this and states,

> When he acquired power, he recovered these valleys, and devastated the country of the Parthians, the territory about Ninus, and that about Arbela. He subjected to his authority the Atropatenians, and the Gordyæans; by force of arms he obtained possession also of the rest of Mesopotamia, and, after crossing the Euphrates, of Syria and Phœnicia.[14]

Strabo is correct. In 86 BCE, Tigranes II did take advantage of the uncertainty within Parthia. However, Tigranes never conquered all of Mesopotamia; he conquered the northern

---

[13] Kaveh Farrokh, *Shadows in the Desert: Ancient Persia at War* (Oxford: Osprey Publishing, 2007), 126-127.
[14] Strabo, *Geography*, 11.14.15.

portion of Mesopotamia and greater Media. When Tigranes entered Media, he made his way to Ecbatana, the capital of Media and the very place where he was held hostage during his youth. It was here in Ecbatana that he let be known to the world, especially to the Parthians, that he, Tigranes II, was the "King of Kings," thus proclaiming his mastery over Asia.

After gobbling up portions of the Parthian Empire, Tigranes moved west towards Syria. In 83 BCE, Syria, which was up until this point a part of the once mighty Seleucid Empire, broke away from their Seleucid masters, who were exhausted by war. The Syrians were not comfortable declaring their independence.[15] Instead, the Syrians sought a new master to protect them, and Tigranes was to be a desirable overlord, protector, and king, being far more stable than the Seleucid regime. The Ptolemies did not hate Armenia nor was Armenia at war with Rome.[16]

As mentioned, Parthia fell into a dynastic power struggle between Gotarzes I and Orodes I, in addition to many other smaller nobles who may have vied for power. The cuneiform tablets mention that Gotarzes I came to power after the death of Mithridates II, who may have been his father or brother, but he only lasted a year on the throne. The tablet mentions that an "Arsaces drove out Gotarzes" from the throne roughly in 87/86 BCE. Orodes I

---

[15] Vahan M. Kurkjian, *A History of Armenia* (New York: Armenian General Benevolent Union, 1958), 63.
[16] Justin 40.1.

retained the throne until 80/79 BCE, when he was driven out by an unknown Arsaces. By the time we reach 77 BCE, an Arsaces identified as Sanatruces holds power.[17] An interesting passage from the ancient writer Lucian concerning Sanatruces states, "Sinatroces, king of Parthia, was restored to his country in his eightieth year by the Sacauracian Scyths, assumed the throne and held it seven years."[18] Sanatruces may have been a younger brother or cousin of Mithridates II. However, the passage is quite clear that he, too, was involved in the early struggle for supremacy with the passing of Mithridates II.

Another point of interest is the fact that the Sacauracian Scyths helped him gain the throne. Where the Sacauracian Scyths came from is unknown, but from their name it would appear that they might have come from the Caucasus and if so, possibly from the provinces of Iberia and Albania. But why would this particular tribe of Scythians help Sanatruces to the throne? The answer could be that the Scythians helping Sanatruces may have been allied at one time with either Mithridates of Pontus or Tigranes II, and after the setback in both kingdoms found the Parthians to be not only a better ally but also a better asset when dealing with the Romans. In other words, they needed a protector. However, it is possible given the period of Sanatruces' restoration to the throne that the Sacauracian Scyths fled from their homelands, possibly

---

[17] Richard Nelson Frye, *The History of Ancient Iran* (Munchen: C.H. Beck, 1984), 214-215.
[18] Lucian, *Long Lives*, 15.

Iberia and Albania, due to Tigranes II's conquest of the provinces after the death of Mithridates II.[19]

Sanatruces' ascension seems to have stabilized Parthia for the time being. However, even with Parthia stable, Sanatruces' presence did not cause Tigranes II to fear him. It was not until Sanatruces' son Phraates III took the throne that signs of respect for one another became evident.

Tigranes' conquests rattled Rome. The Roman statesman Cicero is said to have stated, "He made the Republic of Rome tremble before the prowess of his arms."[20] In one sense this is true: Armenia was the new power on the block and friend of Mithridates of Pontus. However, Rome's fear of Armenia only goes so far, especially when the man Rome defeated and wished to kill or imprison fled to his son-in-law, Tigranes II.

In the spring of 73 BCE, the third and last Mithridatic War occurred. L. Licinius Lucullus was placed in command of the Roman forces in Asia Minor. Mithridates' success against Rome was short lived as Lucullus marched on Pontus quickly, inflicting heavy defeats, causing Mithridates to flee into Armenia in 70 BCE.[21]

---

[19] Frederik Coene, *The Caucasus: An Introduction* (London: Routledge, 2010), 100-101.

[20] Zabelle C. Boyajian, *An Anthology of Legends and Poems of Armenia* (Aram Raffi; Viscount Bryce. London: J.M. Dent & Sons, Ltd. 1916). 117.

[21] Christopher S. Mackay, *Ancient Rome: 1200 Years of Political and Military History* (New York: Cambridge University Press, 2004), 136.

His son-in-law Tigranes II could do little to keep him safe. Tigranes seems to have been unafraid of Rome and rightfully so. His army was rather large due to the many kings who provide him forces in a time of crises; he is the king of kings. However, it is no matter to Rome if you are the king of kings, for what Rome wants Rome gets and Mithridates is a wanted man. Lucullus sent a messenger named Appius to the court of Tigranes and demanded that Mithridates be handed over. If Tigranes refused, a state of war would be declared. Tigranes refused the demand, but offered a large number of gifts, which Appius refused, except for a bowl, which Appius took back with him to Lucullus. The war was on.[22]

When Rome demonstrated how serious they were by declaring war on Armenia for harboring an enemy of Rome, Tigranes II quickly made an appeal to King Phraates III of Parthia to ally with him and Mithridates. When Lucullus got word of this, he sent ambassadors as well. Both parties were competing for Parthia's military support. However, unlike Tigranes and Mithridates, Lucullus made promises to Phraates for supporting Rome along with many threats if Parthia chose to aid the enemy. Phraates agreed with Lucullus to a treaty that kept the peace between the two powers.

Lucullus, curious about the Parthians, sent an officer to Phraates' court named Sextilius. While at the royal court, Sextilius came across some rather startling information. Phraates had also made treaties with Tigranes

---

[22] Plutarch, *The Life of Lucullus*, 19.1, 21. 6-7.

and Mithridates. This brings up another question. What was Sextilius doing at the Parthian court? The Roman Historian Cassius Dio mentions that Phraates was suspicious of Sextilius, stating that Phraates "began to suspect that he was there to spy out the country and his power." This is partially true. Sextilius was probing and collecting intelligence on the Parthians. However, Sextilius mission seems to be that of a military advisory, which Phraates noticed later due to the treaty that was signed between the two powers. Therefore, Sextilius acted on behalf of the treaty by providing military assistance to the Parthians if they desired to go to war against Tigranes and Mithridates.

Phraates had no desire for war, for "he offered no opposition, but stood aloof from both parties, naturally wishing to make neither side strong; for he thought that an evenly-balanced struggle between them would ensure him the greatest safety." Indeed it did. With Rome, Armenia, and Pontus all battling it out, the Parthians were able to regain their strength and reconsider their position later.[23]

Rome's war with Tigranes and Mithridates would be long, harsh, and mutinous. Lucullus achieved many victories, such as capturing Tigranocerta, the capital of Tigranes, in 69 BCE, followed by the city of Nisibis in 68.[24] However, the many victories he achieved came from the harshness in fighting an enemy who gradually resorted to

---

[23] Cassius Dio, *Roman History*, 36, 3.
[24] H. H. Scullard, *From the Gracchi to Nero: A History of Rome 133 BC to AD 68* (London: Routledge, 2010), 86.

guerrilla methods, making victory elusive. Tigranes' move towards unorthodox warfare caused many within the Roman ranks under the command of Lucullus to mutiny, for it was better to go on the defensive than achieve empty victories. However, it is rather odd that a well-trained army would just mutiny. Lucullus did not have the manpower to permanently occupy regions won, and what men could be left behind to garrison certain regions or provinces came under attacks by which they were quickly removed by Tigranes. Had this tug of war continued, Rome would have ultimately left. But this is not the Roman way. Instead, by 66 BCE, the Roman Council removed Lucullus and themselves from the arena and placed total responsibility into the hands of Pompey.[25]

With Pompey now in command, the war would go into full swing. As Pompey began to go on the offensive, he also renewed the neutrality agreement with Phraates. Phraates remained neutral for now, while Pompey came up with an elaborate ruse. While Pompey concentrated his efforts on Mithridates, he would distract Tigranes by making him believe that the Parthians were to attack Gordyene. Pompey manufactured a fine piece of propaganda to cause division in order to conquer. However, the deception would become truth. Phraates had no intention of intervening until the son of Tigranes II, who happened to be named Tigranes and was the son-in-law to Phraates, came forward with an offer. Tigranes the younger pleaded with Phraates to attack Armenia and to

---

[25] Mackay, *Ancient Rome*, 136-137.

place him on the throne after victory. Not a bad offer, for it would allow Phraates to recoup all that territory Parthia lost to Tigranes II. Phraates agreed to the proposal and moved his forces westward.

Tigranes II got word of the coming Parthians and decided that it was best not to meet them in the field. Tigranes' decision shows how weak his forces were by taking to the hills. A smart move, but nonetheless shows that Tigranes has not the manpower to counter such an invasion; and if he were to achieve victory it would be costly, and grant the Romans a decisive victory at a later date. Before taking to the hills, Tigranes makes a smart move. He bolstered the defenses of his capital, Artaxata. When Phraates arrived at Artaxata, he reconsiders, since the Parthian forces were unprepared and unsuited for siege warfare, as we shall see again later. Moreover, Phraates had no time for a protracted war for another reason: a possible coup d'état could be festering in his absence. Therefore, Phraates abandoned Artaxata and headed home. However, he did recoup former Parthian territory during the invasion of Armenia. As for Tigranes the younger's dream of ascending his father's throne, that fell by the wayside. Tigranes the younger stayed in Armenia while the Parthians moved out. Once Armenia was clear, Tigranes II moved his forces out of the hills and drove his son out of Armenia.

Tigranes the younger would flee to Pompey in hopes that Pompey could make his dreams come true. However, Pompey had different intentions. Pompey advanced into Armenia in 66 BCE, accompanied by Tigranes the younger. Given the circumstances of the situation, Tigranes II felt that further conflict was useless and it was best to surrender.[26] As Tigranes made his way towards Pompey, many of his own men fled in fear. These men would turn to Tigranes the younger, in hope that he would seize the throne. When Pompey got word of this, he quickly seized him and put him in chains, particularly since the young Tigranes was trying to stir up the Parthians against Pompey.[27] Pompey treated Tigranes II kindly, allowing him to retain Armenia; but he could not retain his conquests. Those parcels of land now belonged to the Parthians--for the time being.[28]

As for Mithridates of Pontus, his fate came in 63 BCE. According to Appian, Mithridates could not kill himself with poison after many years of building up a resistance to the various concoctions with which he experimented. Thus, he had to have an officer of the Gauls by the name of Bituitus run him through with a sword. Cassius Dio mentions that Mithridates "desired to die, albeit unwillingly, and though eager to kill himself was unable to do so; but partly by poison and partly by the sword he was at once self-slain and murdered by his foes."[29]

---

[26] Dio 36.45, 51-52.
[27] Appian, *The Mithridatic Wars*, 105.
[28] Plutarch, *Pompey*, 33.
[29] Dio 37.13.

The Coming Storm

ROME DECIDES THE BORDERS

After the Mithridatic Wars ended, Phraates quickly sent envoys to meet with Pompey. Pompey's lieutenants were subjugating the rest of Armenia along with parts of Pontus, not to mention that Gabinius then praetor, had crossed the Euphrates River, the very boundary that was once agreed upon as the border between the two powers, and had made it as far as the Tigris before turning back, which caused Phraates to fear the worst. Even though Pompey agreed to the older treaty, and accepted that Phraates did help by invading Armenia, he became more belligerent towards the Parthians.[30]

The issues were provinces and borders, particularly the provinces of Osrhoene and Gordyene. Pompey confiscated the semi-autonomous kingdoms of Osrhoene and Gordyene located in upper Mesopotamia from the Armenians around 65 BCE. However, Parthia also laid claim to both kingdoms.

Phraates demanded Pompey give him back Tigranes the younger, the lost provinces, and respect the Euphrates as the boundary between the two. Pompey replied that, "so far as Tigranes was concerned, he belonged more to his father than his father-in-law; and, with regard to the boundary, that the one adopted would be a just one." Pompey's response to Phraates suggested that Rome makes the boundaries and no other. Pompey

---

[30] Ibid., 37.5.

has clearly violated his own treaty with Parthia by claiming their western provinces as Roman property.[31] As for the fate of Tigranes the younger, Pompey had taken him prisoner and paraded him through streets of Rome.[32]

Rome and Parthia were adamant in dominating Osrhoene due to its strategic purposes. Osrhoene was strategically important, for within lay the fortified city of Samosata, which was on the west bank of the Euphrates, not too far from the fortified town of Seleucia at Zeugma on the east bank of the Euphrates. Pompey saw the value in controlling the kingdom, for it would allow Rome easy access to travel down or cross the Euphrates in times of war, for the function of Samosata was to protect a major crossing point of the river on the east-west trade route. We can see why it was beneficial to the power that controls it. Furthermore, Osrhoene was important since Rome controlled the provinces, directly or indirectly around Osrhoene, except to the south. This gave Rome an umbrella of protection.[33]

The second issue was that both Phraates and Tigranes laid claim to the province of Corduene after the war. However, the province was under Roman hegemony. Someone must not have told Tigranes and Phraates this, because Phraates sent Parthian forces to recoup Corduene

---

[31] Plutarch, *Pompey*, 33.
[32] Ibid., 45.
[33] Stephen Mitchell and James A. Arvites, *Armies and Frontiers in Roman and Byzantine Anatolia: Proceedings of a Colloquium Held at University College, Swansea, in April 1981* (Oxford, England: B.A.R., 1983), 103.

The Coming Storm

in 64 BCE. Once Pompey got word that Parthian forces had entered and laid claim to the province, he became furious, sent ambassadors, held Phraates in contempt, and demanded that the Parthians leave the disputed province immediately. Instead of waiting for an answer, Pompey sent Lucius Afranius with some forces into Corduene and retook it without a fight, according to Cassius Dio. However, Plutarch mentions that there was some sort of conflict. Whereas Cassius Dio says no fight occurred, Plutarch states, "the Parthian king, who had burst into Gordyene and was plundering the subjects of Tigranes, he sent an armed force under Afranius, which drove him out of the country and pursued him as far as the district of Arbela."[34] Plutarch's take on the situation sounds more like propaganda, since the province of Corduene was in fact a semi-autonomous kingdom under Parthian control until Tigranes subjugated Corduene after the death of Mithridates II. When Rome declared war on Armenia, the Kingdom of Corduene decided to exchange Armenian shackles for Roman. Of course, they did not know that their quest for independence was about to be ignored by the very people who sought to liberate them. Once the Parthians left Corduene, Pompey quickly handed over the province to Tigranes.

Phraates was upset, as one would expect. Phraates argued that armed diplomacy was the only method the Romans understood and he was right. However, Phraates

---

[34] Plutarch, *Pompey*, 36.

is guilty of this. Phraates felt wronged by Pompey, he sent ambassadors to make the case that Rome was wrong in their decisions and actions, and even forbade Pompey to cross the Euphrates. Pompey made no reply, which enraged Phraates.

Phraates immediately went on the offensive once spring arrived. His target was Tigranes. The first engagement between the two powers resulted in a Parthian loss, followed by a Parthian victory. Tigranes feared the worse; he knew his army could not stand up to the might of the Parthians and he needed the assistance of Pompey who was in Syria at the time.

Phraates likely knew that Tigranes would seek Roman help and would do the same but in a different manner. Phraates sent ambassadors to Pompey in which they brought forth many charges against Tigranes, condemning the Romans at the same time. Phraates' strategy was to make Pompey feel ashamed and troubled. Pompey ignored Tigranes' request and took no hostile measures against Phraates. Pompey's reason or excuse was that he had not the permission to execute such an expedition and that his mission at the time was to defeat Mithridates of Pontus.

It is true that Pompey had Mithridates to deal with and that any further distraction could impede the current campaign. In addition, he was satisfied with what had been gained and did not want to risk much more.

Pompey also had reason to fear the Parthians at this time. Pompey knew that the majority of his time, effort, and forces, had been concentrated on securing the newly acquired Roman territory that had expanded to the borders of the Ptolemaic kingdom, while the remainder of his forces were concentrated on Mithridates. Due to the Roman east being fragile, Pompey sent arbitrators to the two kings to hammer out a deal, a brilliant move on Pompey's part. Tigranes and Phraates agreed to cease hostilities against one another. Even though the war was over, Tigranes was disappointed and angry with Pompey for not sending aid. Phraates, on the other hand, saw the value in keeping Tigranes in power, for if Rome were to become aggressive against Parthia, Tigranes could prove to be a useful ally and vice versa. Tigranes also saw the value in the relationship and understood that he could not depend on the Romans, and because of this mutual understanding, both men realized that if one were to conquer the other, it would only help Rome subdue the winner.[35]

In summary, Parthia regained its prominent position in the Near East with the crippling of Tigranes' kingdom. When Tigranes surrendered, he was still friends with Mithridates. Soon after, Phraates and Tigranes decided that friendship through arbitrators sent by Pompey was best. Had Phraates and Tigranes allied with Mithridates, Pompey would have to deal with an even greater conflict that possibly could have sent Rome packing for good, or at least for a long while. Even though

---

[35] Dio 37.6-7.

Parthia was once again master of the Near East, they now had an equal. Rome was not going anywhere and the Parthians seemed fine with this so long as the two powers could coexist equally and on peaceful terms. However, this would not be the case. Pompey's response to Phraates over the border was a delayed declaration of war. Phraates, and the Parthian king after him, knew that Rome was anything but friendly. Pompey's actions on that fateful day sealed the fate for many Roman and Parthian woes to come. Pompey could have respected the borders agreed upon before his arrival, but this was not the Roman way and as we shall read, Rome wanted to expand further east in hopes of acquiring the vast resources and trade routes that crisscrossed the Near East for Rome felt that they were the rightful heirs to Alexander's former empire.

The Coming Storm

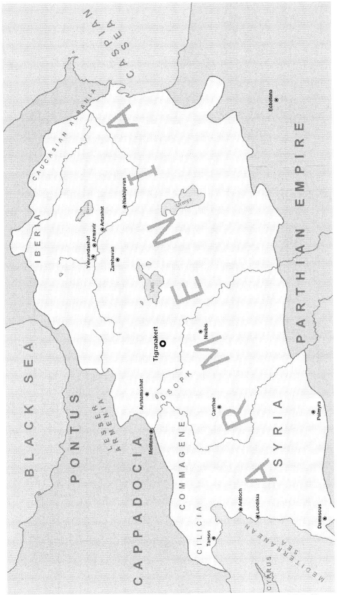

Figure 1 Map of Tigranes the Great's Armenian Empire (c. 80 BC)
Created by Aivazovsky (CC BY-SA 3.0)

Figure 2 Coin with Tigranes the Great portrait (Armenian king, ruled 95 BCE–55 BCE
http://en.wikipedia.org/wiki/Tigranes_the_Great#mediaviewer/File:Tigran_Mets.jpg

Figure 3 Portrait of the king of Pontus Mithridates VI as Heracles. Marble, Roman imperial period (1st century). Louvre. Paris

Figure 4 So-called "Sulla", probably from the time of Augustus after a portrait of an important Roman from the 2nd century BC.

Figure 5 King of Cappadocia Ariobarzanes I 95-63 BC.
(CC BY- SA 3.0)

Leviathan Vs. Behemoth

Figure 6 Coin of Mithridates II of Parthia from the mint at Seleucia on the Tigris.
http://en.wikipedia.org/wiki/Mithridates_II_of_Parthia#mediaviewer/File:Coin_of_Mithridates_II_of_Parthia.jpg

The Coming Storm

Figure 7 Pompey

Figure 8 Coin of Phraates III

2

CLASH OF THE TITANS

With a lukewarm peace established between Rome and Parthia, Phraates III could now cautiously relax at his capital in Ctesiphon, but that was to change.

In 57 BCE, Orodes II and Mithridates III murdered their father Phraates.[1] The motive is unknown, but the desire for power is usually the reason. However, the sons of Phraates may have felt that their father's foreign policy in dealing with the Romans and Tigranes was weak and that a stronger leader was desired by the Parthian autocracy to safeguard the empire's security. It is true that when Parthia and Armenia made amends and noticed Rome's permanent move into the neighborhood, such that Pompey had masterfully conquered and confiscated, whether directly or indirectly, the "Colchians, Albanians, Iberians, Armenians, Medes, Arabs, Jews, and other Eastern nations," only to stop at the borders of Egypt. Pompey had built a unified wall, a Roman coalition, to buffer the Parthians. It was designed to provoke war and to procure wealth. In other words, the Roman Near East was a coercive, fortified cash cow looking to expand beyond the Iranian plateau.[2]

---

[1] Dio 39.56.
[2] Appian, *Mith.* 17.114, 118.

With Phraates died, his son Orodes II ascended the throne as the next Parthian king and installed his brother Mithridates III as king of Media. Orodes' first order of business was to marry. Orodes would marry the Greek Princess Laodice, daughter of King Antiochus I Theos of Commagene.

The kingdom of Commagene was independent and at war with Rome during the Third Mithridatic War (73–63 BCE). The Roman General Lucullus besieged the Commagene city of Samosata.[3] However, once Pompey took command of the Roman forces from Lucullus, we read that Pompey continued to war against Antiochus until he entered into friendly relations. Pompey allowed Antiochus to keep his kingdom independent of Roman rule, at least on the outside.[4]

Among the many monarchs who capitulated to Pompey, Antiochus was regarded the most important. The historian Josephus speaks of this, stating, "Of all the monarchs who owned the Roman sway, the king of Commagene enjoyed the highest prosperity."[5] Even though Josephus is not directly referring to Antiochus of First century BCE, his mentioning of the monarchy's importance tells us a great deal. The reason Antiochus would have owned the Roman sway and enjoyed the

---

[3] Pliny, *The Natural History*, 2.108.
[4] Appian, *Mith*. 16.106.
[5] Josephus, *Wars of the Jews*, 5.11.3.

highest prosperity is in large part due to its natural resources and one of its cities' strategic location.

Commagene not only controlled the crossing point of the Euphrates at Zeugma and Samosata, Commagene had fertile valleys, large iron deposits, and was one of many areas where the Hellenic, Semitic, and Iranian lands met.[1] One can understand why Rome valued Commagene, for failure to appreciate this kingdom could spell disaster. Josephus stresses the strategic importance of Commagene stating, "For Samosata, the capital of Commagene, lies upon Euphrates: and upon any such design could afford an easy passage over it to the Parthians: and could also afford them a secure reception."[2]

Antiochus made a smart political move, which saved him and his kingdom from annexation. However, even though Antiochus swore allegiance to Rome, men like the Roman politician Cicero felt that it was ostensible. Cicero was concerned that Cappadocia was wide open for a Parthian invasion on the Syrian side. The reason for concern was that Cappadocia was not fortified. Because of this, he questions the kings, including Antiochus I, over the wide-open terrain, stating, "even if they are our friends in secret, nevertheless do not venture to be openly hostile to the Parthians."[3] Cicero's concern is further backed when

---

[1] Peter Richardson, *Herod: King of the Jews and Friend of the Romans* (Columbia, S.C.: University of South Carolina Press, 1996), 83.
[2] Josephus, *Wars of the Jews*, 7.7.1.
[3] Cicero, *Letters to his Friends*, 15, 4.

Antiochus I's daughter Laodice marries King Orodes II of Parthia.[4]

The marriage was not only a dynastic union but also a carefully orchestrated political move on Antiochus' behalf. His move to allow the marriage of his daughter to Orodes showed his lack of trust towards Rome and the uncertainty that hovered over the region. Antiochus understood that if Rome was victorious over Parthia in any future wars to come, he was safe. However, if Rome lost to Parthia, he still was safe due to the marriage. Cicero was right in his concern that the kings like Antiochus were philoromanist in secret, but openly in favor of Parthia without saying a word. Orodes likely understood that the marriage to Laodice would be another thorn in Rome's side, another ally you could say, since Tigranes of Armenia also saw Rome as an unwanted guest and had found a new respect for Parthia.

ROMAN INTERVENTION

Orodes' peace with Rome was short-lived. While Orodes enjoyed the luxuries of life, he received word that the Parthian senate had expelled his brother Mithridates, whom he had made king of Media, a Parthian client state, due to his cruelty. The Roman historian Justin does not go

---

[4] Dio, 49, 23. For inscription, see Roger Beck, *Beck on Mithraism: Collected Works with New Essays* (Aldershot, Hants, England: Ashgate Pub, 2004), 299.

into detail about the reasons Mithridates was expelled, but does mention that "after his war with Armenia, he was banished from his kingdom." One could look at Justin's passage here and suggest the expulsion of Mithridates was due to attacking Armenia. However, Justin may have confused Mithridates III with Mithridates II, who did go to war with Armenia. Justin is the only one who mentions this among the many Roman historians. Justin may very well be correct that Mithridates did attack Armenia in an attempt to recover the province of Gordyene, a former province of Parthia until the rise of Tigranes. Tigranes conquered the province only to lose it to Pompey. Once peace was made between Tigranes and Pompey, Pompey gave Gordyene back to Tigranes. Mithridates crossed the line by attacking Armenia after a peace settlement between his father Phraates III and Tigranes II, which would be a clear violation and a dangerous one at best, giving Rome a reason to invade Parthia, at worst. Therefore, the likely reason for Mithridates' expulsion was due to violating the treaty, which would amount to treating your subjects poorly.[5]

When Mithridates received word that he was no longer the king of Media, he went on a rampage. Mithridates likely led his army to Ctesiphon, which was just one of the many Parthian capitals. The reason Ctesiphon should be considered is that Plutarch mentions that Orodes was driven out. Moreover, the city of Ctesiphon was close to the region of Media. After Orodes

---

[5] Justinus, *Epitome of Pompeius Trogus' "Philippic histories,"* 42.4.

had been driven out, Mithridates crossed the Tigris River and captured Seleucia.

From Seleucia, he advances to the southwest and captures Babylon. He now controls a significant amount of territory, but evidently does not have sufficient forces to protect Media and parts of Mesopotamia. Because of his lack of security, the Parthian General Surena in 55 BCE had restored Orodes to the throne by capturing Ctesiphon. From Ctesiphon he crosses the Tigris and besieges the city of Seleucia. Plutarch mentions that Surena was the first to scale the city walls and fight the defenders. Afterwards, Surena marched to Babylon and took the city. However, Mithridates was gone.[6]

Mithridates fled Media and sought political asylum in Roman Syria. The Roman governor of Syria at the time was Aulus Gabinius. Roman Syria was anything but grand. Cassius Dio mentions that Gabinius extorted wealth from the people, "inflicting far more injury upon the people than did the pirates." However, Gabinius was disappointed in the "mere trifles" that he confiscated from the citizens and desired a much richer adventure. He had already been planning to invade, with the goal of confiscating Parthian wealth, if not a portion of Parthia itself. Mithridates' plea for Roman help could not have come at a better time.

Mithridates promised Gabinius riches if he were to restore him to the throne. However, this did not go over well in Rome. As Gabinius and Mithridates crossed the

---

[6] Plutarch, *Crassus*, 21.

Euphrates,[7] Gabinius received a letter from Pompey with instructions to restore the corrupt, violent, and licentious Ptolemy XII to his throne. Ptolemy first contacted Pompey, requesting aid, but Pompey refused. Pompey suggested that he seek out Gabinius. Gabinius accepted and quickly abandoned the Parthian campaign since Ptolemy's bribe paid a portion up front and promised the rest once restored.[8] Gabinius restored Ptolemy to the throne and collected 10,000 talents,[9] besides the money he was able to extort from the locals in Syria.

However, there may be more to this. Going to war with Parthia would understandably cause quite a stir in the Roman Senate. Rome and Parthia had a treaty, but a fragile one. Gabinius did not turn his back on Mithridates due to a lack of interest; rather, Gabinius turned back because the money he was about to receive would fund a much larger army to invade Parthia, potentially obtaining the vast wealth of the region and procuring a triumph in Rome once he returned. However, that would not happen. Gabinius was tried and convicted for not seeking Senate approval, bribery, and abandoning his post in Syria for Egypt.[10]

With Mithridates left high and dry on the east side of the Euphrates, he likely was contemplating to whom he should turn. With no substantial forces to further his cause, he decided to surrender to his brother, Orodes, in 54

---

[7] Josephus, *Antiquities of the Jews*, 14.6.2.
[8] Dio 39, 12-14, 56.
[9] Cicero, *In Defense of Rabirius Postumus*, 21.
[10] Dio 39, 63.

BCE. Mithridates thought that his brother would show mercy, but he was wrong. Orodes gave the order and Mithridates was executed.[11] Orodes now could rest, knowing that his empire was safe. But even though Orodes had no more political opponents to deal with in Parthia, there were those like Gabinius, or Marcus Licinius Crassus on the outside, conspiring to get in.

BUILDUP TO WAR

In 56 BCE, Julius Caesar invited Marcus Licinius Crassus and Gnaeus Pompeius Magnus to Luca in Cisalpine Gaul (Luca is the modern day city of Lucca in Italy) in 56 BCE. Caesar requested that they meet to repair their strained relationship, which was established around 60 BCE and was kept secret from the Senate for some time.[12] During this event, a crowd of 100 or more senators showed up to petition for their sovereign patronage. The men cast lots and chose which areas to govern. Caesar got what he wanted, Gaul; Pompey obtained Spain; and Crassus received Syria.[13] All of this would become official

---

[11] Justin 42.4.
[12] Arthur Boak, *A History of Rome to 565 A. D.* 4th ed (New York: Macmillan, 1955), 169.
[13] Max Cary and Howard Hayes Scullard, *A History of Rome Down to the Reign of Constantine* (London: Macmillan, 1995), 392.

when Pompey and Crassus were elected as consuls in 55 BCE.[14]

Crassus was delighted that his lot fell on Syria. Crassus' grand strategy and desire was to make the campaigns of Lucullus against Tigranes and Pompey's against Mithridates appear mediocre. Crassus' grand strategy and desire of conquest and confiscation went beyond Parthia, beyond Bactria and India, reaching the Outer Ocean--easier envisioned than orchestrated.

Crassus' plan to war with Parthia by launching a preemptive strike caused great commotion among the senators. The Senate did not like the idea because Rome had a treaty with Parthia. However, men with power see things differently. While the Senate was against the idea, Caesar was for it. Caesar sent a letter from Gaul that encouraged Crassus to take on this project. In other words, Crassus received Caesar's blessing. Of course, Caesar would approve of such an undertaking because Crassus was not military material; he was a businessman and nothing more. Crassus may have had financial backing to raise and support an army, but he was not a military mastermind like Pompey or Caesar. Caesar would approve of such an expedition, because with Crassus dead, it would leave just two men to fight over the Republic.[15]

Crassus prepared for his departure to Parthia by making ritual sacrifices on Capitoline Hill in Rome. Of course, the entrails of the beast favored Crassus'

---

[14] Plut, *Crass*, 15.
[15] *Crass*, 16.

campaign---and why not? However, even though the entrails upon examination favored a successful campaign, there were those who did not approve of going to war, like the tribune Ateius. Ateius, along with a rather large crowd, threatened to stop Crassus from going to war with a people who had done no wrong to the Romans. Crassus, who was blocked from leaving the city, requested Pompey's aid Pompey agreed. When Pompey arrived, his face was bright, cheerful, and calm. The crowd immediately went from angry to silent. The masses stepped aside as Pompey led Crassus out of the city, but Ateius verbally attacked Crassus and stood in their way. He even called for the arrest of Crassus, whereupon an attendant seized Crassus. The tribunes would not allow it and ordered that Crassus be released. Ateius made one last protest at the city gate that the war was morally wrong. There he had set up a brazier with fuel and lighted it. As Crassus approached the gate, Ateius threw incense and libations on the brazier, calling down curses.[16] Crassus would leave on November 14, 55 BCE, never to return.[17]

It is obvious Crassus didn't care what the anti-war protesters thought or how the Parthians felt. This was typical of late republic generals. He was hell bent on making a name that would be equal to Alexander the Great at first and go beyond what Alexander had done many centuries before. But also he wanted to show Caesar and Pompey that he was no "flash in the pan" general.

---

[16] Ibid.
[17] Cicero, *Epistulae ad Atticum*, 4.13.2.

When Crassus left Rome, he made his way south to the city of Brundisium. Between Rome and Brundisium, Crassus used his wealth to recruit troops from Lucania. Most of the men recruited were not battle hardened. Crassus would eventually get his battle hardened veterans from Pompey. There is an interesting passage in Plutarch, which mentions that Crassus recruited an unknown number of Pompey's men who had served with Pompey during the 60's.

Pliny the Elder mentions that before Crassus left for Syria, it "rained iron among the Lucanians." Pliny further mentions that the "augurs warned the people against wounds that might come from above." This sounds like something that might have been a meteor shower. Whatever the case, Crassus must have been spooked just a little, for the iron that rained that day can be metaphorically applied to the future barrage of Parthian arrows raining down.[18]

Crassus arrived in Brundisium to winter storms and rough waters, far too dangerous for sailing. But he would not let bad weather hinder his ambitious plans and gave the order to set sail. Many ships were lost. He eventually made landfall and hurried his men through Galatia. Before Crassus made his way into Syria, he turned east, marched to the Euphrates River, built a bridge, and violated the border agreement by crossing over into

---

[18] Pliny, *Nat,* 2.57.

Parthian territory. The Parthians were unaware of the attack, which made the crossing easy for Crassus.[19]

Crassus' first engagement with the Parthians took place near the fortress of Ichnae. The satrap Sillaces was wounded and defeated, then retreated to inform Orodes of the Roman invasion. Crassus' preemptive strike was short-lived, resulting in widespread damage and plundering.

During the mission, many Mesopotamian cities, particularly the Greco-Macedonian ones, like the city of Nicephorium, surrendered without a fight, for they saw the Romans as friends who shared a similar culture and way of life.[20]

However, one city withstood the Roman deliverance: Zenodotia, ruled by Apollonius, a Greek-. Apollonius' small garrison killed about 100 Roman soldiers. The Romans quickly overwhelmed the defenses; the people were sold into slavery and the city was looted. After Crassus' men had totally despoiled the city, "he allowed his soldiers to salute him as 'Imperator', which was not an action that at all redounded to his credit."[21]

Crassus did not proceed any further than Zenodotia. Instead, he turned his forces back and crossed over into Roman Syria for the winter. Cassius Dio mentions that the reason Crassus decided to turn back was his "longing for the indolence of Syria." The consequences of Crassus' decision not to pursue further into Parthian

---

[19] Plut, *Crass*, 17.
[20] Dio 40.12-13.
[21] Plut, *Crass*, 17.

territory were grave. By not capitalizing on the momentum gained, the Parthians had time to muster their forces and coordinate their plan of attack.[22]

Crassus arrived in Syria with seven legions (roughly 35,000 heavy infantry) along with 4,000 lightly armed troops and 4,000 cavalry. Caesar gave Crassus an additional 1,000 Gallic cavalry under the command of Crassus' son Publius. With such forces under his, you would think Crassus would be preparing the men for war, continuing to send scouts, building upon the gathered intelligence, and taking the opportunity to make contact with potential allies, like the cities of Babylon and Seleucia, which were hostile to the Parthians. However, Crassus did none of the above, according to Plutarch. The troops did not muster; there were no athletic contests or physical training. In other words, there was no accountability taken. When troops are left to their own devices, uncertainty creeps in. With no real purpose, the men begin to lose sight of their objective. However, we have to take this with a grain of salt, for it is Plutarch who mentions that Crassus knew little when it came to military affairs. This would be a bit unfair, for even though Crassus enjoyed the luxuries of a wealthy man, we cannot forget that he did defeat Spartacus' slave rebellion, even though Pompey took credit for the victory at the very end. Even though Plutarch paints a negative picture of Crassus, it should be questioned, but not be entirely dismissed.[23]

---

[22] Dio 40. 13.
[23] Plut, *Crass*, 17.

Instead of preparing the men for battle, he went about confiscating wealth from the local Syrian cities, including temples, like the temple treasures of the goddess Atargatis in Hierapolis Bambyke,[24] or making his way further south to the province of Judea and looting the temple in Jerusalem. In Jerusalem, the priest Eleazar offered Crassus a gold beam if Crassus would refrain from taking the temple treasures. Crassus agreed, but decided to take all the gold anyway.[25] Crassus was a fully fledged kleptomaniac. Instead of using his own bankroll to fund the entire campaign, why not use the locals and their temples instead? He treated his campaign as a business venture, weighing the amount of gold and silver day and night on his scales. As they say, "War is Business." However, Crassus forgot about the war part.

Once the winter had subsided, Crassus began to mobilize his forces. While Crassus was preparing to set off for war, ambassadors from Parthia paid a visit. The ambassadors of King Orodes asked a simple question. If the Roman people sent this army then it should be a war to the bitter end. However, the ambassadors understood that the Roman public did not support this war. In a way, one could say that Parthia's military intelligence was far better than the Romans, at least in this case. They understood the difference between a nation declaring war and one man's ambition. Because of this, Orodes displayed a level of respect in his message. Orodes shows his sympathetic

---

[24] Ibid.
[25] Josephus, *War of the Jews*, 1.8.8/ *The Antiquities of the Jews*, 14.7.1.

feelings and is willing to be merciful to Crassus due to his old age. Even the men serving under Crassus were viewed as prisoners by Orodes, and because of this, Orodes was willing to let the soldiers go freely back home. Orodes' message was rather simple: leave and no blood shall be shed. Crassus listened carefully to the king's message and boastfully replied "that he would give them his answer in Seleucia." This caused the ambassadors to laugh, and the eldest ambassador, Vagises, pointed to the palm of his upturned hand and replied, "Hair will grow here, Crassus, before you set eyes on Seleucia."[26] The war was on.

MANDATORY SUICIDE

Before Crassus set off for Parthia, messengers from the Roman-occupied cities in Mesopotamia brought startling news. The Parthian forces were large, terrifying, and well-equipped to fight the Romans. The truth is, while the Parthian ambassadors negotiated with Crassus, Parthian armies were on the move. The general responsible for the devastating news brought to Crassus was none other than Surena, along with Sillaces, who were in Mesopotamia recapturing the provinces lost to Rome.

> These people are impossible to shake off if they are in pursuit, and impossible to

---

[26] Plut, *Crass*, 18.

overtake if they are in flight; they employ a new kind of missile which travels faster than sight and pierces through whatever is in the way before one can see who is discharging these weapons; and their armoured cavalry has weapons of offence which will cut through everything and defensive equipment which will stand up to any blow.[27]

Crassus likely found these reports to be exaggerated. However, the soldiers thought otherwise. The news was depressing and one can see why.

    The soldiers who found the news disheartening were likely those who had never seen combat. These men thought that the Parthians were no different from the Armenians or Cappadocians that Lucullus and Pompey engaged a decade earlier. However, the veterans, those who served under Pompey, likely understood what they were about to face. But even veterans get nervous; they just go about it more professionally. The same goes for officers, but even they showed signs of uncertainty, like Gaius Cassius Longinus, the quaestor, who advised Crassus that it might be smart not to advance and to rethink the whole operation. Crassus would not hear of it. Even the professional prophet's forecast of doom and

---

[27] Ibid.

gloom did not move Crassus to reconsider. Crassus was hell bent and pressed forward.[28]

While Surena was campaigning in Mesopotamia, Orodes was moving towards the Armenian border. Orodes strategy was defensive. Orodes figured that if Crassus were to make his way into Parthia, he would use his ally, Armenia. King Artavasdes II of Armenia offered Crassus safe passage through his country with supplies and provided 10,000 armored cavalry, including the king's personal guard of 6,000 cavalry along with an additional 30,000 infantry, all paid for by the king. Artavasdes' offer to Crassus was great, but also strategic. Artavasdes understood that if Crassus' army were to pass through Armenia, it would give the Romans and the supporting Armenian troops the upper hand since the cavalry-based forces would be somewhat immobile in the mountainous areas. By avoiding the open plains below, the Parthians would be at odds and effectively hamstrung from using their full potential power during engagement. However, Orodes understood this and during his march towards the Armenian border, took mainly infantry with him.[29]

One could look at this and notice that if Crassus did go through Armenia, with the additional Armenian support, the Romans combined with their allied support would total around 88,000 men. This complex force, which had both substantial elements of heavy and light infantry and cavalry, would have been a strong weapons system to

---

[28] Ibid.
[29] Plut, *Crass* 19.

contend with. To think Orodes did not realize this is in error. It is quite obvious by now that Orodes knew what was going on in Rome before Crassus even knew that they knew of his intentions. Furthermore, Orodes was not blind to the presence of the Armenians. He likely knew their strengths and weaknesses and understood what he could and could not do. So, why would Orodes wait for the enemy forces to pour down from the Armenian mountains into Parthia if he did not have a fighting chance? The answer involves Surena and the open plain. Orodes, a very smart strategist and tactician, understood that if Rome had a chance, it would be through Armenia. Once the Roman forces were located, fixed, and engaged on the open plain, it would allow Surena to maneuver around the enemy and attack from behind with his cavalry forces. This was a classic tactic used by many, made popular by Alexander the Great, and was known as "The Hammer and Anvil tactic." However, Orodes' seemingly well-planned coordinated defense measure would not take place. Instead, Crassus, being the business tactician he is, decided to gamble even when the chips were stacked in his favor.

To Orodes' surprise, Crassus turned down the Armenian king's generous offer of safe passage and assistance along the way. Crassus made the decision to march along the Euphrates River. His reason was to reach the "many brave Roman soldiers." Either the intelligence reports Crassus received indicated that some cities were still under Roman control, or he really did not know and felt that the reports that came in from those cities being attacked by the Parthians before he left were mere exaggerations.[30] Either or, Crassus' move exposed his army to immense danger. As for Orodes, who likely was astonished that Crassus did not take King Artavasdes' safe passage and assistance offer, decided to go on the offensive and invade Armenia, leaving Surena to confront Crassus.[31]

Before we go any further, it is necessary that we know who Surena was. According to Plutarch, Surena was "an extremely distinguished man. In wealth, birth, and in the honor paid to him, he ranked next after the king; in courage and ability he was the foremost Parthian of his time; and in stature and personal beauty he had no equal." Plutarch further adds that Surena was "always accompanied by a baggage train of 1,000 camels; 200 wagons carried his harem; 1,000 armored cavalry and still more light armed cavalry acted as his escort." In total, he had 10,000 at his side.[32]

The first point to make is that the name Surena is not his real name. His real name is unknown. Plutarch called him Surena because the Parthian general was of the House of Suren. The House of Suren was located in Sistan. Sistan, or Sakastan, "land of the Sakas," located in what is today southeast Iran bordering the modern-day countries of Afghanistan and Pakistan. Besides being a ruling house in the region, the House of Suren also "struck silver

---

[30] Ibid., 19.
[31] Ibid., 21.
[32] Ibid.

drachms in the Parthian fashion, with the portrait of the king wearing a bejeweled headdress on the obverse and an enthroned ruler on the reverse."[33] This indicates that Surena's family was in the monetary business; and, since they struck coins for the Parthian king, suggests that they had considerable financial control over the empire. In other words, the power of the purse lay with the House of Suren, granting them "the ancient privilege of his family, the right to be the first to set the crown on the head of a King of Parthia at the coronation." This ancient privilege goes back to the 3rd century BC.[34]

As Crassus' army crossed the Euphrates at Zeugma, a storm of great magnitude fell upon them with thunder, lighting, and hurricane force winds. The storm, possibly a sandstorm, made the task of crossing the river daunting. Even the place where Crassus decided to bivouac was smitten by two thunderbolts. This was an obvious sign to the Romans that the campaign was cursed. If that was not enough, the *aquila*, or eagle standard, which was routinely planted in the ground when the army stopped to encamp, had rooted itself so firmly that it would take several men to pull it from the ground. When the Romans moved out, the standard was hoisted, and supposedly it turned about on its own. Once the men settled in, regrouping their thoughts, rations were given out. However, the soldiers were rationed lentils and salt,

---

[33] Vesta Sarkhosh Curtis and Sarah Stewart, *The Age of the Parthians* (London: I.B. Tauris, 2007), 4.
[34] Ibid.

which are a sign of mourning or an offering to the dead. And, to top it all off, Crassus made an ill-fated statement, "I propose to break down the bridge, so that not a single one of you can get back." The men closest to Crassus likely gave him a look of disbelief, and, as the message made its way through the ranks, many were likely distraught by the news of this mandatory suicide. Crassus sure knew how to win his men over, especially during a sacrifice to purify the army. When the seer handed Crassus the entrails, he let them fall out of his hands and hit the ground. His soldiers, once again, were likely in shock and disbelief. Crassus looked to his men and said: "This is what comes of being old. But I can hold on to my sword tightly enough."[35]

After all the spectacles and natural anomalies had taken place, Crassus set off down the Euphrates. As the Romans pressed forward, the usual task was to send scouts ahead of the main body to collect intelligence, maybe even get a glimpse of the enemy scouts and so forth. The scouts would come back with nothing new to offer, other than the path is clear, no sign of danger. However, that was about to change. A report came to Crassus that horse tracks--a great many of them–had been discovered. Crassus was delighted by the news, because to the Romans, it only proved that the enemy will not engage them directly, that the enemy is afraid of the Romans, that the fight will be just as easy as it was for Lucullus and Pompey during the Mithridatic Wars.[36]

---

[35] Plut, *Crass* 19.
[36] Ibid., 20.

But Cassius, who at times was the voice of reason, spoke to Crassus, suggesting that maybe the army should have some time to rest in one of the Roman cities. Cassius understood that it was too quiet. Therefore, they should move to a better location and continue to gather intelligence. If Crassus did not like this option, the next best thing would be to advance to the city of Seleucia, keeping close to the Euphrates in order to receive fresh supplies along the way, and if the Parthians did engage them, they would not be surrounded. In this way, the Parthians would have to fight an upfront battle, making them equal with the Romans. Cassius' advice is good, they should stay close to the river and continue to make their way to Seleucia, if they are not going to make a pit stop at any of the Roman-occupied cities. Now, while his strategy was smart in keeping near the river, his ignorance of the enemy shows. Cassius, like Crassus, and many of his men, assume the Parthians are like any other barbarian Rome had defeated in the past. While Cassius wishes to play it safe, gathering intelligence and keeping to the river, Crassus "throws caution to the wind." So much for trying to reach those "many brave Roman soldiers."[37]

As Crassus was being advised, another man appears, Ariamnes. Plutarch does not speak highly of this man. Instead, he refers to him as a "sly treacherous character." Not much is known about this Arab chieftain other then what Plutarch mentions.[38] However, the

---

[37] Ibid.
[38] Ibid., 21.

historian Cassius Dio calls him by the name of Abgarus, and instead of being an Arab chieftain, he is from the Kingdom of Osrhoene, which was located in northern Mesopotamia, bordering Roman Syria, and was under the suzerainty of both Rome and Parthia during their turbulent times.[39] To avoid confusion, we will call him Ariamnes, since Plutarch's source is much older.

What is known is that Ariamnes had been around the Romans for quite some time, that he benefited from Pompey's kindness, and that Roman soldiers who once served under Pompey, now under the command of Crassus, seemed to trust him. In other words, there is nothing to worry about, because Ariamnes is pro-Roman. What makes him suspect is that he was able to persuade Crassus not to play it safe but to continue to move down the Euphrates River and making an unthinkable beeline across Mesopotamia to attack the enemy, who was supposedly disorganized due to the disappearance of the king. By moving his army away from the Euphrates, Crassus effectively severed his line of supply and communication, and soon would realize that the enemy was anything but disorganized. Crassus' decision exposed his forces to the vultures.[40]

---

[39] Dio 40: 20.
[40] Plut, *Crass* 21.

A DESERT FUNERAL PROCESSION

By taking Ariamnes' advice, Crassus led the Romans into a desert abyss. At first the route taken went well. But as the Romans marched on, the land slowly changed from being easily traversed to trudging your way through ankle-deep sand. It was a level plain with not a living thing or water to be found there. It was a sea of seemingly endless sand. With the mind trying to comprehend this wasteland that surrounded them, the heat beating down on their armor did not let up, nor did their quick pace in order to keep up with Crassus help.[41]

As the Roman army quickly marched on, some within the ranks believed that they had been tricked into going into the desert, but before tempers and finger pointing flared, startling news came to Crassus that King Orodes had invaded Armenia and that King Artavasdes needed his immediate help. Artavasdes advised Crassus that the best solution would be for Crassus to come to Armenia and help defeat Orodes. If Crassus could not aid him, Artavasdes advised Crassus to stay near the mountains to avoid the cavalry. Crassus could either turn around and aid Artavasdes in the fight, or head north towards the mountain ranges and play it safe. Crassus chooses neither option. Crassus becomes angry, refuses to send a reply, and makes it clear to the Armenian messengers that he has no time to help them. He informs that "he would come there and make Artavasdes pay for

---

[41] Ibid., 22-23.

his treachery." Artavasdes message was clear; the Parthians were not disorganized and fleeing for the hills as Ariamnes would have Crassus believe. Crassus seems not to grasp this, but Cassius does.[42]

Cassius, the voice of reason, was not impressed with and "strongly disapproved" of Crassus' harsh words, which evoke war. Armenia was an ally to Rome, and to make such a bold statement threatened the stability of the region, which could in turn cause the Armenians to side with the Parthians. Cassius likely tried in vain to get Crassus to choose one of the two options, but Cassius' words only annoyed Crassus.

Cassius quickly rode off looking for Ariamnes and when he confronted him, he gave Ariamnes a few choice words. "What evil spirit brought you to us, you villain? What drugs and sorceries have you been using to persuade Crassus to pour his army into a great yawning wilderness and to follow a route that is better fitted for a captain of Arabian robbers than for a Roman imperator?" One can understand Cassius' concern. The march is insane and could have been avoided. Many men are suffering due to Ariamnes' advice.[43]

With every quick step in the exhausting heat, their 60 pounds of armor, along with the weight of their weapons and camping equipment, became heavier.[44] Even though Plutarch does not mention any heat-related

---

[42] Ibid., 22.
[43] Ibid.
[44] Vic Hurley, *Arrows against Steel: The History of the Bow and How It Forever Changed Warfare* (Salem, Oregon: Cerberus Books, 2011), 97.

illnesses directly, it can be suggested that this did occur. Plutarch mentions that during the march, some of the standard bearers were unable to hoist the standard because of the weight, which caused them to be "fixed like monuments into the earth." It sounds like heat exhaustion and cramps had already set in, causing muscle fatigue. However, it was not just the standard bearers that suffered from the heat.

Plutarch mentions that Ariamnes rode up and down the Roman lines and "managed the Romans as if they were children." Not only that, he would also help some of them with their tasks. He also mocked the soldiers saying, "Do you think that you are marching through Campania?" He would also tease them about their thirst, saying, "Are you longing for the fountains and streams there, and the shady places, yes, and the baths and the taverns?" Ariamnes' mockery is a clear indication that the Roman army was out of its element, and if the Parthians did not defeat them first, Crassus' impatience, along with the harsh desert sands of Mesopotamia, would. As time pressed on, so did Ariamnes, as he would soon disappear before his ruse was exposed.[45]

---

[45] Plut, *Crass* 22.

THE BATTLE OF CARRHAE

What made matters worse during the march was that Crassus was not wearing the purple robe that Roman generals normally wear. Instead, he wore a black robe, as if he was leading a funeral procession. He quickly changed his robe after he realized the color problem. He should have stayed with the black robe, because as Crassus pressed on, pushing his men harder, the cavalry scouts that were sent ahead came back in fewer numbers. Surena, the Parthian general, had set up an ambush, killing many of the scouts. One could argue that Surena's ambush was intended for the main Roman force and not the scouts. However, the ambush was his calling card, indicating that the ground the Romans were advancing on was the preferred battleground. But this tells us something else: that Surena was able to spread disinformation via Ariamnes. Remember, it was Ariamnes who told Crassus that it was best to avoid Seleucia and head straight into Parthia, because the Parthians had not fully mobilized. Take advantage quickly, because only an advance guard waits and has been placed to check your movements under the command of Surena.[46]

However, that was not the case. As the Roman scouts ventured farther ahead of the main body, they soon found themselves in a trap. The few scouts that made it back reported that the enemy was great in number and full

---

[46] Ibid., 23.

of confidence. Ariamnes' lie seems to have gone unnoticed by Crassus, who was excited and soon became impatient, making inconsistent decisions. Crassus was obviously overwhelmed by the situation until Cassius gave him some advice, which for once did not annoy to Crassus. Cassius suggested that they should form the men into one long line with little depth and that the cavalry should be divided between the two wings. Cassius' plan seemed like the right strategy to choose. However, Crassus decided that it would be best to form the men into one huge hollow square with 12 cohorts on each side and a cavalry detachment next to each cohort. By choosing the hollow square strategy, Crassus felt that it would ensure equal balance for protection. In other words, they could avoid being flanked by the enemy, although they would sacrifice mobility. Cassius would take command of one of the wings, Publius, Crassus' son would command the other wing, and Crassus would command from the middle of the square. They would move forward in this formation until they came to the Balissus stream.[47]

    The men were hot, hungry, thirsty, weak, and weary, and they looked upon the stream as a blessing. The officers advised Crassus it was best to stay next to the stream, set up camp, and allow the men to rest while a new scouting party was formed and sent out to gather intelligence on the Parthian order of battle. Unfortunately for the men, Crassus could not make a sound decision. He agreed that the men should eat and drink, but only

---

[47] Ibid.

standing up and staying in formation. But then Crassus changed his mind, yes, the men can eat and drink, so long as they march. However, Crassus gave a new order: move out. Many of the men likely ate and drank on the move, but many likely could not, because Crassus kept the men at a quick pace to keep up with the cavalry. Crassus did this because his son Publius was eager to press on and engage the enemy.[48]

As Crassus pushed on, the enemy slowly came into sight. Crassus gave the order to halt, and to their eyes the enemy were "neither so numerous nor so splendidly armed as they had expected." However, looks can be deceiving. What Crassus and his army saw was the front rank of just 1,000 cavalry who were covered in skins and coats. Surena's main force was hidden behind the front ranks. While the Romans watched in curiosity, Surena gave the order and a thundering sound proceeded forth from the Parthian cavalry. Many unseen drums covered in stretched animal hide with brass bells attached to the drums roared across the field, vibrating Roman armor as well as their hearts. The use of sound as a psychological weapon before battle manipulated human behavior in both Roman and Parthian armies, affecting all senses. In other words, the home team is pumped up while the away team is losing confidence quickly.[49]

Plutarch mentions that, "before the Romans had recovered from their consternation at this din, the enemy

---

[48] Ibid.
[49] Ibid.

suddenly dropped the coverings of their armour." Once the drums were silent, the Roman army, discombobulated by the intense sound of the drums, besides being physically weak, was in for another surprise. The Parthian heavy cavalry, otherwise known as the cataphract, was charging towards them, with Surena leading the way. As the cataphract thundered across the plain, their coverings dropped from their armor revealing "helmets and breastplates blazing like fire, their Margianian steel glittering keen and bright, their horses armored with plates of bronze and steel."

The Parthian cataphract was the main and most important military force. These mailed cavalrymen were the aristocracy, who could afford the expensive armor. In return for their service, they demanded a greater degree of autonomy from the Parthian king at the local level, thus ensuring a king (sub-king) of their own to governor their territory.[50]

A description of the Parthian cataphract is of interest, particularly the term Plutarch uses to describe their steel in which he refers to it as "Margianian steel."[51] Margianian steel that the Parthians use to produce armor comes from a Parthian province known as Margiana. It was located primarily in what is today Turkmenistan, with portions of this ancient province extending into northern Afghanistan and southern Uzbekistan. It was here in

---

[50] Maria Brosius *The Persians: An Introduction* (London: Routledge, 2006), 116.
[51] Plut, *Crass* 24.

Margiana, rich in metal resources, that the iron ore was mined, and possibly refined not far from the mining site and formed into metal goods, like weapons and armor. Plutarch also mentions that the Parthian heavy cavalry wore bronze plates, if not steel. Tin and copper also were mined in Margiana and likely refined in the province to produce bronze goods.[52] On the surface, Plutarch's passage reads as if the Parthian heavy cavalry wore only plate armor. However, Plutarch later mentions that they used "tough breastplates of raw hide."[53]

Plutarch does not go into great detail concerning their armor design, but does give clues as to how it looked and the material used. However, Justin explains the design of Parthian cataphract armor in one short sentence in which he states, "Their armour, and that of their horses, is formed of plates, lapping over one another like the feathers of a bird, and covers both man and horse entirely."[54] Plutarch mentions the use of "raw hide,"[55] which indicates that they covered the leather with overlapping plates of iron and bronze which were held together by stitching or gluing. As for the arms and legs of the heavy cavalryman, Kaveh Farrokh mentions the possibility of tubular ring-armor to protect arms and legs

---

[52] Christoph Baumer, *The History of Central Asia: The Age of the Steppe Warriors* (London: I.B. Tauris, 2012), 104-106.
[53] Plut, *Crass* 25.
[54] Justin 41.2.
[55] Plut, *Crass* 25.

of the rider. The total weight of the armor may have been around 125lb/57kg.[56]

The helmet the Parthian cataphract wore was steel. Professor Litvinsky mentions that the helmet wore by the Parthian cataphract was a "bowl-shaped helmet with corrugated visor, high crest, and moveable cheekpieces."[57] The weapons carried by the cataphract were the mace, axe, dagger, and long sword.[58] However, these would have been secondary weapons as their primary weapon was the pike/lance[59] and composite bow.[60]

The Romans, who never had seen well-armored cavalrymen, were likely in awe, while the veterans who served under Lucullus or Pompey had encountered this type of cavalry during the Mithridatic Wars. As the cataphract closed in, the legionaries locked shields to create a continuous wall. Surena quickly noticed that the Roman line was steady and firm and they were not going to budge. Surena quickly broke off the charge giving the impression that they lacked confidence in engaging the Romans in a full frontal assault. However, this was just a ruse.

What the Romans see is Surena retreating, giving the false notion that the cataphract is unable to make a

---

[56] Farrokh, 132.
[57] B. A. Litvinsky, "HELMET i. In Pre-Islamic Iran," Encyclopædia Iranica, Vol. XII, Fasc. 2, pp. 176-180; available online at http://www.iranicaonline.org/articles/helmet-i (accessed online at 21 June 2013).
[58] Farrokh, 132.
[59] Plut, *Crass* 25.
[60] Ibid., 30.

difference and therefore lacks confidence. Unseen are 10,000 Parthian horse archers, who quickly surround the Romans, firing on them from all sides. Crassus likely was stunned. He quickly assesses the situation, seeing that his forces are bogged down by unarmored petty horse archers, who were vulnerable to missile attack, and orders his light infantry to engage them. As the light infantry left the safety of the hollow square to engage the enemy, they were quickly showered with arrows as the Parthian horse archers galloped away, causing the light infantry to quickly pull back, crashing through the Roman lines seeking safety. The sight, speed, and agility of the Parthian horse archers spooked the Romans. But what really terrified them was the Parthians' primary weapon, the composite bow.

The bow used by Parthians and their Scythian kin was no ordinary composite bow. It was small, compared with later bows used on the steppe,[61] made of horn or wood,[62] and was strung with animal tendon or horsehair.[63] Horsehair may have been the Parthians' preferred material for stringing the bow, like that of their kin, the Scythians. Horsehair is better than animal tendon strings, which tend

---

[61] Erik Hildinger, *Warriors of the Steppe: A Military History of Central Asia, 500 B.C. to A.D. 1700* (New York and Washington D.C.: Da Capo Press, 2001), 36.
[62] Mark Healy and Angus McBride, *The Ancient Assyrians*, (Oxford: Osprey Publishing, 2000), 11.
[63] Bhupinder Singh Mahal, *Punjab: The Nomads and The Mavericks* (New Delhi: Sunbun Publishers, 2000), 30.

to stretch if they absorb moisture in colder climates.[64] Stringing the bow was a difficult process. In order to string the bow, a Parthian, like a Scythian archer, must utilize both legs and arms.

The limbs of the bow curved outward from the handle grip resembling a "Cupid's bow."[65] Strabo compares the bow's shape to the Black Sea.[66] The tips of bow lacked ears, giving it more flexibility.[67] The length of the Scythian bow is approximately 80 cm (2.6 feet) in length,[68] while other bows found in burial mounds at Pazyryk, Russia, measured 127 centimeters (4.2 feet).[69] Overall, the Scythian double-curved composite bow is small, stiff, hardy, and powerful. But how far could the bow deliver an arrow?

As the Parthian horse archers spread out at Carrhae, attempting to attack the Romans from all sides, they had to be effective in killing or wounding the Romans at a distance of 160 yards; however to be lethal, he had to be at least 160 feet to 200 feet away. In addition, like the Scythians, the Parthians likely carried anywhere between 30, 150,[70] and some estimates say up to 200[71] arrows in

---

[64] Antony Karasulas, *Mounted Archers of the Steppe 600 BC-AD 1300* (Oxford: Osprey Publishing, 2004), 21.
[65] Hildinger, 36.
[66] Ellis H. Minns, *Scythians and Greeks* (New York: Biblo and Tannen, 1971), 66.
[67] Hildinger, 36.
[68] Cernenko and McBride, 11.
[69] Heidi Knecht, *Projectile Technology* (New York: Springer, 1997), 153.
[70] Ibid.

their quivers. When engaged in combat, the archer could release up to 12 arrows a minute,[72] while others suggest 20 arrows a minute,[73] but of course, this would depend on the nature of the battle.

The reason for the high rate of death inflicted upon the Romans was that not only did the hollow square protect them on all sides from frontal assaults or being flanked, it also made them an easy target due to being so densely crowded in together. It would have been impossible for a Parthian horse archer to miss. The Parthians, like the Scythians, were not necessarily looking for one shot, one kill. I am sure they would take advantage if the opportunity had presented itself. The Parthian horse archers at Carrhae likely positioned their bows at a 45-degree angle. From this angle, they could shower the enemy with arrows, to kill if possible, but mutilation would be the main objective from such a distance. Arrows from this distance would fall erratically on top of the enemy. Due to the distance of the shot, the intention would be to demoralize the enemy in hope that the enemy forces would withdraw. If the enemy withdrew, the Parthians, like the Scythian horse archers, could begin to pick apart

---

[71] James R. Ashley, *The Macedonian Empire: The Era of Warfare Under Philip II and Alexander the Great, 359-323 B.C.* (Jefferson, N.C.: Mcfarland & Company, 2004), 66.
[72] Karasulas, 23.
[73] Adrienne Mayor, *Greek Fire, Poison Arrows & Scorpion Bombs* (Woodstock, New York: Overlook Duckworth, 2003), 85-86.

their enemy with individual kills, or they could leave him alone entirely to retreat.[74]

Dr. Kaveh Farrokh suggests that the average Parthian horse archer, with a quiver of 30 arrows, loosed between 8-10 arrows a minute at Carrhae. It would take 2-3 minutes to exhaust his arsenal before needing resupplied. The amount of Parthian horse archers at the battle is estimated at 10,000. Now, if all 10,000 fired away for 20 minutes, the amount of arrows fired by an individual horse archer would have been between 160-200 arrows. Take 10,000 and the amount of arrows fired upon the Roman soldiers are estimated to have been an astounding 1.6-2 million arrows in a 20-minute timeframe.[75]

The Romans soon realized that they could do nothing to alleviate the situation. If they stayed in their rank and file they would be wounded or killed. But if they made an attempt to counter the horse archers they would suffer the same fate. Any attempt to chase after them resulted in the horse archers retreating at a full gallop, and in doing so, they would turn around to shoot at the pursuing enemy. This is where we get the term "Parthian Shot." The Parthians were literally shooting fish in a barrel.

Moreover, the Parthians were exploiting the Roman way of warfare. For the Romans to see the enemy retreat was a sign of defeat. Therefore, the Romans felt that

---

[74] Karasulas, 23.
[75] Farrokh, 133.

they now had the advantage over their nemesis and pursued them. However, they soon realized and learned from this mistake that the enemy fought by an entirely different method. The Romans could do nothing as death from above poured down on them.[76]

Crassus' only hope was that as long as they stood still in their square, the Parthians would soon run out of arrows. Once that happened, Crassus felt that the Parthians would have no choice but to engage the Romans at close quarters. However, that would not be the case. To the astonishment of the Romans, a Parthian camel train was standing by with fresh arrows. Surena proved adept at organization and logistics by using trains of camels to keep his horse archers constantly supplied, keeping continual pressure upon the Romans.[77] This is contrary to Cassius Dio's claim that the Parthians "do not lay in supplies of food or pay." Cassius Dio may have felt that since the Parthians were not good at sieges, it must be due to issues of supply.[78]

Crassus' confidence was deteriorating quickly. He sent a message to his son Publius to join the battle by taking 1,300 cavalry, 500 archers, and eight cohorts from the infantry. Crassus' hope was to draw some of the Parthians away from the square as they were attempting to encircle the Romans. However, two reasons are given for the Parthians to attempt this. The first was to envelop the

---

[76] Plut, *Crass* 24.
[77] Ibid., 25.
[78] Dio 40:15.

Romans completely, that in due time the legions would crowd closer as their numbers dwindled. However, Plutarch mentions that the Parthians had trouble enveloping the Roman rear due to the marshy terrain that made it difficult for the horses to maneuver. The second reason Plutarch gives seems more plausible, and that was to leave a window open just big enough to make the Romans think that they had found an advantage. Deceiving the Romans into thinking that they cannot surround them, Crassus' son Publius takes the bait and charges ahead. However, it was an old steppe trick. Thinking they were retreating, Publius shouted excitedly, "'They are on the run,' and charged after them." The faked retreat worked, Publius was on the move; and the Parthians, stationed farther ahead and well hidden, were awaiting his arrival.[79]

    Publius and the men were full of joy, thinking that they now had the advantage and victory was surely close at hand. But moving farther away from the main body, they soon realized the pursuit was nothing more than a trick when the horse archers wheeled around and were joined by fresh troops. Publius ordered the men to halt as the Parthian cataphract was stationed in front of him. He hoped that they would engage them in close combat. Instead, the horse archers in loose order rode around the Romans, kicking up so much sand that a mini-sandstorm fell on top of the Romans and it became nearly impossible to see the enemy. By using nature as a weapon to disguise

---

[79] Plut, *Crass* 25.

their movements, the horse archers were able to engage the Romans safely. Using nature as a force multiplier gave them the advantage of fighting uninhibitedly. Publius and his men could not see or breathe very well, inciting fear, which soon led to panic. The Romans in their disarray tripped, stumbled, and fell in each other's way. The Parthian horse archers quickly took advantage and the arrow shower began. Publius did what any commander in the field would do and that was to reestablish order among the men. However, it was too late.

> In the convulsion and agony of their pain they would writhe as the arrows struck them; they would break them off in their wounds and then lacerate and disfigure their own bodies by trying to tear out by main force the barbed arrow heads that had pierced through their veins and muscles.[80]

Many of the men would die a slow, agonizing death in this fashion. Publius needed to act quickly. The Romans could not engage the horse archers in close combat while the Parthian chain of command, the cataphract, was nearby. If the Romans could make a break for the cataphract and engage them in close combat, they might have a chance to turn the tide of battle, especially if they could reach the Parthian commander, Surena, and kill him.

---

[80] Ibid.

Publius gives the order to attack the cataphract, but reality sets in. The Roman infantrymen who heard Publius showed him that they were unable to go on any further, for their "hands pinioned to their shields, feet nailed through into the ground, so that they were incapable of either running away or defending themselves." Publius was so in touch with the battle that he was out of touch with his men. Publius likely had a limp, unfocused gaze, when confronted by those who were literally pinned to their equipment and ground. He soon realized the carnage that had been inflicted upon his men. Once Publius assessed the situation, he gathered what remained of his Gallic cavalry and charged toward the cataphract.[81]

Publius' Gallic cavalry was light, wore little armor, and carried small light spears. You would think Publius would have known better than to charge toward cavalrymen who were better armored than his. They would soon realize this as their light spears broke against the breastplate of the cataphract. The Gallic cavalry was no match for the cataphract, which would thrust their long pikes into the horses or riders. In order to overcome, or at least have a fighting chance, the Gallic cavalryman, if the opportunity presented itself, would grab the pike of the cataphract and hope to use his own weight against him by pulling him off his horse. Many of the cataphract were smart enough to know that being weighted down made you clumsy and moving was cumbersome. If there was any fighting chance, it was best on foot or in this case, on

---

[81] Ibid.

his back or knees, as he would get underneath the Gallic cavalryman's horse and thrust his sword into the animal's belly. This would cause the horse to rear up, throwing the rider off, and trampling whoever was underneath or nearby before collapsing. Perhaps even some cataphract died in this fashion. With so many Gallic cavalry now dead, the only option for the Romans was to retreat. What was left of the Gallic cavalry pulled back, taking a badly wounded Publius and what remained of the infantry to higher ground. This would also prove to be a mistake.[82]

Publius and his men retreated to a nearby sandy hill. However, the sandy hill provided little protection. As the Roman infantry was placed in the front, those behind the infantry stuck out like a sore thumb due to the elevation. The horse archers once again pelted the Romans relentlessly with arrows. The Romans could do little more than watch their troops fall.

As the situation quickly deteriorated, two Greeks from the nearby town of Carrhae, Hieronymus and Nicomachus, offered to help Publius escape to a nearby town, Ichnae, friendly to Rome. Publius refused the offer since so many men were either dead or dying on his account. Like a Roman commander, he attempted to take his own life, but was unable since an arrow had pierced his hand. Thus, he ordered his shield bearer to run him through with his gladius.[83]

---

[82] Ibid.
[83] Ibid.

The Parthians eventually made it up the hill after the horse archers had softened the Romans a bit more. Once on the hill, the Parthian cataphract would charge through the Romans, breaking their bodies and spirits. The remaining Romans surrendered; about 500 were taken prisoner. As for the body of Publius, the Parthians took the body and severed his head.[84]

When Publius had gone charging off after the Parthian horse archers in an attempt to give the Roman army some breathing room and time to assess the situation, the Parthians had slacked off from attacking the main body. The reason, of course, was that Publius was a high profile target with little protection. Surena understood that if he could get Publius as far away as possible from the main Roman body, he could fix, engage, and defeat the target, which would send shockwaves throughout the Roman army. Surena was correct in his judgment.

As Crassus waited for his son Publius to return back from the pursuit, he began to gain confidence that his son was doing all right. Crassus placed his men in regular order and moved them to sloping ground. During Publius' engagement, he attempted to send messages to Crassus. The first never made it through, as the messenger was killed, but other messages indicating that Publius needed his help immediately made it through to Crassus. Crassus' hopes that his son was doing well all came crashing down when his son needed him. It was at this point that Crassus

---

[84] Ibid.

was unable to make a clear judgment on what to do: Either he assist his son or stay put. On top of that, he began to lose confidence and feared the worst possible outcome for his army. As Crassus was going through a tug of war in his head, he finally made the decision to move the Roman army in attempt to help Publius; Crassus did not know that his son, Publius, was already dead.[85]

Just as Crassus' army moved forward, the Parthians swooped in again, beating their drums and shouting aloud, but with even greater ferocity than before. As the Roman army prepared for the second wave of attack, some of the Parthian cavalry approached the Roman line. One of the cataphract had a nasty surprise for Crassus; it was the head of Publius on the tip of a spear. But before the battle was to commence again, the cataphract had a message for Crassus saying, "it was impossible, they said, that such a brave and gallant solder could be the son of such a miserable coward as Crassus." If the Roman army had any confidence left in them, that very moment sucked the life's blood out of them.

Crassus, who suffered the most from this tragedy rode up and down the ranks, shouting, "this grief is a private thing of my own. But in you, who are safe and sound, abide the great fortune and the glory of Rome. And now, if you feel any pity for me, who have lost the best son that any father has ever had, show it in the fury with which you face the enemy." Crassus' encouraging speech to fight on and think of their ancestors who fought hard

---

[85] Ibid., 26.

battles did little to lift up the men's spirits, for Plutarch mentions that "while he was speaking these words of encouragement, Crassus could see how few there were who were listening to him with enthusiasm." When Crassus wanted to hear the war cry of his men, it was a "weak, feeble, and unsteady shout." The battle was lost.[86]

As soon as Crassus was done preparing the men for the second wave of battle, the Parthians quickly got to work by surrounding the Romans and showering them with arrows. As the horse archers began to pelt the enemy to death, Surena decided to up the carnage by unleashing the cataphract. The strategy was simple. With Roman confidence withering away, the cataphract would have a much greater chance of driving the Roman infantry closer together and into each other's way. The strategy paid off! With each charge, the cataphract was successful in penetrating the Roman lines and quickly breaking from engagement, which allowed the horse archers to concentrate their arrows on a compacted target.

The Romans were losing men quickly during this second wave of attack as the arrows continually rained down and the cataphract kept crushing and driving back the troops. Crassus had no choice but to retreat; but to do so in the daylight was far more risky, and the night could not come soon enough.[87]

---

[86] Ibid.
[87] Ibid., 27.

INTO THE DARKNESS

As the sun set, the Parthians withdrew from the battle. The Romans could now try to gather their senses and make plans on what to do next. It was during this time that the Parthians sent a messenger informing them that they would give Crassus some space to mourn the loss of his son, but also advised Crassus that it would be best if he go to Orodes unless he desired to meet him dead. Crassus did neither; instead, he was found lying down in the dark with his face covered. The remaining Romans were in a similar state of mind. Not a finger was lifted to help the wounded or bury the dead. As Crassus lay in silent anguish, an officer by the name of Octavius tried to motivate Crassus to get up and take charge of situation. Crassus would not budge, nor did he show signs of concern. Therefore, the Roman officers got together and made the decision to move out. The Romans packed their camp and moved out, leaving behind the maimed and the dead to be picked clean by the vultures. Absolute panic erupted in the camp as those unable to move shouted to their compatriots for help. Some Roman soldiers did help the injured, but many feared for their lives and noisily drowned out the request. As the Roman army moved forward they would alter their course, likely zigzagging at times to throw off the Parthians if they intended to attack during the night march. The march was anything but fluid; rather it was slow and cumbersome, as those who had been wounded slowed down the Romans' progress toward temporary safety. Some men, like Ignatius and his 300 cavalrymen, quickly moved ahead of the main body, and in doing so reached the city of Carrhae around midnight. Once Ignatius was outside the walls, he yelled to the sentinels on the walls in Latin. He informed the sentinels to tell their commander Coponius that there had been a "great battle between Crassus and the Parthians." Afterward, Ignatius moved to the safety of Zeugma, leaving the main body behind and establishing a bad name for deserting Crassus. Coponius was suspicious of the news. Ignatius never gave his name or any detail as to what had happened, just saying that there was a "great battle between Crassus and the Parthians" and riding off in haste. Coponius ordered that his men immediately arm themselves and soon learned that Crassus was on his way. Coponius quickly went out to relieve Crassus and escort the Roman army into the city.[88]

    The Parthians were not ignorant of the situation. They knew that the Romans had fled, but nothing more at the moment. Once dawn broke, the Parthians mustered their forces and moved out to the battle site, where they saw only the dead and wounded. Those who were still alive, 4,000 in total, were killed. Afterwards, the Parthians pushed on, searching for stragglers, and soon found some. Vargontinus, the legate, along with four cohorts, had lost their way during the night and became separated from the main force. Once the Parthians were in sight, the Romans quickly found a small hill where they could make a stand,

---

[88] Ibid.

but they were slaughtered. Only 20 men survived the battle and were allowed to leave for Carrhae, due to their courage.[89]

It was during this day that Surena received a report that Crassus bypassed Carrhae and escaped with the main army and only some stragglers were left in Carrhae. Surena now faced one of two options: either run around the desert looking for Crassus, wasting time and energy, or send one of his own men who could speak Latin to Carrhae to ask questions. Surena decided that the best option was to send a spy to probe Carrhae. Once at the walls, the messenger gave a message that Surena wished to have a conference with either Crassus or Cassius. If they accepted, they would be allowed to leave safely after they had negotiated the terms with the king, to leave Mesopotamia indefinitely. Crassus accepted the invitation and Cassius informed the messenger that the "time and place be fixed for a conference between Surena and Crassus." Parthian intelligence has just paid off. Surena was on his way to Carrhae.[90]

Crassus had hoped that the parley was real as he and his men were desperate to make their way home. However, it was only a trick. There was no truce, at least not as it was initially perceived. The next day, early in the morning, Surena gave the order to move out and head towards Carrhae. The sentinels on the walls notified

---

[89] Ibid., 28.
[90] Ibid.

Crassus and Cassius that the Parthians were near. Cautious joy was likely the response among the men.

Once Surena was outside the city walls, there was no peace offer. Instead, the Parthians began to hurl insults and demanded that if the Romans wished peace, then they must hand over Crassus and Cassius in chains. The Romans were stunned by this request and grew angry. The whole notion of peace talks beforehand had been a ruse. The men were getting frustrated and the officers made it clear to Crassus that he must give up hope that the Armenians would come to their aid. Crassus was in a dire situation. Carrhae could not provide the supplies needed and no Roman troops were available in Syria to come to their aid.

Crassus made the decision that they would slip out during the night once again, since the Parthians were not good night fighters. Crassus' desired destination is the town of Sinnaca, located in Armenia. Reaching the town would be no problem under the cover of darkness, so long as your guide were not a double agent.[91]

Crassus quickly mustered the men and marched towards Sinnaca by night. Their guide towards Sinnaca was Andromachus. All was going well until some of the Roman officers began to notice That Andromachus was leading them in one direction, but then he would make a sudden turn in another direction. They continued on, zigzagging, until they reached an area where it was

---

[91] Ibid., 29.

difficult to move, being an area that was marshy and full of ditches.

Cassius was not comfortable with this route or the guide and quickly went back to Carrhae. While in Carrhae, Cassius consulted his Arab guides, who suggested that Cassius wait until the moon passed the sign of the Scorpion. Cassius replied, "Personally I am more frightened of the Archer than the Scorpion." Afterwards, he and his 500 cavalry rode off towards Syria.

Another Roman officer, Octavius, who had reliable guides, also noticed the bizarre movement patterns and rode off from the main body with 5,000 men to Sinnaca, where he was able to set up a defensive position. As for Crassus, the day came and still no Sinnaca in sight. Instead, he was still meandering around in the marsh with four cohorts, a few cavalry and five lictors.[92]

Andromachus eventually got the Romans on the right road, only a mile and one-half from Sinnaca, but it was too late. The Parthians had spotted the Romans and were charging towards them. Crassus and his men quickly set up defensive positions on a small hill that provided little protection against the Parthian cavalry. However, the inadequate hill had one advantage: it was below Sinnaca and had a ridge that ran from the hill to Sinnaca. Octavius could barely see what was going on down below, but he knew Crassus was in trouble.

Octavius quickly assembled his men and rushed down the ridge to aid Crassus. Once he arrived, the

---

[92] Ibid.

Romans were able to push back the Parthian cavalry just enough to cover Crassus with their shields. Octavius declared to the Parthians "that there was no arrow in Parthia that should touch the body of their imperator, so long as there was one of them left alive to fight in his defense." The Romans were so ferocious in their defense that the Parthian cavalry slowly lost the will to push on and Surena, being a wise tactician, understood that an army with its back against the wall would put up the utmost fight. Instead of pressing on the attack, Surena came up with a new strategy that did not require a sword.[93]

    Surena had a new plan, deception. Once the Parthian attack ceased, Surena met with his council, discussing the peace terms and how Crassus would be treated. However, Surena did this within hearing of the Roman prisoners nearby, saying that he, like the king, wanted nothing more than to end this war with Rome and be friends, and that Crassus would be treated kindly. After the terms had been agreed upon, he freed the Roman prisoners. Surena's strategy was paying off. Allowing the Roman prisoners to hear the desired terms of the Parthians and releasing them to go back to their own camp to tell the good news was nothing more than setting up a Trojan horse.[94]

    Once the freed Roman prisoners arrived in their camp they were excited about the news they had heard

---

[93] Ibid.
[94] Ibid., 30.

and shared it with the rest of the camp. The Romans were overjoyed that finally, this war would come to an end. Surena, accompanied by the nobles, rode to the Roman camp. Surena unstrung his bow and held out his hand, offering the Romans a truce and promising them safe return. The Romans were excited about this. However, Crassus distrusted Surena's offer.

  Crassus had been deceived by almost every native along the way and during the retreat, thus he could not believe that the Parthians would let him and his men go in peace. Because of Crassus' attitude towards Surena's peace proposal, the Romans grew hostile towards Crassus, insulting him in every way and even accusing him of being a coward. Crassus did not take too kindly to these words; rather he was disheartened and frightened, but understood the men's feelings. Therefore, Crassus approached Surena, but was terrified. Before he spoke a word to Surena, he turned around, looked at the men, and said, "Octavius and Petronius and all you other Roman officers present, you see that I am being forced to go this way. You are eye-witnesses of the shameful and violent treatment which I have received." Crassus made it clear that he did not want his officers to think that his own men through their desire for peace handed over Crassus to the enemy, rather the enemy was so good and decisive that they were able to capture Crassus through deception.[95]

  In the end, Crassus would make his way down the hill to meet with Surena. The Romans were on foot and the

---

[95] Ibid.

Parthians were on horseback. Surena was so shocked that Crassus, the imperator of Rome was on foot that he quickly offered him a horse, but Crassus declined the offer, saying he was merely following the custom of his own country. Surena quickly went straight to the point and informed Crassus that peace existed between King Orodes and the Romans. In order to make this deal final, an agreement must be signed near the Euphrates River. Surena than spoke to Crassus and said "We find that you Romans have not got very good memories about the terms of treaties." Afterwards, Crassus called for a horse and suddenly Surena offered him a horse with a golden bridle as a present. The grooms lifted Crassus up onto the saddle and ran alongside the horse, whipping the horse to make the animal go faster. Octavius quickly charged after Crassus and got hold of the bridle. Petronius, along with the men, quickly surrounded the horse to slow the animal. It was during this struggle with the horse that a brawl broke out. It seems that the grooms of the horse did little to slow the beast down, so Octavius drew his sword and killed one of the grooms; this in turn caused himself to be killed. Petronius also would be struck, but his breastplate saved him. Crassus would also be killed during this struggle by a Parthian named Pomaxathres.[96] However, Cassius Dio expresses that Crassus did not die by the hands of a Parthian, rather a fellow Roman killed him to prevent him from being captured alive.[97] What is most

---

[96] Ibid., 31.
[97] Dio 40. 27.

important and overlooked is that Parthia had a body but no treaty.

A GREAT TRIUMPH!

While Crassus lies dead, Surena ordered the rest of the men to come down from the hill and have no fear. Not every Roman trusted Surena's word. Many stayed put, waiting for night to fall. Under cover of darkness, they scattered. Some of the Romans reached safety, while many others were killed or captured by the Parthians. In all, 20,000 Romans were killed, while another 10,000 were taken prisoner.[98]

While Plutarch does not mention the fate of the prisoners after their capture, Pliny the Elder mentions that the prisoners were taken to the province of Margiana, possibly settled in the city of Merv, to protect the Parthian frontier. "This is the place to which the Roman prisoners taken in the disaster of Crassus were brought by Orodes."[99] The lyric poet Quintus Horatius Flaccus, better known as Horace, who wrote during the time of Augustus, adds a bit more detail in one of his poems in which he mentions that the prisoners married into the native population.[100] As for the body of Crassus, Surena had his head and right hand cut off and sent to King Orodes, who

---

[98] Plut. *Crass.* 31.
[99] Pliny, *Nat*, 6.47.
[100] Horace, *Odes*, 3.5.5.

happened to be in Armenia; more on this shortly.[101] However, Cassius Dio tells an entirely different story that "the Parthians, as some say, poured molten gold into his mouth in mockery."[102]

Surena decided to have a little fun with the event and sent messengers to Seleucia, the same city that had been hostile to Parthia from time to time and likely hoped for Crassus' arrival. Surena's messengers informed the powers that be in Seleucia that he was bringing Crassus alive. The man to be paraded through the streets of Seleucia was Gaius Paccianus, who was picked to play Crassus because he happened to look like him. Surena had Paccianus put on a queen's dress, placed him on a horse, and when addressed, he should answer that he is the Imperator Crassus. In front of this mock Crassus were trumpeters and a few lictors on camelback. However, it was the lictors who displayed the most gruesome sight. The lictors carried the Roman fasces with purses hanging from the rods and freshly severed Roman heads hung from the axes. Bringing up the rear of the parade were women singing songs about the coward named Crassus. It was a parade of death and a warning not only aimed at Rome but to the Grecian city of Seleucia, which had hoped for Roman occupation. However, Plutarch's take on the parade should be taken with a grain of salt, for it is quite possible that the events as described by Plutarch did

---

[101] Plut. *Crass.* 31.
[102] Dio 40. 27.

happen; on the other hand, it is also possible that the story was nothing more than Roman propaganda.[103]

As for King Orodes, he was busy feasting and drinking with his new ally, King Artavasdes of Armenia. Artavasdes agreed to allow his sister to marry Orodes' son Pacorus, thus sealing Armenia's dependence on Parthia. As the kings feasted while watching the Greek performance of Bacchae of Euripides, an officer by the name of Sillaces arrived with a war trophy; it was the head and hand of Crassus. In usual tradition, Sillaces, bowed down low before his king and then threw the head of Crassus onto the stage. King Orodes told Sillaces to stand up and take a seat at the banquet. It was at this moment that one of the actors named Jason of Tralles, who had been playing the part of Pentheus during the play, grabbed the head of Crassus, switched costume and put on the attire of Agave,[104] who according to the story happened to murder her own son Pentheus, severing his head and then carrying his head back to Thebes on a stick.[105] While holding Crassus' head, Jason sang loudly to the audience:

> "We bring from the mountain
> A tendril fresh-cut to the palace,
> A wonderful prey."

---

[103] Plut. *Crass*. 32.
[104] Ibid., 33.
[105] Euripides, *The Bacchantes*.

The audience was happy. King Artavasdes, likely was delighted that the Romans had been beaten, but he understood that the victory obtained was just the beginning, for the Romans would be back, and his kingdom once again would be in the crosshairs of both empires. With Crassus' head held high for all to see, Jason of Tralles shouted to the audience one last time:

(Chorus) "Who slew him?"
(Agave) "Mine is the honour,"

A great applause thundered forth from the audience while both kings hid their uncomfortable delight. Artavasdes was uncomfortable because his protector, Rome, represented by Crassus, was now dead. Orodes, the new master over Armenia, was also uncomfortable, because Surena stole his victory. Shortly after, due to his supposed jealousy and fear of Surena's growing reputation after the battle, he had Surena executed.[106] Orodes not only lost his greatest general, who was not even 30 years of age, but lost an even greater opportunity to possibly expand his borders, had he allowed Surena to live. Instead of expanding his borders, Orodes chose to immortalize Surena.

---

[106] Plut. *Crass.* 33.

AFTERMATH

The victory at Carrhae placed Parthia on an equal, if not superior level with Rome, at least for a brief moment. But one must be careful, for even though Surena looks like a military genius, he simply was better prepared than Crassus, for the Parthians did keep track of the events and movements of the Romans through double agents, whereas the Romans had a lack or better yet, a breakdown in military intelligence. In other words, Crassus was fighting in the dark.[107]

There is a persistent myth of Parthian military superiority due to their victory at Carrhae. It is true that the Parthian cavalry and their use of the bow had just wiped out the foundation and backbone of the Roman military system, the infantry. Does this make the Parthian war machine superior to the Romans? The answer is no. There are two ways of looking at this. The first is that the Romans understood the military tactics of the east. One example is the Battle of Magnesia 190 BCE in which Antiochus III fielded 3,000 cataphracts, which did little to dent the Roman army. In other words, there was nothing grandiose about cataphracts' presence or effect. The second example is the Battle of Tigranocerta on 6 October 69 BCE, where the cataphract were ineffective once again. However, at Carrhae, the cataphract are vindicated, but are they really? In fact, the Parthian cataphract played a

---

[107] Rose Mary Sheldon, *Rome's Wars in Parthia: Blood in the Sand* (London: Vallentine Mitchell, 2010), 39.

minute role. Remember, they did not engage until later in the battle, first against Publius once he was in a limited withdrawal, and second, when the Romans were demoralized due to the death of Publius. The real victors in this battle were the horse archers.

Even though Carrhae was a major setback for the Romans in terms of losing men and resources along with exposing their eastern territories, they soon understood that in order to protect their centerpiece of warfare they had to give the legions the support they needed by adding cavalry. Julius Caesar had done this a few years before Carrhae and understood the importance of having a well-rounded military with elements of Gallic and Germanic cavalry alongside the Cretan and Numidian archers with his legions in Gaul. Therefore, the Roman military apparatus was not a failure. Rather, it was the man leading the military expedition. If Rome is going to compete for supremacy in the region with this eastern giant, it had better begin by learning, adapting, and incorporating elements that would counter the Parthian way of war.

Last, and most important, are the deaths of Crassus and Surena. Earlier it was mentioned that after the death of Crassus, Parthia had a body but no treaty. The treaty Surena presented to Crassus provided that "a state of peace existed between King Orodes and the Romans; it was necessary, however, to go forward as far as the river and have the terms of the agreement put into writing."[108] However, Crassus never signed a treaty with Orodes

---

[108] Plut. *Crass*. 31.

because he died in Surena's custody. In other words, the war was still on. Remember, King Orodes sent messengers to Crassus when he was in Syria, knowing that it was Crassus who had declared war on Parthia and not the Roman people. But all this changed once Crassus was dead.

This brings up another issue. Did Orodes execute Surena due to his growing reputation? The answer is complicated, but it seems rather odd that Orodes would execute his greatest general from fear and jealousy. Another alternative is that Orodes did not execute Surena for those reasons; rather, he executed Surena because Crassus was allowed to die. Crassus was supposed to sign a treaty with the king to ensure that the battle just fought was a war between Crassus and Parthia. Not Rome and Parthia. For Orodes understood from the beginning that when Crassus arrived in Syria it was a personal war.[109] Therefore, allowing Crassus to die gave Rome a new reason to continue its war with Parthia.

Even though news of the disaster did little to provoke war fever among the Senate in Rome, as we shall read later, it did among a few, particularly Julius Caesar. Crassus' personal crusade was now going to be justified, as in a just war. Avenging Crassus would be the excuse to facilitate war to further political ambitions.

---

[109] Ibid., 18.

Figure 9 Orodes II
http://www.cngcoins.com/
(CC BY-SA 3.0)

Figure 10 Marcus Licinius Crassus
http://commons.wikimedia.org/wiki/Category:Marcus_Licinius_Crassus#mediaviewer/File:Crassus_Kopenhagen.jpg

Figure 11 Statue thought to represent Surena at National Museum of Iran

Figure 12 Crassus campaign route to Carrhae. The Growth of Roman Power in Asia Minor." From The Historical Atlas by William R. Shepherd, 1923.

Figure 13 Crassus defeated by the Parthians. By Alfred John Church, Helmet and Spear: Stories from the Wars of the Greeks and Romans, p. 300.

3

PARTHIAN COUNTER ATTACK

The disaster at Carrhae left the Roman East, particularly Syria, exposed, but not completely defenseless, since Gaius Cassius Longinus led the surviving 10,000 legionaries back into Syria. However, their tattered presence could not sufficiently defend the province if the Parthians counterattacked. If Parthia were to attack, only the Roman province of Cilicia could send support; but even that would be problematic, for Cilicia had less than 15,000 men, not enough to aid and defend both Syria and Cilicia if the Parthians launched a two-prong invasion with Armenian aid. Moreover, sending a substantial number of troops to aid Syria could cause rebellion in Cilicia due to the lack of security in the province. There was only one solution to the problem: Rome must send fresh troops immediately or possibly lose all that was confiscated by Lucullus and Pompey due to the debacle at Carrhae.[1]

Back in Rome, the news of the defeat caused little concern. This is not to say that there was no concern; however, those who might be able to do something about it, Caesar and Pompey, were in a fight of their own, a

---

[1] Gareth C. Sampson, *The Defeat of Rome in the East: Crassus, the Parthians, and the Disastrous Battle of Carrhae, 53 BC* (Philadelphia: Casemate, 2008), 148.

political and provincial fight. When news of the 53 BCE disaster reached Rome, Caesar was far too busy quashing the discontent among the Gaul's due to his armies plundering the locals and forcing the local chieftains to conscript men to create auxiliary troops. Pompey during this time was in charge of managing the affairs in Rome. However, the Senate could do little with Pompey present and obstructing them from going forward with any new political issues. With Pompey in the way, the Senate resorted to infighting, settling old scores, and trying to obtain high offices by any mischievous means. With the Senate in chaos, it is not surprising that when news arrived of the disaster at Carrhae, it was met with apathy. Those in power may have viewed the disaster at Carrhae as a private matter, one between Crassus and the Parthians, thus leaving Roman pride intact since it was not Rome that had declared war on Parthia.[1]

Because of Rome's inability to send additional forces to the region due to political turmoil back home, the Parthians were preparing for a counterattack. In 52 BCE, Parthian forces were on the move, but in very small numbers, as they began to probe, collect intelligence, and test the defenses of Roman Syria through a series of raids. Their raids, desultory and confused, were repelled by Cassius and the remaining Roman troops who were at Carrhae, but they still caused concern among the Romans in the region. While Rome observed these raids as something possibly bigger to come, others, like the Jews

---

[1] Cary, 360, 386, 392.

under Roman hegemony saw the defeat of the Romans at Carrhae, the re-conquest of Mesopotamia, and Armenia turned once again into a Parthian dependency, as a sign of hope that the Parthians would drive the Romans out of the Near East, thus allowing Judea, among the many other regions under the sphere of Roman influence, to be rid of Rome once and for all.[2] While the natives of the Levant looked on in anticipation and hope, the Romans looked eastward with caution. All was quiet on the eastern front until 51 BCE.

ALL QUIET ON THE EASTERN FRONT

In May 51 BCE, Marcus Tullius Cicero, better known as Cicero, was made proconsul of the Roman province of Cilicia, located in what is today the southern (Mediterranean) coast of Turkey. The proconsul of Cilicia was vacant, and a new governor was needed to replace the outgoing governor. Cicero, likely wishing to escape the political circus in Rome, allowed his name to be considered and was appointed Cilicia by lot. Cicero's first order of business was to write a letter to Appius Claudius Pulcher, who was the current and outgoing governor of Cilicia. Cicero started his correspondence from Brundisium in good faith with concern. Cicero understood

---

[2] Jacob Neusner, *A History of the Jews in Babylonia: The Parthian Period* (Chico, Calif: Scholars Press, 1984), 28-29.

of the risks of being governor of Cilicia since the province was next door to Parthia and its ally Armenia. Cicero's first concern was the numbers of troops stationed in Cilicia. He had heard that the outgoing governor had disbanded a number of troops, which turned out to be false.[3] Even though Cicero was assigned 12,000 infantry and 2,600 cavalry, the social conditions of the province to which he had been assigned was far worse. His mission, according to Plutarch, other than safeguarding the Roman province of Cilicia, was to "keep Cappadocia friendly and obedient to King Ariobarzanes."[4] In other words, Rome was keeping a close eye on its neighbors it had hegemony over due to the instability caused by not only the disaster at Carrhae but also by corrupt provincial governors like Pulcher, not to mention the lack of forces in the Roman east to provide stable security.[5]

Cicero's mission was to keep the peace and maintain good relations with nearby kingdoms friendly to Rome, as well as collecting intelligence before his arrival in Cilicia and during his governorship on the movements and whereabouts of the Parthians. Most, if not all, of the reports coming in were from Rome's allies like Antiochus of Commagene. The reason for their cooperation is that they fear a Parthian invasion.[6] In a series of letters, Cicero expresses his desire that the Parthians remain peaceful and

---

[3] Cic, *Fam*, 3.3.
[4] Plutarch, *Cicero*, 36.1.
[5] Cic, *Att*, 5.16: *Fam*. 3.10.6: *Fam*. 3.7.2-3.
[6] Sheldon, 51.

rightfully so. Any information on the Parthians was vital as he journeyed towards Cilicia.

His first letter concerning the Parthian movements, whereabouts, and intentions, was first written on July 6, 51 BCE, from Athens, stating, "I don't hear a word about the Parthians. For the rest, heaven preserve us!"[7] Cicero is cautious in his letter, while he shows concern due to their silence, he has hope that they have no intentions to escalate the war. On July 22, Cicero showed his frustrations as news reaches him of dire conditions in Cilicia, not only socially, even though the social condition is far from stable due to Pulcher's corrupt administration. When Pulcher had heard of Cicero's arrival, he had "hurried to the most distant part of the province."[8]

Not only was the province a shambles, but so was the military. Three days later, on July 27, he writes from Asia Minor his hope for peace between the two countries: "Meanwhile, however, the following items of news of a welcome nature have reached me: first, that the Parthians are quiet." As far as Cicero is concerned, no news of the Parthians is enough said.[9] On the 3rd of August, Cicero writes from Laodicea: "I arrived at Laodicea on the 31st of July. From this day, therefore, count the beginning of my year. Nothing could be more warmly, more affectionately welcomed, than my arrival."[10] The warm welcome given to Cicero is heartwarming. However, the warm feeling is

---

[7] Cic, *Att*, 5.11.4.
[8] Ibid., 5.16.2.
[9] Ibid., 5.14.1: *Fam.* 3.7.2-3.
[10] *Att*, 5.15.1.

short lived once he arrives and assesses the situation in Cilicia in person.

Once in Cilicia, Cicero looks over his security forces. His reaction to what he saw was dismal:

> And that, while our friend has that great army, I should have nominal command of two wretched legions! But the fact is, that it is not such things as these that I miss. But I will endure it as best I may, provided that it does not last more than a year.[11]

Cicero had much work to do to whip his men into shape. Knowing full well that the Parthians could attack at any time, and even if the Parthians never were to attack, it was imperative that his forces be at their maximum potential to ward off any attack, whether foreign or domestic.

By mid-August, Cicero sends a curious report to Rome: "About the Parthian not a word: but, nevertheless, some who come from those parts announce that some cavalry of ours have been cut to pieces. Bibulus even now is not so much as thinking of approaching his province. People say that he is acting thus because he wishes to leave it somewhat later."[12] These rumors of Roman cavalry being cut to pieces are just that, rumors. There is no indication that it did take place and if it did, the Parthians are not mentioned as the culprits. Even though these are just

---

[11] Ibid.
[12] Ibid., 5.16.2.

rumors and not official reports, Cicero takes no chances and dispatches a report to Rome. Cicero also mentions a man by the Marcus Calpurnius Bibulus. Bibulus was elected to govern Syria the same time Cicero was elected to govern Cilicia while in Rome. Bibulus decides to delay his appointment to Syria due to political reasons involving Julius Caesar back in Rome, thus leaving Gaius Cassius Longinus, who was at Carrhae, in charge of Syria for a little longer.[13]

THEY'VE CROSSED THE EUPHRATES

Fourteen days later, Cicero's concerns turn into a nightmare. On August 28, 51 BCE, ambassadors of Antiochus of Commagene arrived at Cicero's camp near Iconium with starting news:

> the son of the king of the Parthians, whose wife was the sister of the king of the Armenians, had arrived on the Euphrates with a very large force of Parthians, and a great host of other nations besides, and had actually begun the passage of the Euphrates, and that it was reported that the

---

[13] Hildegard Temporini and Wolfgang Haase, *Aufstieg und Niedergang der romischen Welt: Geschichte und Kultur Roms im Spiegel der neueren Forschung* (Berlin: Walter de Gruyter, 1976), 897.

> Armenian king was about to make a raid upon Cappadocia.[14]

Not only does he anticipate the Parthians, but he awaits the arrival of the Armenian response. In doing so, Cicero will eventually place his forces between Cappadocia and Cilicia. However, even Cicero shows his doubts of an Armenian invasion of Cappadocia. Cicero knew that King Artavasdes of Armenia straddled the political fence line and desired to keep in good faith with both Rome and Parthia.[15] But for the time being, Cicero will wait. As for the unnamed son of the king of the Parthians, his name is reveled to Cicero in another letter dated September 20:

> the Parthians have crossed the Euphrates under Pacorus, son of the Parthian king Orodes, with nearly all his forces. I have not yet heard of the arrival of Bibulus in Syria. Cassius is in the town of Antioch with the whole army.[16]

The legates of king Antiochus of Commagene bring Cicero the startling news, which Cicero takes cautiously, awaiting a more trustworthy source before moving out to intended defensive positions.[17] However, Pacorus is not the one leading the Parthians; rather, it is the Parthian general

---

[14] Cic, *Fam.* 15.3.1.
[15] Sampson, *The Defeat of Rome in the East*, 157.
[16] Cic, *Att*, 5.18.1-2.
[17] Cic. *Fam.* 15.1.1-2.

Parthian Counter Attack

Osaces. The reason why Prince Pacorus is not leading this army is due to his age. Cassius Dio explains that Pacorus "was just a child."[18] The age of Pacorus is hard to determine. Cassius Dio may be correct that Pacorus was just a child. However, Cassius Dio may be using the child analogy due to Pacorus' lack of military experience. Either-or, Pacorus is not the one leading this campaign. He is just a student, an observer, with limited military involvement.

As the Parthians move, their objective is not quite clear to Cicero. Cicero learns that he is in Cappadocia with his army near Cybistra, which is near Cilician Gates, a pass through the Taurus Mountains. The Parthians have moved south into the Syrian province of Cyrrhestica. Cicero informs the senate to take a closer and careful look and consider sending additional forces. The reason is that Cicero's legions are weak and so are the legions stationed in Syria. Cicero is not desperate but understands that if Rome wishes to hold its eastern provinces, it might very well consider sending more legions along with Pompey. However, Rome must put aside its political differences and focus for a moment on what is truly in turmoil.[19]

While Cicero was preparing for the oncoming onslaught, the Parthians bypassed Cilicia entirely. Cicero was relieved by this but remained cautious. On September 22, Cicero informs in a dispatch that he received a letter from Tarcondimotus, a former pirate from the Amanu

---

[18] Dio 40.28.
[19] Cic, *Att*, 5.18.2.

Mountains who was settled in Cilicia by Pompey[20] and is revered by Cicero. Tarcondimotus provides valuable military intelligence concerning the Parthian movement indicating that they were heading straight for northern Syria:

> Pacorus, son of Orodes, the king of the Parthians, had crossed the Euphrates with a very large body of Parthian cavalry, and had pitched his camp at Tyba, and that consequently a very serious commotion had been caused in the province of Syria. On the same day a despatch on the same subject reached me from Iamblichus, phylarch of the Arabians, who is generally considered to be well-disposed and friendly to our Republic.[21]

Iamblichus, a petty tribal chief among the Arabs, brings the same message as Tarcondimotus, but it's the ending that concerns Cicero. Even though Iamblichus is loyal to Rome, Cicero shows skepticism:

> Though I was fully aware that, on receipt of this information, our allies were unsettled

---

[20] Thomas Grunewald, *Bandits in the Roman Empire: Myth and Reality* (London: Routledge, 2004), 78.
[21] Cic. *Fam.* 15.1.2-3.

in their feelings and wavering from the expectation of political change.[22]

The reason for the questionable loyalty is the lack of open hostility towards the Parthian invasion. Cicero mentions that "a very serious commotion had been caused in the province of Syria." This commotion is obviously not pro-Roman; rather it is pro-Parthian and has Cicero as well as the outgoing governor of Syria, Cassius, on edge.[23] The Parthian invasion is not seen as unwanted, it's rather a liberating sight to many in Syria and to those mini-kingdoms near Syria under Roman hegemony, as Cicero clearly points out that their feelings were due "to the harshness and injustice of our rule."[24] Gareth C. Sampson in his book "The Defeat of Rome in the East" sums up the reason for this pro-Parthian reaction by the natives, stating, "There would have been many inhabitants in Syria, who believed that they had more in common with Mesopotamia and the east than with the inhabitants of Italy."[25] Even though the inhabitants of Syria see the Parthians as liberators, those mini-kingdoms outside of Syria sit on the political fence, waiting for the outcome. If there was one man Cicero could trust to aid Rome with the necessary forces, since Rome was unable to provide

---

[22] Ibid.
[23] Ibid.
[24] Ibid.
[25] Sampson, 157.

legions due to political squabbling, it was King Deiotarus of Galatia.[26]

While Cicero awaits the outcome in Syria, he expects one of two possibilities at this point. The first is a Parthian thrust from Syria into Cilicia via Cappadocia. The second is the rumored Armenian attack aimed at Cappadocia. As we read earlier, Cicero doubts an Armenian invasion, remaining cautious. By straddling the rugged borders between Cappadocia and Cilicia, Cicero avoids the Parthians and Armenians in a head-on open field battle. Cicero mentions that he could have defended Cilicia itself, stating:

> the natural strength of Mount Amanus—for there are only two defiles opening into Cilicia from Syria, both of which are capable of being closed by insignificant garrisons owing to their narrowness, nor can anything be imagined better fortified than is Cilicia on the Syrian side.

There is another reason that Cicero chose the location: distrust. Cicero mentions that he was "disturbed for Cappadocia, which is quite open on the Syrian side, and is surrounded by kings, who, even if they are our friends in secret, nevertheless do not venture to be openly hostile to the Parthians."[27]

---

[26] Cic. *Fam.* 15.1.3, *Fam.* 15.4
[27] Ibid., 15.4.3.

Parthian Counter Attack

In early October 51, Cicero received a dispatch while in Cybistra, Cappadocia, that "the Parthians and Arabs had approached the town of Antioch in great force." While the main Parthian force converged on Antioch, some Parthian detachments were sent north and towards Cilicia. Cicero quickly gathers his forces and moves out, stating, "I therefore marched rapidly into Cilicia by the "Gates" of Taurus. I arrived at Tarsus on the 5th of October. Thence I pressed on to Mount Amanus, which divides Syria from Cilicia by the line of its watershed."[28] While Cicero waits for the Parthians, Cassius and his legions have walled themselves up within the city of Antioch. The Parthians could do little to a walled city since their whole army consisted of cavalry. With Cassius walled in, the Parthians began to raid the nearby villages and suburbs of Antioch. Cassius will remain behind the safety of the walls, drawing up his plans and waiting until the Parthians have gone. The Parthians eventually leave Antioch and make their way to a place called Antigonea. According to the historian Cassius Dio, the Parthians had trouble with Antigonea, stating:

> the neighbourhood of this city was overgrown with timber, and they did not dare, nay were not even able to penetrate this with cavalry, they formed a plan to cut down the trees and lay bare the whole place, so that they might approach the town

---

[28] Cic. *Att.* 5.20.2.

> with confidence and safety. But finding themselves unable to do this, because the task was a great one and their time was spent in vain.[29]

While the Parthians were occupied in finding a way into Antigonea that would allow them to utilize their cavalry, other Parthian detachments ventured elsewhere looking for loot.

On Oct. 7, Cassius decided to make a break for it and engage the enemy.[30] Cassius is not going to confront them head on, which would be futile. Therefore, he must use asymmetrical tactics, the preferred tactics of his enemy. Cassius begins by harassing the Parthian units that had scattered abroad. His strategy is a success. By harassing the smaller units, he is able to effectively drive them further away from the main force. This allows Cassius to focus on the main Parthian force without being harassed by the smaller detachments. Cassius quickly gets to work by taking advantage of a road the Parthians are using to depart. Cassius sets up an ambush by stationing a small number of infantry on each side of the road. His next objective is to bait the Parthians with a feint retreat using cavalry.[31] The Parthians take the bait. The Roman cavalry makes a run for it; once the Parthians are between the hidden Romans, they strike. Cassius' strategy works, a

---

[29] Dio 40.29.
[30] Cic. *Att.* 5.21.2.
[31] Sextus Julius Frontinus, *The Stratagems*, 2.5.35.

Parthian Counter Attack

number of Parthian cavalrymen are killed, and[32] General Osaces is wounded during the engagement and dies from his wounds a few days later.[33] The Roman ambush was so affective that the remaining Parthians under Prince Pacorus are said to have abandoned the campaign.[34] However, Cassius' ambush was rather weak. Cassius does not provide numbers as to how many died during the ambush and he could very well be exaggerating the intensity of the engagement. Second, the Parthians never abandoned their supposed campaign. All reports indicate that this was not a campaign bent on conquest.

On Oct. 8, Cicero was at his camp near Mopsuhestia. The former governor of Cilicia, Appius Claudius Pulcher, asks about the Parthians. Cicero's response, "I think they were not Parthians at all. The Arabs who were there, wearing with a semi-Parthian equipment are said to have all gone back. People say that there is no enemy in Syria."[35] When Cicero wrote this letter, he had already begun assaulting the towns of Amanus a day after Cassius victory from the 7-13 of October. Cicero's assault was because "a large body of their horsemen, which had crossed into Cilicia, had been cut to pieces by some squadrons of my cavalry and the praetorian cohort then on garrison duty at Epiphanea."[36] However, Cicero has not encountered Parthian, but Arab horsemen, according to his

---

[32] Dio 40.29.
[33] Cic. *Att*. 5.20.2.
[34] Dio 40.29.
[35] Cic, *Fam*. 3.8.10.
[36] Cic. *Att*. 5.20.2; Cic. *Fam*. 15.4.7.

letter on Oct. 8. Cicero likely knew that the main Parthian force had left the area around Antioch on Oct. 7, but did not leave Syria, and that small units--Arab detachments—were conducting raids that were partially equipped in the Parthian fashion. So why did Cicero assault Amanus? For starters, it is obvious that the inhabitants of Amanus are hostile to Rome and friendly toward Parthia. Had the inhabitants of Amanus not allowed the enemy to travel through, Cicero might not have acted so harshly. Cicero needed to stop the flow of enemy forces from entering Cilicia as well as any recurrences thereafter.[37] The truth is there was no large body of Parthian horsemen, merely a small Arab raiding party of Parthian allies. Thus Cicero is attempting to create an image and event that is equal to Cassius' victory over the Parthians. Why? Because Cicero needs a victory of his own that would downplay Cassius' victory. It's all politics.

    Cicero later writes to his friend Marcus Caelius Rufus on Nov. 26 that "our friend Cassius, to my great joy, had repulsed the enemy from Antioch."[38] Indeed the Parthians were repulsed from Antioch but not the areas around Antioch and evidently not from Syria. Shortly after, Caelius responded to Cicero and is not so thrilled by Cassius' report. Caelius explains to Cicero that he is "disturbed by the dispatches of C. Cassius and Deiotarus. For Cassius has written to say that the forces of the

---

[37] Cic. *Fam.* 15.4. 4.
[38] Ibid., 2.10.2.

Parthian Counter Attack

Parthians are across the Euphrates."[39] However this is not true. The notion that Cassius' victory caused the Parthians to retreat across the Euphrates is unfortunate. This is mere propaganda and misinformation. The truth is that Cassius targeted Osaces, won the engagement, and likely lost many men. Moreover, the victory does not seem to faze or hamper the Parthian operations in Syria. Therefore, the Parthians were done raiding the rich villages surrounding Antioch and spreading discontent among the natives for that year. They officially left western Syria around late October or early November. Even though the Parthians stopped raiding, their Arab allies continued to conduct raids in Syria and Cilicia.

After Cassius' great victory over the Parthians, the man elected to take his place, Bibulus, arrived to replace him as governor[40] sometime in mid-October, shortly after Cassius' victory. Once he arrived, he quickly sought glory of his own and was denied. Cicero reports that Bibulus, "lost the whole of his first cohort and the centurion of the first line" and "It was really a very galling blow both in itself and in the time of its reception."[41] Dispatches reporting great victories, along with ignorance of the enemy he was to face, made Bibulus overconfident. He shut himself up behind the walls of Antioch after losing to

---

[39] Ibid., 8.10.1.
[40] Ibid., 2.10.2.
[41] Cic. *Att.* 5.20.2-4.

an enemy he neither knew nor understood, all in hope of "exerting himself to get a triumph."[42]

Even though the Parthians ceased their operation in Syria, they still were present. Prince Pacorus decided not to leave Syria that winter of 51 BCE. Instead, he led his forces to Cyrrhestica in northern Syria for the winter. Cyrrestica is a district that lies between the plain of Antioch to the east and the Euphrates to the west.[43]

While the Parthians take up winter quarters in Cyrrhestica, Cicero travels to Laodicea and temporarily places Cilicia in the hands of his brother Quintus. While in Laodicea, Cicero makes the case that if something is not done to ease the situation taking place in Syria, "a most serious war is impending."[44] While in Laodicea, Cicero corresponds with his friend Caelius. Caelius hears Cicero's concern and is concerned himself, but makes it clear that the situation in Syria is just as difficult as the situation taking place in Rome, that no one person can agree on who to send, let alone who would be willing to go:

> One man is for sending Pompey, another against Pompey's removal from the city, another for sending Caesar with his own army, another the consuls; no one, however,

---

[42] Ibid., 6.8.
[43] Strabo, 16.2.8.
[44] Cic. *Att.* 5.21.2.

is for sending any who are in Rome without office by a senatorial decree.[45]

Caelius in his letter makes it clear that the generals and the politicians in Rome are hesitant to leave their seats of power. Some politicians in Rome have suggested that the war was invented by Cassius, that it was Cassius and not the Parthians who attacked his own province, claiming that Cassius, "sent some Arabs into the province, and told the senate that they were Parthians." It was this kind of information that caused the senate to hesitate and question what was really going on there. One would think that the senate would have trusted Cicero's dispatches. However, Caelius has an answer for that and advises Cicero "to describe minutely and cautiously the state of things in your part of the world, whatever it is, that you may not be said either to have been filling some particular person's sails, or to have kept back what it was important to know."[46]

After much deliberation in Rome, the senate agreed "that one legion should be sent by Pompey, and another by Caesar, to the Parthian war."[47] While Cicero waits for the arrival of Pompey, Cicero begins strengthening his defenses with the aid of Deiotarus. On February 22, 50 BCE, Deiotarus agrees to aid Cicero in full force and brings with him "thirty cohorts of four hundred men apiece,

---

[45] Cic. *Fam.* 8.10.1-2.
[46] Ibid.
[47] Julius Caesar, *Commentarii de Bello Gallico*, 8.54.

armed in the Roman fashion, and two thousand cavalry." Not only will Deiotarus aid Cicero, he will also take charge of the campaign until Pompey arrives. Cicero is certain that Orodes will soon join his son Pacorus in Syria and take command of the Parthian forces. However, this is all speculation and rumors on Cicero's part.

While Rome strengthens their defenses, the Parthians stay put in Cyrrhestica for the time being. The likely reason as to why the Parthians are not moving is that they are guarding the Euphrates river crossing.[48] By staying put for the winter, the Parthians are cautiously preparing to return home while keeping an eye on the western horizon. Moreover, by staying put, the Parthians are preparing for a possible Roman counterattack. When considering the location of their encampment, this would be the preferred terrain of the Parthian cavalry when encountering a Roman army predominately consisting of infantry.

Spring, 50 BCE, the season when armies are on the move, Cicero decides that it is time to leave Laodicea after spending the winter in intense debate making his case for additional reinforcements. Cicero departs on May 15 and is en route to Cilicia. Before Cicero leaves, he asks for prayers as he journeys, since the actions of the Parthians in the weeks ahead are uncertain. Cicero will arrive at the capital, Tarsus, on June 5. Once he arrives, he is disturbed by accounts of war in Syria and banditry in Cilicia.

---

[48] Sheldon, 55.

Parthian Counter Attack

While Cicero insists that Rome send reinforcements, the new governor of Syria, Bibulus, uses diplomatic deception as his weapon to stop the next invasion. Bibulus does this by winning the trust of the satrap Ornodapates, who was not fond of King Orodes. Bibulus plan was simple. If you want revenge against King Orodes, Ornodapates, join Prince Pacorus and support his bid for the throne.[49] However, that did not happen. Orodes soon got wind of the affair and recalled Pacorus to Parthia.[50] The Roman poet Horace gives an alternative as to why the Parthians did not conduct a second raid, and that was political division -- not in Parthia, but Rome. Horace makes the case in a poem, without mentioning King Orodes, that the Parthians withdrew their forces back across the Euphrates to allow Pompey and Caesar to have their civil war. After the squabble was over, the Romans would be so weak that the Parthians would march back into Syria and have their way.[51] Whatever the reason is, the Parthians were done with Syria and did not return in 50 BCE. The mini-war was over.

REFLECTION

There are some issues at hand when looking closely at the Parthian campaign into Syria. There is no doubt that

---

[49] Dio 40.30.
[50] Justin 42.4.
[51] Horace, *Epodes*, 7. 1-3.

Cicero's letters and Cassius Dio's histories, among the many others who write on the events that took place between 51-50 BCE show us a very clear picture of the events that transpired during that time. The first issue is Cicero's concern of a massive Parthian invasion engulfing the Roman Near East, which never took place.

In the first place, the reason the Romans never encountered a massive Parthian invasion is that King Orodes did not call for a full mobilization. Instead, he called on some nobles from the nearby provinces to provide troops to assist his son Pacorus while being led under the direction of General Osaces.

Second, Cicero had every reason to be concerned about a Parthian invasion after the disaster at Carrhae. The Parthians knew that the Romans were weak and would be unable to put up a strong defense. However, the invasion Cicero feared was not an invasion bent on conquest. Rather, it was merely a raid targeting rich villages around Antioch and a training exercise to baptize young Prince Pacorus by fire and nothing more.

It would be in error to think that the Parthians had no ulterior motive or that their objective was just to raid a dozen or so rich villages around Antioch. Rather, the Parthians were hoping to incite the Syrian natives to rebel against their Roman masters. If the insurrection was successful, the Parthians would have an indirect hegemony over Syria. I use the word indirect since Parthia did not need to liberate Syria through conquest in order to find an ally with a common cause. Their presence was just enough to rattle the Roman authorities.

If a victor must be declared on the Roman side, it must be Bibulus, who successfully defeated the Parthian forces, not with legions, but with diplomacy. Even though Bibulus' strategy of pitting a prince and king against one another did not materialize, the effect of the message did. One must be careful in choosing winners, because the sources presented in this chapter show that the Parthians never intended to conquer Syria--at least for now--and to continue raiding was a waste of time after their first round in 51 BCE.

Figure 14 Cicero

Parthian Counter Attack

Figure 15 Pacorus I of Parthia
http://en.wikipedia.org/wiki/Pacorus_I#mediaviewer/File:Coin_of
_Pacorus_I_of_Parthia.jpg

Figure 16 Classical Syria during Roman times

4

CALM BEFORE THE STORM

While the Parthian invasion that Rome expected never happened in 50 BCE, in the west, the Great Roman Civil War in 49-45 BCE exploded. It was a politico-military conflict that pitted Pompey against Caesar until Pompey's death in 48. It was during this time that Pompey may have sought Parthian assistance, although one would think that Pompey would avoid any type of assistance from Rome's nemesis in the east.

However, Pompey had no choice in the matter, for he had not the armies he once had. Instead, Pompey had the "senatorial and the equestrian order and from the regularly enrolled troops, and had gathered vast numbers from the subject and allied peoples and kings." Pompey had a quagmire of experienced and inexperienced forces, all of which swayed in loyalty. Caesar had the legions of the state, a uniformly battle hardened, well-armed, professional fighting force. The odds were against Pompey and caused him to look elsewhere for financial aid. Pompey's military handicap and lack of wealth caused him to look elsewhere for financial aid to acquire additional forces.[1] In the words of Plutarch,

---

[1] Dio 42.55.

> Pompey had now to plan and act on the basis of existing circumstances. He sent messengers to the various cities, and sailed to some of them himself, asking for money and for men to serve in his ships.[2]

Of the many messengers Pompey sent, one of them visited Parthia. Pompey's interest in seeking Parthian help was due to the fact that they were the "most capable of both receiving and protecting [Pompey] them in their present weakness and later of helping them to build up their strength and sending them out to fight again with a large force." His advisor, Theophanes, suggested that Egypt was a safer bet, because the Ptolemies were indebted to Pompey for his kindness. If Pompey chose Parthia over Egypt, he would be playing second fiddle and would be at their mercy. Pompey likely had already made up his mind that Egypt was a safer bet, but decided to send an envoy to Parthia anyway. This visit to the court of Arsaces caused Julius Caesar to become suspicious; Caesar mentions that "it was hotly argued in their discussions whether Lucilius Hirrus, who had been sent by Pompeius to the Parthians."[3] Caesar knows that Pompey sent an envoy, but speculates as to whom Pompey sent. Cassius Dio provides more detail in the matter:

---

[2] Plutarch, *Pompey*, 76.
[3] Caesar, *Civil Wars*, 3.82.

Calm Before the Storm

> I have heard, indeed, that Pompey even thought of fleeing to the Parthians, but I cannot credit the report. For that race so hated the Romans as a people ever since Crassus had made his expedition against them, and Pompey especially, because he was related to Crassus, that they had even imprisoned his envoy who came with a request for aid, though he was a senator.[4]

What Cassius Dio cannot credit is whether or not Pompey considered political asylum if the situation turned bleak. However, even though it cannot be verified, the possibility remains. Moreover, Cassius is wrong about the Parthians hating the Romans. In chapter two, it is mentioned that King Orodes made it quite clear to Crassus that if this army was sent by the Roman people, it shall be a war to the bitter end. However, the ambassadors were smarter than that. They understood the difference between a nation declaring war and one man's ambition.[5]

Cassius Dio further mentions that Pompey's envoy, who happened to be a senator, was imprisoned. The unknown envoy who was imprisoned may have been Lucilius Hirrus. Even Caesar speculated whether or not Hirrus was sent to Parthia on behalf of Pompey. According to Cicero, Hirrus was a poor politician who spoke with a lisp and was the brunt of Cicero's jokes. Cicero once called

---

[4] Dio 42,2.
[5] Plut, *Crass*, 18.

Hirrus a "would-be-noble."[6] It is evident that Cicero didn't think highly of Hirrus. Cassius Dio mentions that the Parthians hated Pompey because he was related to Crassus.[7] However, Hirrus happened to be a cousin of Pompey, which may have been the reason for his imprisonment. But this seems unlikely. What may have gotten Hirrus imprisoned was his "fatuous conceit."[8] It may have been this fatuous conceit that got Hirrus into trouble with Orodes. In other words, once Hirrus arrived at the court of King Orodes, he laid out Pompey's terms. Orodes evidently agreed with the terms and was willing to forgive and "promised to be his ally," but on one condition. Pompey must hand over Syria. This did not go over well with Hirrus, who spoke on Pompey's behalf. Knowing full well that Pompey was not about to let go of his prosperous and strategic province likely caused Hirrus to insult Orodes, which led to his imprisonment. However, this is mere speculation, as there is no concrete proof Hirrus ever visited the court of Orodes. But one thing is certain; an envoy was imprisoned, not for his relationship to Pompey, but more likely for his demeanor during negotiations.[9]

The news of the imprisonment likely caused a stir among Pompey's advisors and likely caused Pompey to choose Egypt as his base of operation. It is also

---

[6] Erich S. Gruen, *The Last Generation of the Roman Republic* (Berkeley: University of California Press, 1974), 111.
[7] Dio 42.2.
[8] Gruen, 111.
[9] Dio 41.55.

understandable that Pompey would choose Egypt over Parthia due to cultural similarities. Whatever the case may be, Pompey's refusal was a potential game changer that could have saved his life and secured his place of power in Rome, for after he was defeated at the Battle of Pharsalus on 9 August 48 BCE, he fled to Egypt a month later, where his life ended after he stepped foot on Egyptian soil.[10] On the other hand, it is possible that if Pompey had gone to Parthia seeking financial and military assistance, he may very well have gotten what he needed to battle Caesar… or he could have ended up being displayed as a trophy in the court of Orodes. However, Pompey went to Egypt, where he was assassinated, and Caesar rose to a higher, previously unseen level of power in the Roman Empire. Pompey's alternative course in history, perhaps with the Parthians, was never realized.

What likely got Caesar's blood boiling over the Parthians was some circumstances concerning a man named Caecilius Bassus. In 48 BCE, Bassus, a Pompey supporter, fled to Syria and found safety in the city of Tyre after Pompey had been defeated at Pharsalus. The reason Bassus fled to Tyre was because of its former governor, Metellus Scipio, who supported Pompey and afterwards the optimates' (Aristocrats or Populists) cause. However, Scipio did not return to Syria, because he was present at the battle of Pharsalus and afterward decided to flee to Africa. Bassus' goal was to lay low and survive while in Syria. As time passed, Bassus began to reassociate himself

---

[10] Plut, *Pompey*, 76.

with the soldiers, particularly the soldiers of the newly appointed governor in 47 BCE, Sextus Julius Caesar who happened to be Julius Caesar's cousin.

Bassus quickly got to work and was able to spread disinformation about Caesar in Egypt, which allowed him to gain the support of some of Sextus' soldiers. Because of Bassus' disinformation, he was able to stir up a silent rebellion that allowed him to gain a political foothold in Syria. Sextus grew suspicious of Bassus due to the large influx of soldiers joining him. In his defense, Bassus made it clear that the soldiers he was recruiting were intended to aid Mithridates the Pergamenian for an expedition against Bosporus Kingdom. This was a lie, of course, but Sextus believed him and allowed him to continue.

Shortly after Bassus was let go, he forged a letter, claiming that the previous governor, Scipio, had informed him that Caesar had been defeated and killed in Africa and that Bassus had been appointed as the new governor of Syria. However, it was just the opposite, for Caesar defeated and killed Scipio in Africa at the Battle of Thapsus in 46 BCE. Sextus refused to believe this and prepared for war. It became clear to Sextus that Bassus had been collecting soldiers all this time to take over the governorship of Syria. Bassus immediately went to Tyre and gathered his forces. Bassus then advanced with his forces and engaged the legions of Sextus. Bassus was defeated and wounded. It was a great victory for Sextus, but Bassus was not finished. After Sextus had won, Bassus was able to win over the hearts and minds of some of

Sextus' soldiers, who rose up and assassinated Sextus in 46 BCE.[11]

In December 46 BCE, Quintus Cornificius, governor of Cilicia, was awarded the governorship of Syria by Caesar, a post he would officially take the following year in 45 BCE. However, if Cornificius wanted to occupy his new post, he would have to fight for it.[12]

Because of this altercation, Gaius Antistius Vetus, appointed Quaestor pro praetore of Syria by Caesar, was sent into Syria to engage Bassus. Vetus had the upper hand over Bassus. Bassus had no choice but to take refuge behind the walls of Apamea. While Vetus lay siege to Apamea, an Arab mercenary by the name of Alchaudonius had been called on behalf of both Vetus and Bassus. Now, since both Vetus and Bassus desired his services, Alchaudonius decided that it was best to stay between the city and the camps. His goal was to start a bidding war: the person who offered the most would win his forces. Bassus won the bid and Alchaudonius quickly got to work and had a great deal of success against Vetus. It was also during this time that Bassus sent a message to the Parthian court seeking assistance. King Orodes of Parthia agreed and sent a small force to aid in lifting the siege. With Parthian assistance, Bassus was able to claim victory. However, it was only temporary, as the Parthians quickly returned home due to the approach of winter. In the end, Bassus was only able to buy safety temporarily, for shortly

---

[11] Dio 47.26.
[12] Cic. *Fam.* 12.19.1.

afterward, forces loyal to Caesar would once again be marching into the province of Syria and beating on the gates of Apamea.[13]

It is obvious that Caesar's hot anger was not so much due to Bassus' takeover of Syria, but that Bassus invited the Parthians into what was largely a Roman affair. From Caesar's standpoint, the Parthians had no business getting themselves involved. Bassus' request for Parthian aid was asking for more trouble than Caesar wanted. Syria was already weak and Rome as a whole was deeply divided. Caesar's concern was that if Parthia were to commit to the war on the side of the optimates, the optimates could undo everything Caesar had thus far accomplished. Furthermore, Caesar understood that if this were to happen, Rome as a whole would become far more unstable. If the optimates won with Parthian support, Rome would be far weaker defensively, thus encouraging a full-scale Parthian invasion of the Roman East. Caesar understood that to rely on Parthia, whether pro or con, was risking much.

With Pompey dead and the optimates defeated, Caesar was now vying for dictatorial powers in Rome and inevitably acquired them from the Senate on February 14, 44 BCE, making Caesar Dictator for Life.[14] Caesar, possessing absolute power, prepared for his next grand campaign, one that he had been planning for a long time, a campaign to conquer Parthia.

---

[13] Dio 47.26.
[14] Cary, 415.

Calm Before the Storm

While Pompey sought to embrace Parthia as a potential ally, Caesar wanted to invade them, which gained support among the Romans. Cassius Dio mentions that "a longing came over all the Romans alike to avenge Crassus and those who had perished with him."[15] Those Romans who favored an ample revenge were the politicians who supported Caesar. But Caesar had one problem stopping him from conquering the Parthians, he was not a king. According to Plutarch, "a report that from the Sibylline books, it appeared that Parthia could be taken if the Romans went up against it with a king, but otherwise could not be assailed." Julius Caesar refused to call himself king, but instead chose the name Caesar.[16] Caesar understood that the notion that he must be a king in order to defeat the Parthians was irrelevant, for titles are just a facade and the real power behind the title is what matters. Caesar could care less about the Sibylline books and rightfully so. Here was a man who conquered Gaul, defeated Pompey, and defied the Roman Senate by crossing the Rubicon. What makes the Parthians so much more special than the rest? Besides, the Sibylline report was a mere article of political propaganda. The report does demonstrate a high level of respect for the Parthians.[17]

In another act of political theater, Caesar is given total "command of the war ... and made ample provision

---

[15] Dio 43.51.
[16] Plut, *Caesar*, 60.
[17] Sheldon, 63.

for it."[18] Caesar's first order of business was to send sixteen legions along with 10,000 cavalry across the Adriatic Sea.[19] The destination of these Roman forces is Illyria, where they would gather at Apollonia. Six of the legions along with archers, light infantry, and cavalry would stay in Apollonia[20] while another legion was sent to Syria.[21] Caesar's objective was to take the forces through Lesser Armenia, allowing Caesar safe passage and to gather additional forces from Armenia. Armenia is just the launching point for Caesar's true desire, to "invade Scythia; and after overrunning the countries bordering on Germany and Germany itself, to come back by way of Gaul to Italy, and so to complete this circuit of his empire, which would then be bounded on all sides by the ocean."[22] In order to fund the early stages of the expedition, Caesar sent large amounts of gold to Asia Minor to pay for the expenses,[23] and weapons were sent in advance to the port city of Demetrias in Thessaly.[24]

What the Senate failed to understand was that in Caesar's mind, avenging Crassus was just an excuse to facilitate Caesar's desire for further expansion whether foreign or domestic. This is not to say the Senate was totally oblivious to Caesar's grand ambition; however, one

---

[18] Dio 43.51.
[19] Appian, *The Civil Wars*, 2.110.
[20] Ibid., 3.24.
[21] Ibid., 4.58.
[22] Plut, *Caesar*, 58.
[23] Nicolaus of Damascus, *Life of Augustus*, 18.
[24] Plut, *Brutus*, 25.

has to wonder how much they understood. Invading and conquering Parthia was not impossible, but going beyond Parthia was fanciful. It is possible that Caesar never intended to invade Parthia. Rather, Caesar being the shrewd politician who understood the power of image, intended to intimidate rather than engage Parthia by sending legions along the Euphrates.[25]

Even though Caesar had many supporters in the Senate, there were those who grew tired of Caesar's continual expansion and overreach of powers, which ultimately led to his assassination in 44 BCE. Even in death his plan to invade Parthia would not be swept aside, as one of his trusted men, Mark Antony, would pick up the gauntlet and accept the challenge.

With Caesar dead a Second Triumvirate was formed on November 27, 43 BCE. This new Triumvirate consisted of Octavian, Marcus Aemilius Lepidus, and Mark Antony.[26] Since Rome had three new masters to watch over them, the Liberators, consisting of Brutus and Cassius, who participated in the assassination of Caesar, fled eastward. Cassius and Brutus both understood the need of alliances and were hoping to gain the support of Parthia, so they sent General Quintus Labienus to the court of King Orodes "to secure some reinforcements."[27] After Labienus presented the request for assistance, Orodes decided to detain him and wait for the outcome of the

---

[25] Sheldon, (see note 50.)
[26] Cary, 430.
[27] Dio 48.24.

battle before he issued an order for mobilization. However, Orodes had a change of heart and sent a small contingent to aid the Liberators.[28] Orodes may have respected Cassius due to past conflicts, thus showing he is a worthy general.[29]

On first impression, Orodes may have sent military aid to Cassius and Brutus. The reason for this is that Parthian cavalry were present at the Battle of Philippi in October 42 BCE. It is unknown how many troops took part in the battle; however, Brutus had a total of 6,000 cavalry, of which 2,000 consisted of "Thracian and Illyrian, Parthian and Thessalian." Brutus may have had 500 Parthian cavalry under his command. Cassius also had 6,000 cavalry under his command, of which 4,000 consisted of "Arabs, Medes, and Parthians." Of the 4,000 cavalry, roughly 1,300 or 500 are Parthian. However these are just guesstimates.[30]

Nevertheless, the Battle of Philippi was a failure for Cassius and Brutus. When news of the defeat reached Labienus, he decided to stay in Parthia, hearing that the victors would spare no one who fought against the Triumvirs.[31]

---

[28] Ibid.
[29] App, 4.59.
[30] Ibid., 4.88.
[31] Dio 48.24.

ANTONY BEATS THE WAR DRUMS

Once the dust cleared at Philippi, Antony went on a tour of the newly acquired eastern provinces. Besides sightseeing, Antony needed money and lots of it. However, Cassius and Brutus had depleted the wealth of Asia, leaving Antony with scraps of capital.

During his confiscation tour, Antony made it clear to all of Asia that those who aided Cassius and Brutus were to be heavily taxed. Antony states: "For what you contributed to our enemies in two years (and you gave them the taxes of ten years in that time) will be quite sufficient for us; but it must be paid in one year, because we are pressed by necessity." The Greeks after hearing this news "threw themselves upon the ground," pleading with Antony to understand that they did not contribute willingly, but were forced to give much more than just money. After hearing their plea, Antony presented a new deal in which his subjects should pay "nine years' taxes, payable in two years. It was ordered that the kings, princes, and free cities should make additional contributions according to their means, respectively."[32] Moreover, Antony made sure his provinces throughout Asia would "pony up" capital by appointing agents with the help of soldiers to collect the taxes by threat of force.[33] The purpose of the double tax was not only to pay his men

---

[32] App, 5.5-6.
[33] M. Rostovtzeff, *The Social and Economic History of the Roman Empire, 2 vols.* (Oxford: Oxford University Press, 1998), 1006.

and resupply the ranks, but was used to fund his upcoming Parthian campaign.[34] The amount of money Antony is said to have extracted from his subjects was in the range of 200,000 talents.[35] This maybe an exaggeration, because if Antony had 200,000 talents, why the need for Cleopatra's wealth?

    It is obvious that Antony never banked 200,000 talents or a portion of that in a year or two, for if he had a fraction of that amount, he would have bypassed Cleopatra on his way to Parthia. However, he has not the amount mentioned and this is where Cleopatra comes into play. In 41 BCE, Antony summoned Cleopatra to meet with him in Cilicia to answer the charges made against her for funding Cassius during the war. Antony knew that Cleopatra had stayed out of the war and had the financial means to assist his future expedition against Parthia. But Cleopatra decided to ignore him and his messenger's request. Instead, she made them beg her.[36] Eventually she agreed to meet with the messenger and would sail to Antony in extreme opulence. Whatever charges were made against her were quickly forgotten after to her luxurious entrance into Tarsus. At first, the relationship between Antony and Cleopatra was merely political. But Antony began to spend quite lavishly to win over Cleopatra. However, Cleopatra won, causing Antony to forget his duties. Antony was lust-struck and decided to

---

[34] Cary, 440.
[35] Plut, *Antony*, 24.
[36] Ibid., 25-26.

Calm Before the Storm

go back with her to Alexandria. Even though Antony was mesmerized by her supposed beauty and charm, he acquired what he needed badly, capital.[37]

While in Syria, Antony had appointed a new governor by the name of Lucius Decidius Saxa[38] and relocated two defeated republican legions to Syria.[39] It was also in Syria where Antony would unintentionally rekindle the conflict between Rome and Parthia. Before Antony left for Alexandria, he had ordered his cavalry to raid the wealthy city of Palmyra, Syria, and to press charges upon the population for not choosing a side. The reason was that the city of Palmyra was independent and remained neutral when it came to international disputes due to being primarily a frontier city of merchants who sold foreign goods. But word soon reached the city that a raid was to be expected. The inhabitants of Palmyra quickly gathered their belongings and moved across the Euphrates River, into Parthian territory. Once across, they set up a defensive position on the riverbank. When the Roman cavalry entered the city of Palmyra, they found nothing and returned to Antony with nothing to show for their efforts. Antony then decided to impose heavy taxes on the Syrians.[40]

This heavy taxation, along with the failed Palmyra raid, caused a wave of Syrian refugees to seek asylum in

---

[37] Plut, *Antony*, 25-28.
[38] Dio 48.24.
[39] Kevin Butcher, *Roman Syria and the Near East* (Los Angeles: J. Paul Getty Museum, 2003), 37.
[40] App, 5.9; Pliny, *Nat*, 5.21.

Parthia. While in Parthia, the Syrian tribal leaders made their case against the Romans before King Orodes. Antony was oblivious to the situation he had created. Even taking further steps to divide his army for the winter, while ignoring the Syrian outcry over the rise in taxes, for he had no time for that, it was time to leave and be with Cleopatra in the winter of 41 BCE.[41]

      General Labienus, who still lived among the Parthians, spoke to King Orodes after word reached him that Antony had gone. Labienus informed Orodes that Antony's forces "were either destroyed utterly or impaired." The information Labienus received was partially correct. What he did not know was that Antony had divided his army for the winter. But one bit of information Labienus had proved correct, and that is the "remainder of the troops were in a state of mutiny and would again be at war." Labienus knew that the two defeated republican legions Antony had placed in Syria might join sides to get revenge if the Parthians were to invade and show support. Furthermore, if Orodes agreed and mobilized his forces, the objective of this campaign would not be a massive raid, but the subjugation of Syria and adjoining provinces of interest. Labienus persuaded Orodes to allow him to take personally responsibility in leading the Parthian forces. Besides subjugating Syria, Labienus also requested that he be allowed, if everything went well in Syria, to help free the various provinces in opposition to Roman rule. Orodes agreed and entrusted

---

[41] App, 5.10.

Labienus with his son Prince Pacorus, along with a large Parthian force.[42]

While Antony played lover to Cleopatra in Alexandria during the winter of 41-40 BCE, the Parthians began to mobilize their forces, likely a partial mobilization of Parthia's western provinces. It would take time to assemble before setting off in the spring 40 BCE.

SHOCK AND AWE

Once spring 40 BCE had arrived, the Parthians, led by Labienus and Prince Pacorus, crossed the Euphrates River and advanced in Syria. Once in Syria, the Parthian force, consisting of cavalry and a hefty supply train, headed straight for the city of Apamea.[43] While in Alexandria, Antony received word that the Parthians had invaded Syria. Immediately he set out with two hundred ships. As Antony neared the province of Phoenicia, he receives startling news; his wife Fulvia and his brother Lucius have waged war against Octavian and lost. Antony takes no responsibility for their actions and sets his course for Italy to settle the issue. As Antony heads towards Italy, his wife Fulvia escapes and sets sail to meet him, but as she is en route, she falls sick and dies.[44] If Antony didn't have a

---

[42] Dio 48.24-25.
[43] Ibid., 25.
[44] Plut, *Antony*, 30.

headache now, he gets word that Calenus, his governor in Gaul had died, and that Octavian quickly rushed in to confiscate the province along with the legions stationed there. Not only does Octavian take Gaul, he also confiscates Antony's province of Spain along with the legions. This was a clear violation of the agreement among the triumvirates. Antony rushes to the shores of southern Italy but is denied access once he arrives at Brundisium. Antony decides to land his troops elsewhere and they blockade a city. Once Octavian's legions arrived, war seems inevitable. However, the men and officers refused to fight, thus forcing Antony and Octavian to hammer out their differences.[45]

In September 40 BCE, the Treaty of Brundisium was agreed upon. Octavian gained all the lands west, while Antony possessed all the lands east and their border was the Ionian Sea.[46] Even though the treaty declared a border between the two men, Antony lost a good number of legions and resources, legions that Antony likely sought to transport to the east to push back the Parthian tide.

Once the Parthians reached the city of Apamea, they were able to subdue only the suburbs of Apamea. The Parthians were not equipped to conduct siege warfare and left Apamea knowing full well that as long as they were present in Syria, the city would eventually submit. While Apamea was besieged with fear, the republican legions once under the command of Brutus and Cassius soon got

---

[45] App, 5. 61/Cary, 436-437.
[46] Dio 48.28.

word and joined Labienus. Saxa, the governor of Syria, mustered his forces to meet the Parthians head on. It was an utter disaster. Saxa's forces were obliterated. While Saxa lay low in his camp, arrows delivering messages began to pour in. Labienus' messages were simple, join us! Saxa, who refused to join the Parthians, became paranoid that his associates would and secretly fled the camp. Labienus would soon after enter the camp, killing many of the men, while sparing others. Labienus soon after learned that Saxa had fled to Antioch. Labienus quickly marched on Apamea again, only this time Apamea surrendered without a fight for they believed Saxa was dead. Saxa likely got word of the surrender and decided to abandon Syria as a whole, which allowed Labienus to take Antioch without a struggle. Labienus continued to purse Saxa in the province of Cilicia, where he was put to death.[47]

With Saxa dead and Syria subjugated, Pacorus declared himself master of Syria except for the city of Tyre. The citizens of Tyre were sympathetic to the Romans, and the Parthians could do little since they had no ships at their disposal. Most of Syria seems to have welcomed Pacorus as a liberator, for those of Sidon, as did Ptolemais called Acre today, welcomed him with open arms. With Syria under Parthian control, phase one was complete. Phase two was about to get under way and it involved the province of Judea and the region of Asia Minor. Pacorus and Labienus would divide their forces. Pacorus would

---

[47] Dio 48.25.

head for Judea while Labienus continued further inland from Cilicia.[48]

THE INVASION OF JUDEA

Once Syria was secured, a man by the name of Antigonus asked to meet with Pacorus. Antigonus Mattathias was the son of King Aristobulus II of Judea. His mission was simple: Offer Pacorus a thousand talents and five hundred women if he would depose the current king, Hyrcanus, who happened to be Antigonus' uncle and friend to Rome. Pacorus agreed to the terms as it would be beneficial and comfortable to the Parthians to have an anti-Roman king on the throne of Judea.[49]

Pacorus then divided his forces. Pacorus would proceed down the coast until he reached the border of Judea, while another commander, Barzaphames, would approach the province through the interior. Once Pacorus reached the border, he sent in scouts to check out the area before proceeding further. After the scouts reported to Pacorus that all was clear, the invasion began.[50]

Antigonus led the Parthian forces to a place called Mount Carmel, a strategic location and a good place to assemble and hide forces before proceeding further into Judea. It was here at Carmel that Antigonus was able to gather the Jews who lived in the area. With a ragtag Jewish

---

[48] Ibid; App, 5, 65.
[49] Josephus, *Jewish Antiquities*, 14.13.3.
[50] Ibid.

Calm Before the Storm

army along with professional Parthian support, Antigonus entered the city of Jerusalem.[51]

However, the Parthians did not enter Jerusalem with Antigonus' forces, at least not yet; this was a Jewish affair. Instead, the Parthian forces remained in the countryside until further notice. Once in Jerusalem, Antigonus men quickly made their way to the palace and besieged it. However, two men were able to hold off Antigonus' forces. Those two men were Phasaelus and the soon to be famous king, Herod. Both Herod and Phasaelus came to each other's assistance, and after a brief fight in the market place, were able to hold off the forces of Antigonus. Antigonus controlled the temple but nothing more. Once Jewish reinforcements arrived, Antigonus felt that he could take the palace. However, Herod and Phasaelus were able to drive the enemy away once again. It seemed that there was no hope of taking the palace or Jerusalem.[52]

Antigonus, growing tired of the seesaw battle, looked to the Parthians for help. Pacorus decided that the best way to end this was through negotiation. Pacorus sent a cupbearer, also named Pacorus, along with many horsemen. Once they entered the city, Pacorus offered talks to end the crisis. Phasaelus liked what was said and agreed to the terms and so did King Hyrcanus. Pacorus left two hundred horsemen and ten "freemen" behind as he escorted the men to Barzapharnes' camp in Galilee as an

---

[51] Ibid.
[52] Ibid.

embassy with Phasaelus acting as ambassador. As for Herod, he refused to leave. Before the two left with Pacorus, Herod pleaded with them before they considered the terms. Herod insisted it was a trap, and decided to hold out as long as possible. Once they arrived, they were received with open arms and presented with gifts. The atmosphere suggested anything but deception; however, it was all a ruse.[53]

Phasaelus and Hyrcanus were soon led to the seaside city of Ecdippa (Az-Zeeb) to meet with Antigonus and Prince Pacorus. Evidently all went well, no suspicions, no second-guessing, not until Phasaelus overheard that Antigonus had offered Pacorus a thousand talents and five hundred women in exchange for the throne. It was at this moment that they realized that Herod may have been right. Those who sympathized with Phasaelus requested that he flee by horse but he refused. Phasaelus was still skeptical of the whole plot until a man named Ophellius approached him. Ophellius made it clear to Phasaelus that everything he had heard was true, and that he had this disturbing information from the richest man of all Syria, one Saramalla. Saramalla sympathized with Phasaelus, offering him ships to flee by sea. However, Phasaelus refused the offer, for he would not leave Hyrcanus' side nor abandon his elder brother Herod.[54]

Phasaelus decided to meet with Barzapharnes and approached him with an issue he had heard. Phasaelus

---

[53] Ibid., 14.13.4.
[54] Ibid.

made it clear that it would be wrong for Barzapharnes to break his oath since they were there to negotiate. He even went as far as to offer to bribe Barzapharnes much more than what Antigonus was offering. Barzapharnes likely laughed at the offer and made it clear to Phasaelus that what he had heard was lies. Afterwards, Barzapharnes left to meet with Pacorus. [55]

Phasaelus was likely confused and rightfully so, but that skepticism soon passed when he and Hyrcanus were placed in chains. Phasaelus was able to get a message out to Herod, informing him that it was all true, that he was right. Herod was likely a mixed bag of emotions after hearing the news. He had to get out of Jerusalem quickly.[56]

Herod gathered his family members, some soldiers, eight hundred followers, of which five hundred were the wives of Hyrcanus, the same wives promised to Pacorus, and left Jerusalem. Once the Parthians realized Herod was gone, they plundered the city of Jerusalem. Once they had exhausted the Holy City of its valuables, they plundered the countryside, even destroying the city of Marissa (Marisa).[57]

However, the Parthians were not done, they still had one mission left to fulfill before they left, and that was to restore Antigonus to the throne. Pacorus would escort Antigonus into Jerusalem. Antigonus was likely hated more than Herod due to his associates plundering the city.

---

[55] Ibid.
[56] Ibid., 14.13.6.
[57] Ibid., 14.13.9.

However, Antigonus had two other people the Jews despised, the former King Hyrcanus and Herod's brother Phasaelus. However, the two men were still in the custody of the Parthians. Even though the Parthian horsemen had their fill, Prince Pacorus still awaited the thousand talents and five hundred women promised to him. Antigonus had neither to offer. Fearing that Pacorus might restore Hyrcanus to the throne, Antigonus cut off his ears. By doing so, Hyrcanus was now permanently ineligible for the priesthood under Jewish law. However, he would live, as the Parthians escorted him to the city of Babylon where he would live for four years among the Jewish population. Herod would invite him back into Jerusalem only to kill him in 30 BCE. As for Phasaelus, he took his own life. With his hands bound, the only option was to bash his head against a stone, thus ending his life. While Antigonus may have been rid of one person, Hyrcanus was still alive and in Parthian custody. In a sense, Hyrcanus is an insurance policy to Pacorus if Antigonus does not find favor with the Parthians.[58]

      As for Herod, he took refuge in Egypt where he met with Queen Cleopatra as he looked for Antony. Cleopatra insisted that he stay. She had been planning a military expedition of her own. She offered Herod a commission to lead the expedition, which he refused, insisting he must get to Rome quickly. Eventually, Herod arrived at Rome and told Antony all the bad news. Antony was moved by Herod's message and made it clear to the

---

[58] Ibid., 14.13.7-8, 10.

Senate and to Octavian that it was in Rome's best interest during this war with Parthia to make Herod a king. The vote was unanimous and Judea had a new unofficial king.[59]

THE INVASION OF ASIA MINOR

While Pacorus was busy playing "the game of thrones" in Judea, Labienus was obtaining the allegiance of Cilicia. After Cilicia had been secured, the Parthians and former republican legions began to pour into the interior of Asia-Minor. It is mentioned that many of the cities submitted without putting up a fight. The likely reason is they could not afford to fight after Antony drained the local treasuries, which led to the Parthians being welcomed as liberators. However, the momentum of this force was moving so rapidly and with relative ease, that it tells us that the Romans have few or no garrisons that could put up a sufficient defense to stem the tide. Even the governor of Asia, Lucius Munatius Plancus, not only fled his capital at Ephesus but fled the province of Asia and set sail for one of the islands.[60] Unfortunately, there is no information concerning Parthian troop movements between Cilicia and the western portion of Asia-Minor.

As Labienus approaches the western edges of Asia Minor, the reports begin to come in. Two out of three cities

---

[59] Josephus, *Wars of the Jews*, 1.14.2-4.
[60] Dio 48.26/ Strabo, 14.2.25

that are mentioned by Cassius Dio have been devastated by the Parthian forces. Those two cities were Mylasa and Alabanda.

The city of Mylasa located in the province of Caria was taken without conflict and even accepted Parthian troops to garrison the city. Once Labienus pressed on with his campaign, the citizens of Mylasa held a festival. It was during this festival that an orator by the name of Hybreas spread discontent among the inhabitants, which quickly turned into open rebellion in which the Parthian garrison was slaughtered. The same situation occurred at the city of Alabanda in the province of Caria, where Labienus left a garrison that was slaughtered by the citizens. Once word reached Labienus, he quickly marched on the cities. The city of Mylasa had been abandoned by the time the Parthian forces arrived, but they looted the city of its valuables before destroying it. The citizens of Alabanda also suffered for their rebellion, for they were slaughtered and their valuables looted. However, the citizens of Stratonicea (Caria) were able to holdout against the Parthian invasion. Once the campaign had ended, Labienus had conquered so much territory that the Parthian Empire now extended from the borders of India in the east to the shores of the Aegean Sea in the west. To commemorate his great victory over the Romans, Labienus adopted the title, Parthicus Imperator (Parthian Emperor).[61]

---

[61] Ibid.

Calm Before the Storm

It's no surprise that while Labienus was conquering Roman-held territory in Asia Minor, he acted no differently when it came to confiscation, like Antony, Brutus, and Cassius before him. Labienus went about levying taxes and plundering temples for wealth. If Parthia had meant to show that they were liberators, far different from the previous occupiers, it seems that even under Parthian rule nothing had changed.[62]

REVERSING THE TIDE

While Antony was dealing with Octavian over political squabbles, he kept a close eye on the reports coming in from Asia Minor. As mentioned earlier, the Treaty of Brundisium defined who possessed what under the Second Triumvirate. However, Antony had little to work with since most of his legions had been stripped away by the treaty. Antony, limited in manpower, decided to take a gamble and gave the order to invade Asia Minor.

In 39 BCE, Antony assigns General Publius Ventidius Bassus the mission to retake Asia-Minor. Ventidius is probably one of the most overlooked if not forgotten generals in military history. Ventidius grew up poor like most Romans. He was said to have sold mules and wagons before joining the Roman army. While serving, Ventidius would go on to have a distinguished

---

[62] Dio 48.26.

military career as he would accompany Julius Caesar during his campaign against Gaul and would take part in the Roman Civil War. Afterwards, Ventidius took up Caesar's offer of the post of plebeian tribune after Caesar reorganized and expanded the senate in 45 BCE.[63]

In 39 BCE, reports reached Antony while in Greece that the Parthians were finished with their campaign in Asia Minor for the year. Antony likely received these intelligence reports from the province of Asia, which was loyal to Rome. It was from these reports that Antony was able to draw up his plans. Antony likely knew that the majority of the Parthian army would return home for the winter to their respected nobles, thus leaving local militias with questionable loyalty to garrison the cities throughout Asia Minor. In addition, Antony understood the need to attack at once to inhibit the Parthians' spring plans. Antony saw this as a perfect opportunity to surprise the enemy. Once the coast was clear, Antony placed a few legions under the command of Ventidius. Ventidius set sail for the province of Asia. His mission is simple: establish a beachhead at the province of Asia and push inland.[64]

---

[63] James E. Seaver, "Publius Ventidius. Neglected Roman Military Hero." *The Classical Journal*, Vol. 47, No. 7 (Ap., 1952). pp. 275-280.
[64] Dio 48.39; Plut, *Antony*, 33.

Calm Before the Storm

BATTLE OF THE CILICIAN GATES

In 39 BCE, Ventidius' landing was unexpected. This shows the lack of intelligence gathering on the part of Labienus.[65] Once the Roman forces were accounted for, Ventidius quickly began to push eastward in a search and destroy mission. Word spreads rapidly that Romans have arrived. His scouts quickly deliver the message to Labienus. Labienus is startled and terrified for he "was without his Parthians." The only troops available to Labienus were neighborhood militia. Labienus quickly fled the province of Asia and headed east seeking military support from Pacorus. Ventidius took a chance, abandoned his heavy troops, and pursued with his lightest forces.[66]

Eventually Ventidius caught up with Labienus and cornered him near the Taurus Mountains. Ventidius took the high ground, from which he could look down upon Labienus' encampment. However, there was another reason why Ventidius took the high ground; he feared the Parthian cavalry. It was a standoff as both generals encamped for several days waiting for the arrival of their main forces. As the main forces from both sides arrived, they hunkered down for the night. At daybreak, the Parthians, overconfident by their numbers and past victories, decided to start the battle before joining forces with Labienus. These hard charges were obviously not

---

[65] Sheldon, 58.
[66] Dio 48.39.

Parthian horse archers but cataphract. Once the cataphract were at the length of the slope, the Romans charged down on top of them and easily repelled the enemy, for the Romans had the momentum. However, even though the Romans were able to kill and maim many of the cataphract, the cataphract were doing a better job at killing and maiming themselves. For the cataphract at the top of slope, where all the fighting took place, would retreat, and in doing so, run into their own men coming up the slope. Instead of coming down the slope to rally around Labienus, they bypassed their general and headed straight for Cilicia. It was absolute chaos.[67]

    Ventidius, seeing that the Parthians were scattering all about and fleeing, decided to bring his men down from the hill and marched on Labienus' camp. Both armies were now face to face but Ventidius decided to stay put due to information he collected from the deserters. Ventidius was informed that Labienus was going to flee the camp come nightfall. Ventidius found that it was better to set up ambushes rather than have an all-out pitched battle, losing many men and resources during the process. At nightfall, the ambushes set in place killed and captured many, except for Labienus, who was able to escape by changing clothes. His destination was Cilicia. However, Labienus could not hide for long, for he was arrested by Demetrius, a former slave, now a "freedman" turned bounty-hunter.

---

[67] Ibid.

After being turned over to the Roman authorities, Labienus was quickly executed.[68]

BATTLE OF AMANUS PASS

With Labienus dead, Ventidius was able to secure the province of Cilicia. However, the mission was far from finished. While Ventidius was in Cilicia, he devised a plan to trick the Parthians. Ventidius sent an officer by the name of Pompaedius Silo with cavalry to scout out the Amanus Pass. The mountain pass connects the province of Cilicia with Syria and was of strategic importance. Not far behind Silo would be Ventidius along with a small contingent of troops to aid in the fight. Pacorus understood that if the pass was not secured, the Romans would march through it and invade Syria. Therefore the best method was to station a garrison there to bottle up the pass. While Silo was on his way, Pharnapates, a lieutenant, and considered the most capable general of Orodes, was stationed by Pacorus at the pass, waiting for the Romans to pour through. Once Silo reached the pass, he was engaged immediately. However, as mentioned, it was a trick. Silo's mission was to lure the Parthians away from their strongest defensive position. In doing so, Ventidius would either attack at the flank or from the rear. In a sense, the Romans were giving the Parthians a taste of their own

---

[68] Dio 48.40; Plut, *Antony*, 33.

medicine by using the feint tactic that worked so well against them at Carrhae. With many of Pharnapates' cataphract lured away, Ventidius fell upon the Parthians unexpectedly. Pharnapates, along with many of his men, perished during the engagement. With the Amanus Pass now clear, the invasion of Syria was imminent.[69]

THE BATTLE OF MOUNT GINDARUS

With the Amanus Pass secured, Ventidius pushed south into Syria. Pacorus was done fighting, at least for now, and abandoned the province to the Romans in late 39 BCE. With the Parthians out of the way, Ventidius led his forces to the province of Judea.

Ventidius' mission to Judea was simple and lucrative: rid the province of any remaining Parthians and the anti-Roman King Antigonus and restore Herod to the throne. However, Ventidius did neither. Instead, he bypassed Herod's royal family who were besieged by the troops of Antigonus on the top of Masada and went straight to Jerusalem, where he camped outside the walls. Ventidius was playing psychological warfare with Antigonus by making him think that he was going to take Jerusalem. However, it was a ruse. Ventidius decided to use fear and trickery, promising not to attack Jerusalem unless he received vast amounts of wealth from the king.

---

[69] Dio 48.41; Plut, *Antony*, 33; Sheldon, 58.

Calm Before the Storm

Antigonus capitulated to Ventidius' demands. Make no mistake, Ventidius was still going to support Herod and place him on the throne, but while Herod was still far away and his brother besieged, he might as well make some money while they wait. After Ventidius' coffers were filled, he took the bulk of his forces and headed back to Syria, leaving Silo in charge to deal with the Jewish problem. However, Antigonus would come up with a ploy; he would bribe Silo multiple times. Antigonus' reason was to buy time and hope that the Parthians would come to his assistance while he kept the Romans at bay. However, this would not happen.[70]

As Ventidius returned to Syria, he sent the bulk of his forces beyond the Taurus Mountains to Cappadocia for winter quarters.[71] It was during this time that Pacorus was planning another invasion of Syria and began to mobilize a substantial number of cavalry from the nearby provinces. Word of Pacorus' intentions soon spread reaching the ears of loyal Roman informants, who then relayed the information to Ventidius. Not only was this information crucial for preparation, the information also informed Ventidius of a Syrian noble, Channaeus (also called Pharnaeus), who pretended to be a Roman ally but was in fact a spy and Parthian loyalist. Ventidius likely invited Channaeus over for dinner and during their meeting, Ventidius made it clear that he feared the Parthian would abandon their normal route "where they customarily

---

[70] Josephus, *Wars of the Jews*, 1.15.2-3.
[71] Sextus Julius Frontinus, *Stratagems*, 1.1.6.

crossed the Euphrates near the city of Zeugma." Ventidius acted concerned over the issue, making it clear that if Pacorus were to invade Syria much further to the south he would have the advantage over the Romans, for it "was a plain and convenient for the enemy." After the meeting was finished, Channaeus returned to his home and quickly sent messengers to inform Pacorus of Ventidius' fears.[72]

In early spring 38 BCE, Pacorus, unwilling to let go of Syria, led his forces south along the Euphrates River based on Ventidius' supposed fears of engaging the enemy on a plain. Once they came to the point of crossing, Pacorus realized that the construction of a bridge was needed due to the banks being widely separated. It took many men and materiel, and the construction of the bridge was complete after forty days. This is exactly what Ventidius wanted. Ventidius' disinformation bought much-needed time to allow his legions to assemble.[73]

Once the Parthian forces were in Syrian territory, Pacorus likely expected an immediate attack during the bridge construction or during the crossing, but neither materialized. With no sign of the enemy, Pacorus became overconfident and began to believe that the Romans were weak and cowardly. Eventually Pacorus would find Ventidius at the acropolis of the city of Gindarus, which is in the province of Cyrrhestica.[74]

---

[72] Dio 48.41; Frontinus, 1.1.6; Sheldon 59.
[73] Dio 48.41; Frontinus, 1.1.6.
[74] Dio 49.20; Strabo, 16.2.8.

Calm Before the Storm

Ventidius has been at Gindarus for three days preparing his defenses when Pacorus showed up. One would think that Pacorus would carefully prepare a plan of action, but no. Instead, Pacorus and his officers tossed out the combined arms strategy of utilizing both heavy cavalry and horse archers in unison that had worked many times, thinking they could take the high ground with little trouble. Due to the arrogance and overconfidence of Pacorus and his nobles, who did not like those commoners, the horse archers, stealing the show as they did at Carrhae. They decided to sally up the slope as they did at the battle of the Cilician Gates. Once the cataphracts were within five hundred paces of the Romans, Ventidius took advantage of their elitism and rushed his soldiers to the brim and over until both armies met at close quarters on the slope. Ventidius' strategy here is simple--engaging the elite Parthian cavalry gave him cover from the Parthian horse archers. You would think the Parthians would have learned from experience what not to do. The result of this knee-jerk reaction was as devastating for the Parthians as expected. As the cataphract advanced up the slope, they were quickly repelled into those troops coming up behind them, inflicting great suffering to riders and mounts not to mention that those who did make it to the brim were met and repulsed by heavy infantry. If the heavy infantry did not get them, the slingers would. Ventidius' use of slingers was because dependence on infantry on the battlefield as at Carrhae 53 BCE, was useless unless they had a force multiplier that could support each other's function in order to effectively deter heavy or light cavalry. The Roman slingers, likely atop the hill and eventually making their way down the slope, were equipped with deadly metal pellets. These pellets, when released, became devastating projectiles that could outdistance the horse archer's bow and penetrate the cataphract's armor. These slingers were likely on the left and right side of the Roman infantry, giving them a deadly arc of crossfire. This very well could be the reason we do not hear of the Parthian horse archers taking part in the engagement, since any attempt to rush toward the front would put them in grave danger.[75]

Even though the cataphracts put up a stiff fight at the foot of the hill, it was not enough. Roman infantry likely swarmed the cataphracts, forcing them into hand-to-hand combat, and with their horse archers neutralized from the fight due to the slingers; there was nothing that could be done to rescue the situation. Pacorus, in the ensuing chaos, likely tried to make one last push in which he along with some men, made an attempt to take Ventidius' defenseless camp, only to be met by Roman reserves. Inevitably Pacorus lost his life during the melee.[76]

As news spread that Prince Pacorus lay dead, a scramble to recover his body was attempted. While those trying to recover Pacorus' body met the same fate, the vast majority of Pacorus' army quickly retreated. Some attempted to re-cross the new bridge but were caught by

---

[75] Dio 49.20.
[76] Dio 49.20; Just 42.4.7-10.

Calm Before the Storm

the Romans and put to death while many others fled to King Antiochus of Commagene for safety. This victory shocked Syria, and to make sure the Syrian would never rebel again Rome, Ventidius took Pacorus' corpse, severed the head, and ordered that the head be sent to all the major cities of Syria. It was a gruesome sight to behold, but the effect it had on the native Syrians was other then negative. Instead, "they felt unusual affection for Pacorus on account of his justice and mildness, an affection as great as they had felt for the best kings that had ever ruled them." As for the Parthians who sought refuge in Commagene, Ventidius was coming for them. But Ventidius could care less about the Parthian refugees and more about how much money he could confiscate from King Antiochus by besieging Samosata, capital of Commagene, in the summer of 38 BCE. Antiochus offered Ventidius a thousand talents if he would just get up and go, but Ventidius refused the offer and proposed that Antiochus send his offer to Antony. Once Antony got word of the situation, he quickly made his way to the scene of the action. Ventidius was about to make peace and take the lucrative offer but Antony barred him from making such a deal. Instead, Antony removed him from his command and took over the operations from there. Antony was jealous of Ventidius and wanted in on the glory. Instead, Antony inherited a protracted siege that went nowhere, which would hurt him in the end, for when Antiochus offered peace, Antony had little choice but to accept the now lowered offer of three hundred talents. After the extortion of Commagene,

Antony ventured into Syria to take care of some domestic issues before returning to Athens. As for Ventidius, he went back to Rome, where he received honors and a triumph, for "he was the first of the Romans to celebrate a triumph over the Parthians."[77]

As Ventidius celebrated his triumph in Rome, Antony idled in Athens. Across the Euphrates in Parthia, King Orodes was in grief over the loss of his son and army. Orodes lost the will to speak and eat and after several days began to talk to Pacorus as if he was alive. It was during this time that the many wives of Orodes began to make bids for Orodes to choose their son for next in line to the throne, and rightfully so. Each mother understood that there was this nasty habit that once a new king was elected, he would murder his brothers/rivals to secure the safety of his reign. Orodes eventually would make his choice and settled on his son Phraates to succeed him. Soon after Phraates was chosen heir to the throne, he began plotting against his father Orodes. Phraates first attempt to murder his father was with a poison called aconite that failed since Orodes was suffering from a disease called dropsy (edema), which made the poison of little effect. Phraates then took a much easier route and strangled his father to death. To make sure his throne was safe, he murdered his thirty brothers and any of the nobility that detested him or questioned his motives for his acts of cruelty. Phraates was here to stay.[78] But while

---
[77] Ibid.
[78] Just 42.4.11-16; Plut, *Crassus*, 33.

Phraates went on a vicious campaign to secure his throne, Mark Antony, jealous of the success that Ventidius had against Parthia, was planning an invasion of his own. It was now Antony's turn to avenge Crassus to fulfill Caesar's dream.

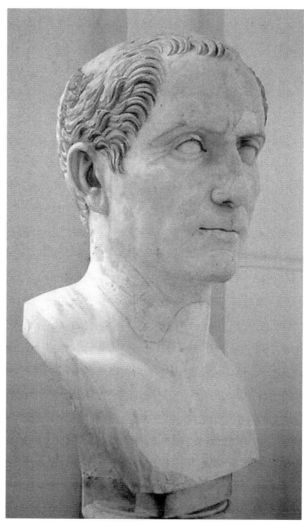

Figure 17 Gaius Julius Caesar (100-44 BCE)
http://commons.wikimedia.org/wiki/File:GiulioC
esare.jpg

Figure 18 Assassination of Pompey

Figure 19 Gaius Octavius
http://commons.wikimedia.org/wiki/File:Augustus_Bevilacqua_Gly
ptothek_Munich_317.jpg

Figure 20 Marcus Aemilius Lepidus
http://www.cngcoins.com/Coin.aspx?CoinID=93378 (CC-BY-SA 3.0)

Figure 21 Mark Antony

Figure 22 Antigonus II Mattathias

Figure 23 Quintus Labienus Parthicus. Herbert A. Grueber. Coins of the Roman Republic in the British Museum. London: Printed by order of the Trustees, 1910.

Calm Before the Storm

Figure 24 General Publius Ventidius Bassus

Figure 25 The Parthian invasion of Judea

5

ANTONY'S WAR TO AVENGE CRASSUS TO FULFILL CAESAR'S DREAM

In 37 BCE, Antony began preparations for war. However, his first act was a campaign to squash, replace, and consolidate many of the regions in Asia-Minor and along the Levant that were sympathetic to the republican cause or to Parthian rule. Antony made sweeping changes throughout the regions, establishing Darius in Pontus, Herod in Judea, Polemon in Cilicia, and Amyntas in Pisidia. However, these were just a fraction of the many changes that took place. Once his western flank was secure from possible rebellion, Antony set his eyes on Armenia.[1]

After Antony secured the various provinces in Asia-Minor under Roman hegemony, he still had one basic issue stopping him from proceeding with his Parthian campaign: money. Antony was cash-strapped. Even those rulers in Asia-Minor Antony had established that were pro-Roman could offer little funding, for Asia was bankrupt. In order to acquire the funds needed to pay for his grand expedition against Parthia, Antony turned to the

---

[1] Daryn Graham, *Rome and Parthia: Power, Politics, and Profit* (North Charleston, South Carolina: CreateSpace Independent Publishing Platform, 2013), 60-61.

age-old practice of debasement by mixing the silver denarius with iron.[2] But even this was not enough. If taxation and inflation could not provide the funds Antony needed, his last option was borrowing. As he made his way towards Syria, he requested that Cleopatra, his love and financier of war, meet him in Antioch. Once Cleopatra reached Antioch, Antony exchanged provinces for money, particularly the provinces of "Phoenicia, Coele Syria, Cyprus, and a large part of Cilicia; and still further, the balsam-producing part of Judaea, and all that part of Arabia Nabataea which slopes toward the outer sea."[3]

      Once Antony procured the much-needed money to fund his war, his second act was to force pro-Parthian Armenia to submit to Roman rule. In theory, Rome and Armenia were in a state of war against one another due to the alliance Armenia had with Parthia.[4] Antony sent an invasion force into Armenia led by General Publius Canidius Crassus.[5] Once the Roman legions entered Armenia, King Artavasdes II immediately submitted to Roman rule.[6] With Armenia now in the Roman sphere of influence, Antony had a base to launch his war against Parthia. In order to strengthen his objective, Antony gave Canidius Crassus another mission: to invade and subjugate the provinces of Iberia and the adjoining country

---

[2] Pliny, *Nat*, 33.46.
[3] Plutarch, *Antony*, 36.
[4] Plutarch, *Antony*, 37.
[5] Dio, 49, 24.
[6] Plut, *Antony*, 37.

of Albania in order to protect his rear once the Parthian campaign was under way.[1]

While Antony was stabilizing his territorial holdings and expanding into others, King Phraates of Parthia went on a murder spree, targeting Parthian nobility who conspired against him or might do so. Many fled Parthia seeking a place of safety. Of those, a Parthian noble and officer by the name Monaeses took refuge among the Romans.[2] Monaeses was a wealthy man who recently had taken part in the Parthian invasions of Judea and Asia Minor.[3] Once behind Roman lines, Monaeses sought the ear of Mark Antony and made it clear that if Antony were to place him in command of the Roman forces, he would not only successfully invade and defeat the Parthian forces, in which he felt that many would join his side without a fight, but would conquer most of Parthia. Antony so loved Monaeses' offer that he gave him three temporary cities, Larissa, Arethusa, and Hierapolis, until he finished the war. If everything went well, Antony promised him, Parthia would be his reward.[4]

Many Parthians during this time looked upon Monaeses' flight from Parthia with favor. Phraates had issue with the growing popularity of Monaeses within Parthia. He understood that if a Roman army entered Parthia with Monaeses at its head, it was very likely he'd become the next king of Parthia. Phraates decided to send

---

[1] Dio 49, 24.
[2] Plut, *Antony*, 37.
[3] Horace, *The Odes*, 3.6.9.
[4] Dio 49.24; Plut, *Antony*, 37.

an envoy offering friendship to Monaeses in hope of settling their differences. Monaeses agreed to return to Parthia for negotiations. Antony was angry when he found out. But Antony saw an opportunity; he agreed to Monaeses' return and even sent along a Roman envoy to accompany him with a message. Give back the captured standards, release any survivors of Carrhae, and agree to peace. Phraates likely thought long and hard about this, but he was no fool. Phraates knew that if he were to agree, Antony would still attack. But how would Phraates know this for sure? Even though Monaeses portrayed himself as an enemy of Phraates to Antony, which he very well could be, he may in fact have been a double agent. Why else would Phraates mobilize additional forces and place them along the Euphrates unless he had ample information concerning Roman troop movements? Depending on guides without investigating them seems to be the Achilles heel of the Romans, starting with Crassus.[5]

  With Cleopatra's financing and his territorial holdings stabilized, Antony began the process of assembling his massive juggernaut, consisting of 60,000 Roman infantry, 10,000 Iberian and Celtic cavalry, and 30,000 troops comprised from other nations–not to mention the massive amount of resources needed to grease the wheels of the army.[6] There should have been an additional 20,000 legionaries sent to Antony under a deal struck between him and Octavian at Tarentum but they

---

[5] Dio 49, 24; Sheldon, 67.
[6] Plut, *Antony*, 37.

never materialized.⁷ In total, Antony had 113,000 troops at his disposal, if not more, twice the size of Crassus' invasion force of 53 BCE, poised for immediate action.

ANTONY'S PARTHIAN WAR

However, this is where Antony got into trouble. The Roman forces mobilized for war were tired and needed to rest, especially the main body, the Roman infantry, which had just marched a thousand miles, not to mention that when they arrived it was the winter of 37-36 BCE. Antony's reason for starting the war before spring was his desire to be with Cleopatra. Once Antony and Cleopatra reached the Euphrates, he had to make a decision: take the path Crassus took or head north and invade Media Atropatene, a Parthian client state, via Armenia. Antony chooses to head north towards Armenia. Once he made his decision, he sent Cleopatra back to Egypt. The reason for Antony's choice is obvious. Phraates has beefed up his defenses along the Euphrates and they are watching Antony closely.⁸

With Cleopatra heading back to Egypt, Antony heads northward from Zeugma on the advice of King Artavasdes of Armenia that the forces of King Artavasdes of Media Atropatene were with the Parthian forces

---

[7] App, 5.95.
[8] Dio 49, 25; Josephus, *Wars of the Jews*, 1. 18.5.

guarding the Euphrates. Thus, if you want to enter Parthia, then Media Atropatene is their brief blind spot—take advantage of it quickly. Moreover, Media Atropatene is rugged terrain, which would negate the use of cavalry, thus forcing the horse-proud Parthians and their allies into hand-to-hand combat with the Roman legionaries. As Antony made his way into Armenia, Artavasdes proudly displayed and offered Antony "6,000 thousand horses drawn up in battle array in full armor and 7,000 foot."[9]

Informants among the Romans and those nearby watching the progress of their movements relayed the information to Phraates. Knowing that the Romans soon would enter the Parthian client state of Media Atropatene, Phraates sends a message to 400 Parthian nobles to assemble their forces, which would total 50,000 cavalry, and prepare to forestall, frustrate, and divert, if not ultimately destroy, the Roman forces.[10]

As the Roman forces moved towards Praaspa the capital of Media Atropatene, they did so without hindrance. One would think Antony would grow suspicious, since he had not encountered the enemy on such a long journey deep into enemy territory. But then again, he trusted his guides without question and never once considered that maybe he's walking into a trap. This is where Antony would commit his second blunder. Antony, growing impatient with the speed of his forces, decides to divide his army.

---

[9] Strabo, 11.14.9; Farrokh, 144.
[10] Justin 41.2.

Antony was growing tired of the sluggish pace. It was not his infantry or cavalry causing the slow movement, but the siege engines and baggage train. The reason for their slow movement goes beyond being weighted down with supplies when you factor in the terrain. Antony led his army through the dense forests of Media Atropatene, easy for infantry and cavalry to maneuver through, but the large cumbersome wagons, along with siege engines, on narrow roads likely required tree removal, which is a task unto itself.[11] Antony had 300 wagons to carry the siege engines, one of which was a battering ram eighty feet long. If the siege weapons were captured or destroyed, they could not be replaced in time, and even if they had time, the wood in the region was not sufficiently long or strong.[12] On top of that, you have the baggage train of valuable supplies, such as food, weapons, clothes, officer's tentage, and medical supplies. Overall, the baggage train was the lifeblood of the army.[13] Antony decided to split his army in two. Antony would take the bulk of the force and place the baggage and siege engines under the command of Oppius Statianus with a security force consisting of two legions.[14] Once Antony detached himself from his burden, it was full steam ahead.[15]

---

[11] Farrokh, 145.
[12] Plut, *Antony*, 38.
[13] Beth F. Scott, James C. Rainey, and Andrew W. Hunt, *The Logistics of War* (Maxwell AFB, Gunter Annex, Ala: AF Logistics Management Agency, 2000), 2.
[14] Velleius Paterculus, *Roman History*, 2.82.
[15] Dio 49, 25; Plut, *Antony*, 38.

Antony was confident that he could take the city of Praaspa with ease. Once outside the city walls, the Romans quickly began the grueling task of building earth mounds in preparation for the arrival of siege equipment, particularly the towers. As the earth ramps moved closer to the walls, one can only imagine the carnage suffered by the Romans below. But as time passed, there was no sign of the siege equipment. With no siege equipment in sight, Antony gives the order to assault the walls; one can speculate that the Roman infantry likely was using makeshift ladders or other ineffective climbing devices. But the numbers of men participating in the assault were ineffective since the walls were strong and heavily defended.[16]

With no success in gaining a foothold on the walls, nor siege engines in sight, Antony grows weary, impatient, and wants to know why the delay. Then Antony receives terrible news: the baggage train under the command of Statianus was attacked, the two legions assigned to escort the train were slaughtered, and the siege equipment destroyed. Many men were taken prisoner, including Polemon, king of Pontus, who was later released on ransom. The person responsible for this was none other than King Phraates himself. While Antony busied himself with the siege of Praaspa, the Parthians kept a close eye from afar on both the besiegers and the vital baggage train. Once Antony's forces were dug in, Phraates took

---

[16] Dio 49, 25; Neilson Carel Debevoise, *A Political History of Parthia* (Chicago, Ill: University of Chicago Press, 1938), 126.

Antony's War to Avenge Crassus to Fulfill Caesar's Dream

advantage of the situation by sending in a large number of cavalry for a surprise attack. But when considering the dense forests of Media Atropatene, it is likely that the cavalry were aided by Median infantry. In some ways, the attack of Antony's baggage train is similar to the Battle of the Teutoburg Forest in 9 AD, in which the Romans were moving through a dense German forest and not marching in combat formation, making them subject to attack. The legions assigned to protect the baggage train under Statianus likely were not marching in combat formation since in addition to providing security, they had to move wagons, and clear trees, dead brush, and the occasional rocks along the way. In addition, notice there was no cavalry assigned to Statianus to scout ahead and keep a close eye on their surroundings nearby. It seems plausible that the Romans were attacked with a barrage of arrows, after which Median infantry charged in and cut the Romans to pieces.[17]

Meantime, where was King Artavasdes of Armenia? Evidently, Artavasdes' mission was to support the rear with Statianus. Plutarch mentions that Artavades left due to "despairing of the Roman cause."[18] Cassius Dio says that he responded to the "message sent to him by Statianus, to go to his assistance, was nevertheless too late, for he found nothing but corpses."[19] Both sources seem to be correct when placed in context. Artavades likely did

---

[17] Plut, *Antony*, 38; Dio 49, 25; Farrokh, 145.
[18] Plut, *Antony*, 39.
[19] Dio 49, 26.

respond, and when he saw the number of corpses, burnt wagons, and the smell of death in the air, became distressed at all he had witnessed. It's likely he felt that Antony and the remains of the Roman forces also had been destroyed. Thus, it was best to turn around and head for home before he and his forces ended up the same way. But even this account is lacking. Considering that Antony did not provide Statianus cavalry to scout out the area, one would think that it would have been Artavasdes' duty to send out cavalry scouts and inform the legions escorting the baggage train of any oncoming enemy attacks, and to take part in the defense, if not a counterattack. It becomes evident that Artavasdes was nowhere near the legions escorting the baggage train and his retreat to Armenia looks as if he had betrayed Antony. If there was one person who could speak on behalf of this disaster, it would have been Polemon, king of Pontus; but his testimony remains silent.

With the siege engines destroyed, two legions massacred, and the food running low, Antony had to make quick decisions. Food was his top priority, but as if matters could not get any worse, the Parthians arrive in full battle array and begin challenging the Romans by shouting insults. Antony understood that if he were to sit still, the Parthians would increase in number and harry his men with hit and run attacks. Antony quickly makes a decision to go forage for food. He takes "ten legions and three praetorian cohorts of men-at-arms, together with all his cavalry." But he has another motive, to get the Parthians to engage in a pitched battle.[20]

After a day's march, Antony sets up camp, but soon he has to take it down, for scouts bring information that the Parthians are on the move. They know where the camp is and are quickly moving in to envelop him. Once the Roman forces assembled, Antony gives the order to move out. Antony seeks to avoid battle, but makes it clear that if the enemy comes within range, the cavalry will charge out against them. The Parthians did come within range and the Roman cavalry quickly scattered them. After seeing the success of the cavalry, the Roman infantry joined the charge and frightened the Parthian horses by yelling and clashing their weapons against their shields, causing them to flee.[21]

Antony quickly took advantage of the situation and pursued the enemy. However, it was all for nothing. The infantry and cavalry were exhausted, they could not keep up with Parthian cavalry, and, to make matters worse, they had nothing of substance to show they had been victorious. Their great efforts produced 80 dead and 30 captured. The Romans were beside themselves after losing 10,000 men along with their baggage train and siege engines, when compared to this measly victory, if one could call it that. But in fact, it was not a battle or a victory. Rather, the Parthians were testing the waters by conducting guerilla hit and run attacks, tactics that the

---

[20] Plut, *Antony*, 39.
[21] Ibid.

Romans had a hard time understanding when facing the Parthians.[22]

The next day, Antony gave the order to head back to Praaspa. While on the move, the Romans encountered a few enemy forces, but as they continued on, their encounters with the Parthians increased until the whole body showed up, challenged them, and attacked from all directions. Antony keeps moving to avoid disaster. Eventually the Romans made it safely back to Praaspa. The Parthian forces that attacked Antony were likely conducting hit and run attacks, for their goal was not to destroy the Roman forces, but rather to demoralize them. In other words, they were tenderizing the Roman forces before commitment to full-scale attack later.[23]

Once Antony made it back to the siege at Praaspa, he received startling news. While he was away, the Median defenders were able to successfully attack the Roman besiegers, dislodge them from their positions and safely return behind the walls of the city. This went on for some time. Antony, enraged by the lack of discipline due to his men not standing their ground, decided to take a disciplinary measure known as "decimation," in which one of every ten soldiers were executed. As for the rest of the besiegers, their punishment was that they would receive rations of barley instead of wheat.[24] But with food running low and Roman foraging parties bringing back

---

[22] Ibid.
[23] Ibid.
[24] Ibid.

more dead and wounded than food, Antony had to do something quick if he wanted his army to survive. Phraates felt the same way about his own forces. Summer was gone, the air was getting colder, and he, like Antony, did not want to encamp for the winter. Unlike Antony, he was afraid that many of his men would desert due to the winter distress.[25]

As the siege continued, some Parthians, who admired the Romans for their bravery and strong will, were able to ride up next to the Roman cavalry, where they would talk of peace and explain to them that Antony was a fool if he were to stay. Phraates was offering to escort them out of Parthian territory peacefully, not to mention that winter and famine was upon them. However, this would also be a problem for the Parthians, excluding famine of course. Winter was upon them and it was time to move out. King Phraates wanted to end this stagnated war before winter arrived. Antony received the news and considered their proposal, that if they agreed to Phraates' kind gesture of escorting them out of Parthian lands peacefully, they will do so. Antony agreed and sent an envoy to meet with Phraates. When they arrived, he was "seated upon a golden chair and twanging his bowstring." The Romans agreed to peace, but delivered their terms. Phraates must return the Roman standards they had in their possession if he desired peace. Of course, Phraates objected to this and assured Antony of a safe escort home. Antony likely thought long and hard over this, but he had

---

[25] Ibid, 40.

no other option. The walls of Praaspa were too strong, he had no siege equipment, food was running extremely low, and any attempt to search for a meal resulted in death. If starvation does not kill you, the winter surely will. Antony made the decision to leave. This was not easy for Antony and it was hard for him to explain this to the men, so he had Domitius Ahenobarbus deliver the speech. Antony felt like a failure in this great endeavor, but even he understood that it was best to fail while alive and the majority of his men intact than end up like Crassus at Carrhae.[26]

ON THE ROAD TO HELL

Once the Romans were in battle formations, the Medes came out, destroyed the makeshift siege equipment, and scattered the mounds.[27] As Antony was about to give the order to march, a Mardian, faithful to the Romans, advised Antony to keep close to the hills on the right, for exposing any part of the legions on an open tract would invite disaster. Moreover, there were many villages that could provide provisions for the journey. Antony agreed. He knew the Parthians were watching and that any meeting might cause the Parthians to become suspicious and distrust his intentions. Antony agreed to the Mardian's proposal and asked for his pledge in good

---

[26] Ibid.
[27] Dio 49.28.

faith. The Mardian agreed to "be put in fetters until he should bring the army safely into Armenia."[28]

Once the Mardian was placed in fetters, the Romans marched for two days without hindrance. On the third day, Antony decided to march in a looser order. The Parthians were the furthest thing from his mind and it seemed that they had lived up to their bargain. All was well until they came upon a flood that covered the road, which halted their crossing. While the Romans looked on at the burst dike that had dammed the waters, the Mardian was quick to notice that this was no accident. He warned Antony that Parthians had done this; it was a trap to delay their movement. Antony quickly gave the order to assemble into battle formation. As Antony was getting the legionaries into position, the Parthians were able to surround and ride around the Romans, hoping to cause confusion and disorder within the ranks. As the legions were getting into formation under a hail of arrows, the Roman light infantry moved through the Roman ranks attempting to pursue and engage the horse archers, but were met with death due to the high number of arrows fired upon them. Once the slingers and javelin-throwers made their way through the ranks and took their positions, they were able to inflict casualties on the Parthians. The Parthians soon retreated and regrouped. As the Parthians were coming back for round two, Antony had to decide whether to let his slingers and javelin-throwers shower the enemy with projectiles and face arrows in return, or send

---

[28] Plut, *Antony*, 41.

out his Celtic cavalry to counter them. He decided that in order to save lives it was best to send out the cavalry. Once the Celtic cavalry were loosed, Antony likely gave them cover fire using his slingers as they advanced. As they approached, the Parthian horse archers quickly retreated, which suggests that, the leaden missiles delivered by the slingers was enough and to engage the Celtic cavalry would be costly. The Romans would not see the Parthians for the remainder of the day.[29]

After the enemy had left the field of battle, Antony decided that it would be best to march in a hollow square formation with slingers and javelin-throwers covering his rear and flanks. By doing this, Antony would have short and long-range firepower, protection that was greatly needed, since slingers can outrange archers, and if the horse archers or cataphract made their way through the hail of projectiles, the javelin-throwers would be able to counter them. In addition, Antony gave strict orders to his cavalry to rout the enemy horsemen, but not to pursue them. Antony was taking every precaution since he was now in a similar situation as Crassus had been some 20 years earlier.[30]

Two days later, the Parthians returned to harass the Romans. Flavius Gallus asked Antony if he could spare some light-armed infantry from the rear and some cavalry. Antony agreed to the request. Gallus pressed on, attacking the Parthian cavalry, but made a vital mistake. Instead of

---

[29] Ibid.
[30] Ibid., 42.

leading them back towards the legionaries, he followed after them. Gallus fell right into the Parthian trap. The rear guard, seeing that Gallus had pursued the enemy so far that he was separated from the main body, began to shout in a vain attempt to call him back. In the ensuing battle, a quaestor by the name of Titus grabbed hold of the standard, tried to rally the men back, and abused Gallus for wasting so many lives. Gallus returned the favor and abuse to Titus for questioning him. Titus would have no more of it and withdrew, leaving Gallus and his men behind. Gallus, confident that he could take the enemy, continued the attack, forcing his way through the enemy, only to be enveloped. To make matters worse, more Parthian cavalry were converging on the scene. Gallus quickly sent a message to Canidius for aid. Canidius would send a small detachment to help in the effort to free Gallus and his men, only to see that detachment decimated. The Romans, who were not acquainted with Parthian tactics, kept sending detachment after detachment to fight the enemy only to lose them. Antony had to do something quickly before he lost his army and quickly sent in the third legion, which was able to break the Parthian momentum during the battle, causing them to flee.[31]

Even though the Romans were able to break free from the Parthian grip, they lost much: 3,000 men were dead and another 5,000 wounded, including Gallus, who took four arrows to the chest and soon would die. Antony

---

[31] Plut, *Antony*, 42.

was said to have "tears of sympathy in his eyes" as he visited the men who were wounded. The many wounded "seized his hand and exhorted him to go away and take care of himself, and not to be distressed. They called him Imperator, and said that they were safe if only he were unharmed." With another 8,000 men out of action, Antony was still far from safe.[32]

With night fast approaching, Antony decided that it was best to camp for the night. While the Romans set up camp and temporary defenses, the Parthians celebrated their small victory as they bivouacked not far from the Roman camp and prepared for an early morning attack. As the sun began to peek over the eastern horizon, the Parthians were gathering in greater numbers, some 40,000 horsemen along with the king's royal guard. As Antony and his men were preparing to move out, Antony asked for a black robe to look more pitiful in their eyes. His friends quickly rejected this for it was a morbid symbol. Antony agreed to their objections and came forward with a purple robe upon his shoulders, a much better symbol and morale booster.

As the Romans moved out, the Parthians were on their way to plunder the Romans.

The Parthians were in for a surprise. The Roman forces were fresh and better organized. When they saw the Parthians charging towards them, they unleashed their projectiles, striking many of the horse archers. The Parthians were in shock and quickly went from pillaging

---

[32] Plut, *Antony*, 43.

mode to battle formations. While the Romans were well prepared for the coming fight, the Parthians quickly looked for opportunities in an attempt to avoid defeat. One opportunity the Parthians found involved the Romans marching up and down hills. As the Romans were slowly descending the hills, the Parthians began showering them with arrows, a primary target no doubt, but the Romans also had a plan as well. In order to avoid death by arrows, the Romans quickly wheeled around their light-infantry and enclosed them by dropping to one knee, in which they would hold their shields out in front of them. The second rank would hold their shields out over the heads of the first rank and so forth until they had a wall and roof of shields protecting every vantage point; basically, the Romans were in the testudo or tortoise formation. The Parthians, thinking the Romans were tired, ceased fire. The Parthians soon dismounted, tossing their bows aside in favor of a dagger or spear, and approached the Romans. Once they were close enough, a battle cry went up and the Romans sprang to their feet and easily cut the Parthians to pieces. A lightly armored horse archer is no match for a heavy infantryman, especially in hand-to-hand combat. The Parthians soon realized that it was a trap and quickly returned to their horses and rode away.[33]

The testudo formation provided a platform of success that the Romans from this point on would use, with the baggage, light infantry, and cavalry in the center

---

[33] Plut, *Antony*, 44-45; Dio 49. 29-30.

of the army.³⁴ While the testudo provided ample security during their long march home, it could not protect Antony's forces from famine. "An army marches on its stomach" Napoleon Bonaparte once said, and rightfully so.³⁵

One of the drawbacks Antony's forces faced was that even with little grain in possession, they had no tools for grinding. Those were abandoned due to the loss of pack animals. Those pack animals still alive were now transporting the sick and wounded on wagons. With food dwindling, the Roman troops resorted to buying and selling within their camp to alleviate their hunger. Plutarch mentions, "one Attic choenix (about a quart) of wheat brought fifty drachmas; and loaves of barley bread were sold for their weight in silver." However there were soldiers who could not afford wheat or barley and resorted to eating "vegetables and roots, they could find few to which they were accustomed, and were compelled to make trial of some never tasted before." If the Parthians did not kill you, hunger would, for many of the men who ate plants unknown to them began to slip into a world of fantasy and madness. Plutarch mentions that those "who ate of it had no memory, and no thought of anything else than the one task of moving or turning every stone, as if he were accomplishing something of great importance." These poor souls would have no sense of direction, except

---

³⁴ Dio 49.30.
³⁵ Martin L. Van Creveld, *Supplying War: Logistics from Wallenstein to Patton* (Cambridge: Cambridge Univ. Press, 2009), 40.

that they would be found "stooping to the ground and digging around the stones or removing them; and finally they would vomit bile and die, since the only remedy, wine, was not to be had."[36] The likely herb that caused such symptoms is the deadly nightshade, Atropa Belladonna.[37] If eating poisonous plants did not kill you, the Parthians would, as they continued to conduct hit and run attacks on the Romans, causing Antony cry out "O the Ten Thousand!" Antony, hoping he could reach safety like Xenophon's army, found only death.[38]

If anything positive can be gained from Antony's retreat, it is that the army stood its ground and stayed unified throughout this endeavor, so much so that the Parthians took notice. Roman soldiers searching for "fodder or grain," would be approached by Parthian cavalrymen with bows unstrung, indicating that they were no threat. Many of the Roman soldiers would come back to camp and report their encounters, in which the Parthians informed them that they would be leaving soon, for this, was "the end of their retaliation." But even as the Romans moved out, the Medes would follow, but did so as observers while others rode ahead to inform the locals of the approaching Roman army and advising them to be calm, courteous, and respectful as the Romans passed through. Once the Romans approached the various

---

[36] Plut, *Antony*, 45.
[37] John Lindley and Thomas Moore, *The Treasury of Botany; A Popular Dictionary of the Vegetable Kingdom* (London: Longmans, Green, 1876), 104.
[38] Plut, *Antony*, 45.

villages, the locals engaged them in a friendly manner. However, looks can be deceiving. The Medes that stayed close by were observing their movements, collecting intelligence, and even approaching them with a friendly attitude. The tactic was simple, kill the Romans with kindness and build up their trust, causing the Romans to lower their guard. This worked so well that Antony began to consider changing direction and moving his army across the plains.[39]

While it is evident that the Romans were oblivious to the ruse, a man by the name of Mithridates, who happened to be cousin to Monaeses, approached the camp, wishing to speak with Antony, but he needed a translator who could speak the Parthian or Syrian tongue. Antony's friend, Alexander of Antioch, would translate for Mithridates. Mithridates asked Alexander and Antony if they could see those hills ahead and both men said yes. Mithridates went on to inform them that "the Parthians with all their forces are lying in ambush for you." As mentioned, the Parthians and their allied forces hoped that their acts of kindness would cause Antony to change direction and enter into the open plain. Mithridates made it clear to Antony that it was best to move along the mountains to avoid the Parthian cavalry, even though it would cause "thirst and hard labor." But Mithridates gives a dire warning: if Antony chooses the other road and "proceeds by way of the plains, let him know that the fate

---

[39] Ibid., 46.

of Crassus awaits him." Afterwards, Mithridates left.[40] Antony, at the crossroads of a major decision, calls for a meeting with his officers and the Mardian guide. While there is much debate, it comes down to what the guide thinks, the Mardian agreed with Mithridates' advice. Antony agreed with him and ordered his men to carry as much water as they could, for the road ahead was dry for at least a day. Many of the men had no vessels to carry water and resorted to using their helmets, while others used skins.

The Parthians kept a close eye on Antony's forces, once they saw them move out under the cover of night. The Romans lowered their shields, since the rugged terrain that lay ahead was not favorable to the testudo formation and they did not expect the Parthians to attack while it was dark. It was during this moment that the Parthians drew up their plans against them.[41]

While the Romans moved ahead, feeling safe from attack, but worried about thirst, the Parthians, who normally did not move at night, followed. As the sun rose over the eastern horizon, many of the Romans were tired, exhausted, and thirsty after marching 30 miles over harsh, rugged terrain. They were disillusioned of safety once they saw the Parthians charging towards them from the rear. It was nothing more than a hit and run attack, but it had a profound impact on the Roman forces, for they not only

---

[40] Ibid., 46-47.
[41] Ibid., 47.

had to continue moving forward but also had to turn around and fight.

But as one can imagine, the brief hit and run engagements made the Romans even thirstier. The Parthians knew this and their surprise attack was meant to push the Romans forward to quench their thirst at a nearby river. The Romans further ahead, away from the engagement, came to a river; the water looked clear and potable. Many indulged to relieve their dry mouths, only to succumb to "pains, cramping of the bowels and an inflammation of one's thirst."[42] The reason for the discomfort was due to the water being salty, for the water they drank was likely coming from the Caspian Sea. Pliny mentions that the "running waters near the Caspian Gates for instance, which are known as the 'Rivers of Salt.' The same is the case, too, in the vicinity of the Mardi and of the people of Armenia."[43] Once word reached the soldiers further back that water had been found, there was a mad rush to relieve their thirst. The Mardian guide tried to stop the men from drinking the poisonous water, because, being from the area, he knew that the stream was a poisonous and likely referred to it as the "Rivers of Salt." No matter how hard they tried to stop the men seeking water, it was no use; many drank and died. Antony now put his foot down and ordered his men to wait, promising

---

[42] Ibid.
[43] Pliny, *Nat* 31.39.

them that there was drinkable water ahead, and to relax, for the terrain ahead was not suitable for cavalry attacks.[44]

After the ordeal at the river, Antony ordered his men to pitch tents and rest. While Antony himself likely relaxed, Mithridates had reappeared. Mithridates informed Alexander that it was best to rest for a little while, for a river with drinkable water was not far away, and once crossed, the Parthians were not likely to pursue. Alexander quickly relayed the message to Antony, who agreed and allowed his men a little rest before making the call to move out. This information so pleased Antony that he rewarded Mithridates with "golden drinking-cups in great numbers, as well as bowls. Mithridates took as many of these as he could hide in his garments and rode off."[45]

As the Roman forces packed their tents away and moved out, the Parthians continued to keep a close eye on them. The Parthians did not attempt to attack the Romans while it was still daylight, instead, waiting for nightfall. When the Romans marched, feeling semi-safe under the cover of night, the Parthians fell on them and attacked: "those who had gold or silver were slain and robbed of it, and the goods were plundered from the beasts of burden; and finally the baggage-carriers of Antony were attacked, and beakers and costly tables were cut to pieces or distributed about."[46] The description Plutarch provides points to a well-planned raid. But how would the

---

[44] Plut, *Antony* 47.
[45] Ibid., 48.
[46] Ibid.

Parthians know where to attack and why did they conduct a raid? The answer points to the mysteriously appearing and disappearing Mithridates. Remember, for his advice, he was rewarded with golden vessels and he took as much as he could carry. Moreover, he was the cousin of Monaeses, the disgruntled Parthian. Mithridates was likely a spy, collecting intelligence and relaying information to the Parthians.

While the Parthians were pillaging the Roman army of its valuables, the Romans fell into a state of shock. The attack so surprised the Romans that it caused great confusion, which rippled through the ranks. Even Antony thought that he was about to meet the same fate as Crassus. Antony was preparing for the worst and ordered his bodyguard, Rhamnus, on his command, to run him through with a sword and cut off his head. Antony wanted to make sure that if he were defeated, the enemy could not take him alive or recognize him dead.

Once the attack was over, realization set in among the Roman ranks that it was a raid. Even though many were wounded and killed, there likely was great relief among them. Antony was tired; his men were in tears; and the Mardian gave encouragement not to give up, for the river they sought is near. Antony, decided at that point that it was best to make camp and regroup before proceeding.

As the sun began to show its face over the eastern horizon, the Romans awoke to a shower of arrows in the rear ranks. The Romans in the rear jumped to action and formed a testudo, which they had done many times before in warding off arrow attacks. With the Parthians being present and a nuisance, Antony ordered the entire army to form the testudo formation and to proceed little by little in this fashion until they reached the river. Once the river was in sight, Antony sent the sick and wounded across first, which would allow them to get water. As the Romans slowly poured across the river undisturbed, the Parthians unstrung their bows and "bade the Romans cross over with good courage, bestowing much praise also upon their valour."[47]

Six days later, the Romans came to the river Araxes, which served as the boundary between Media and Armenia. Before the Roman forces crossed the river, a report was given that indicated that the Parthians were waiting in ambush for the Romans to cross before they made their attack. Antony, tired, like his men, knew that they had no choice but to cross, for if they sought a different route, they faced the possibility of total annihilation. Therefore, Antony will take the chance, cross the river, and see what happens, because if they cross, at least some, will be free from the terror that lurks behind.[48]

---

[47] Ibid., 49.2
[48] Ibid., 49.

ARTAVASDES MUST PAY!

Once the Romans were across the river, the men began to weep as great joy and sorrow overcame them, relief to be alive and sadness for those left behind, rotting in the wilderness. However, another enemy awaits the Romans: disease. As the Romans continued to push on home through the mountainous districts of Armenia during the harsh winter, many fell ill and died of dysentery and dropsy.[49] The wounded were suffering from the cold temperatures.[50] Antony, like any general after battle, decided to hold a review of the men, and found that out of 113,000 troops at his disposal, 20,000 infantry and 4,000 cavalry had died. This does not include the number of wounded. More than half of the deaths were caused by disease.[51] Eventually Antony refused to receive any more reports concerning deaths and illnesses. There is no doubt that Antony was troubled by these reports. However, Antony may have refused to hear these reports for political reasons. Antony, as does any general in the field, was sending dispatches back to Rome. He is aware that his watered-down dispatches will arrive alongside the brutal truth, which will be dispensed in rumors. Therefore, Antony must keep the truth to a bare minimum and

---

[49] Ibid.
[50] Dio 49.31.
[51] Plut, *Antony* 50.

humor the rumors, for any confirmed negative reports would quickly shift the power struggle to favor Octavian.[52]

While Antony and his men suffer from exhaustion and starvation, King Phraates commemorates his victory over Antony by issuing coins. One of the coins depicts the capture of Antony and Cleopatra as the spoils of war.[53] Another coin issued depicts an eagle crowning the head of Phraates with a wreath.[54]

While in Armenia, Antony could not stop thinking about King Artavasdes, the man who he felt robbed him of victory by fleeing when he was most needed to protect the baggage train and supplies. It has been twenty-seven days since they marched from Praaspa, during which the Parthians engaged them eighteen times. Antony's men want to take revenge on Artavasdes. Antony decided to keep calm and not make any hasty decisions, for his army was weak and badly in need of supplies.[55]

With his army lumbering through the rugged Armenian terrain, Antony gave the order to halt and encamp. Antony realized that his men could go on no longer; he had lost another 8,000 men due to the harsh winter and lack of supplies.[56] Therefore, Antony heads off to pay the king of Armenia a visit, likely wanting to give the king a tongue-lashing, if not personally kill the man

---

[52] Dio 49.31.
[53] Debevoise, 131-132.
[54] Warwick Wroth, *Catalogue of the Coins of Parthia* (London: Printed by the Order of Trustees, 1903), xl
[55] Plut, *Antony* 50.
[56] Plut, *Antony* 51.

himself. Instead, Antony flattered the king and was able to procure a loan and much-needed supplies for his men. Moreover, Antony also persuaded Artavasdes to allow his men to stay in Armenia, for he was planning another invasion of Parthia in the coming spring.[57]

Afterwards, Antony left Armenia with a small company of men and headed for a place called White Village, which was situated between Berytus and Sidon in Syria. It was here that Antony waited for his beloved Cleopatra. He waited impatiently, for her arrival was taking too long. Because of this, Antony began drinking, and he would occasionally spring up to see if she had arrived in port. Once Cleopatra had arrived with money and clothes, Antony was happy.[58] Each Roman soldier was paid "four hundred sesterces" while the rest received "a proportionate allowance." Antony handed out so much money that he soon ran out and had to dive into his own coffers to pay the men. In order to recoup his loses, Antony solicited money from his friends, while taxing his allies.[59]

While Antony's men remained in Armenia, he would return to the bosom of Cleopatra in Alexandria for a short time. There, Antony licked his wounds. He was not ignorant; he knew that the Roman Senate knew of the disaster that had taken place, for as many color-coded dispatches as Antony had sent, rumors giving the opposite story had followed. However, Even though he and others

---

[57] Dio 49.31.
[58] Plut, *Antony* 51.
[59] Dio 49.31.

investigated the matter, Octavian did nothing, keeping the public in the dark for the time being. Octavian had other matters at hand and the information he had on Antony was damning enough; but now was not the time to use it against him.[60]

While Antony understood the possible repercussions back in Rome, from his failed campaign, his mind was set on getting some payback from the man who abandoned them when he needed him most. While Antony wintered in Egypt, back in Parthia, the king of the Medes argued over the spoils of war with Phraates. However, the Median king soon began to worry that his disagreement with Phraates might cost him his throne. Therefore, the Median king did what many had done in the past: run to the Romans seeking assistance. The Median sent an ambassador named Polemon to seek an alliance with Antony. Antony was delighted by the news and accepted and rewarded the ambassador handsomely by giving him the province of Lesser Armenia.[61] Antony could now make plans, for he now had the horsemen and archers he lacked during the first campaign against Parthia. This sounds familiar, for Antony had Armenian horsemen capable of using the bow once before and they abandoned him. Nevertheless, Antony formed his plans, similar to his plans for Armenia, except this time he had to travel a little further east to meet up with his new Median

---

[60] Ibid., 32.
[61] Ibid., 33.

ally. From Media, they would together cross the Araxes River and push into Parthia for another round of war.[62]

While Antony was preparing for his second Parthian campaign, he also summed Artavasdes to come to Egypt as a friend. Of course, it was a deception. Artavasdes was no fool, at least at first, but quietly ignored Antony's request. Antony, instead of getting angry, sought other means. Once Antony had left Egypt to join his men for the second Parthian campaign in the spring of 34 BCE, word reached him that his second wife, Octavia was on her way to Egypt with gifts. Antony quickly returned to Egypt. Octavia, while in Athens, received letters from Antony. Antony made it clear that she was to stay away, but he would accept the fine gifts he requested. Octavia was devastated.[63]

Antony left Egypt soon after, seeking a way to lure Artavasdes with the least amount of trouble. Antony sent Quintus Dellius to make a deal. Antony suggested the daughter of Artavasdes and his son Alexander should marry. Artavasdes smelled a plot and decided to ignore Antony no matter how many gifts he would receive due to the marriage proposal. Antony decided to send Dellius again to Artavasdes as a diversion while Antony rapidly marched towards the Armenian capital of Artaxata. Antony's gamble paid off; he kept the king occupied long enough to sneak in unexpectedly with a show of force. Artavasdes' advisors pleaded with him to go out and meet

---

[62] Plut, *Antony* 52.
[63] Plut, *Antony* 53-54.

Antony, which is what Antony had hoped. Artavasdes was immediately taken into custody upon arrival. Antony decided not to place the king in fetters, as he did not want to alarm the public. Antony's reason is understandable: control the situation and you will control the crowd. But he also had another reason besides safeguarding the lives of his men, the gold, and Octavian. Antony ordered Artavasdes to lead him to the forts where he kept his gold. Antony is said to have "professed to have arrested him for no other purpose than to levy tribute upon the Armenians for the safeguarding of the king and to maintain his sovereignty."[64] Antony not only arrested the man who betrayed him, for not protecting the baggage train under the command of Statianus and for robbing the country of its wealth in order to keep it out of Octavian's hands. Before Antony arrested the king of Armenia, Octavian had been in correspondence with Artavasdes in hope that they could work together; but Octavian also wanted to injure Antony by denying him his triumph. If war between the two were to follow, Octavian would need a powerful military and monetary ally.[65]

---

[64] Dio 49.39.
[65] Ibid., 41.

ANTONY'S DEFEAT IS OCTAVIAN'S VICTORY

Antony would leave his army in Armenia and give a portion of Armenia to the Median king. In return, the Mede returned the military standards lost by Statianus and agreed to Antony's request to betroth his son Alexander to Iotape, the daughter of the Median king. Afterwards, Antony headed back to Egypt to celebrate a triumph. He entered Alexandria in a chariot to the sound of a cheering crowd, bringing Artavasdes, his family, and the wealth of Armenia before Cleopatra, who was seated among the populace on a gilded chair on a silver-plated platform. Artavasdes refused to pay homage to Cleopatra before the crowd and was soon after placed in prison.[66]

Even though Antony rode in as a conquering king, he had failed to capture Artaxes, the son of Artavasdes, whom the people of Armenia had elected to be their king. Artaxes escaped and rode off into Parthia seeking the help of King Phraates. Antony's triumph would be short lived, for soon after his grand parade through the streets of Alexandria, Octavian was building his case against Antony.[67]

Once the Second Triumvirate expired in 33 BCE, Octavian went on a propaganda campaign and did everything in his power to convince the Roman people that Antony was an enemy of Rome. He first tried to

---

[66] Ibid., 39-40, 44.
[67] Ibid.

convince the senate that Antony had divided Eastern Roman territory; of course, this was not disputed, even though Octavian provided the evidence that Antony had divided Rome's territorial holdings along with titles in the east among his and Cleopatra's children and even gave territory and title to the only child born between Julius Caesar and Cleopatra.[68] However, the senate and the people were not convinced. Even though Octavian brought forth charge after charge against Antony, it still was not convincing to the Senate or the Roman people. Octavian decided to take a different route and blamed Cleopatra due to her dangerous influence on Antony. In other words, Octavian sold the Senate hook, line, and sinker that Cleopatra was the real power. Since she holds the power, she will use it to undermine and take Rome at some future point. But what really got the Senate in a war fervor was the fact that Antony's will, which was obtained illegally by Octavian, provided that he be buried beside Cleopatra in Alexandria. The Senate went wild and agreed to declare war, not on Antony, but on Cleopatra. Octavian wanted to "avoid" civil war, but knew that by declaring war on Cleopatra, Antony would join her side, thus ensuring a civil war.[69]

In 32 BCE, King Phraates was likely following the situation between Antony and Octavian. Phraates knew that he could not launch an offensive campaign in the presence of Roman soldiers; for now, he stayed on the

---

[68] Plut, *Antony* 54.
[69] Dio 50.3-4.

defensive. But when civil war became a reality, Phraates waited for that moment when Antony would be taking the bulk of his forces westward into Asia Minor. Once Antony was far enough away not to make an impact, Phraates and Artaxes launched a surprise attack, likely probing the Roman and Median forces. The attack failed as the Medes and Romans soundly defeated the Parthians. . Not long afterward, Antony summoned his men back with except a few who remained behind. Once word reached Phraates that Media was defenseless, he gave the order to attack, and this time, Antony would lose his ally, Armenia, and a little later his life, after the Battle of Actium in 31 BCE against Octavian.[70]

While Artaxes was exercising his kingly rights by killing the remaining Roman soldiers in Armenia, Phraates was now in a bit of trouble himself. Long known for his cruelties, Phraates caused quite the upheaval in his own empire when a certain Tiridates II challenged him for the throne and drove Phraates into exile. Nothing is known about Tiridates, but it's quite possible that he may have been the general who successfully drove Antony out of Media Atropatene and back into Armenia. Whatever the case may be, he held a considerable amount of power and popular support. But while Phraates was in exile, he was able to gain the service of the Scythians in 30 BCE. When word reached Tiridates that Phraates, along with a powerful Scythian force, was on the way, a battle likely ensured. It was during this struggle that both men felt the

---

[70] Ibid., 49.44, 51.16.

balance of power tip against them, which caused them to seek Roman help.[71]

Octavian was in the province of Asia at the time and paid no attention to the two men jousting for throne and empire. Octavian was busy dealing with various subject nations; one could say that he ignored the request of both men, for he wanted the Parthians to exhaust themselves before he considered any deals. Eventually, Tiridates would be defeated and would flee to Syria, taking with him Phraates' youngest son.[72]

Octavian brought the boy and Tiridates before the Senate; envoys from Phraates were present as well. Phraates demanded that Octavian give him his son and Tiridates back. Octavian decided to keep Tiridates, who tried to persuade Octavian that he would be Rome's puppet if Rome were to restore him to the throne. Octavian declined and decided that he would neither give Tiridates over to Phraates nor give any assistance to Tiridates against the Parthians. Instead, he permitted Tiridates to live in Syria. Octavian understood that so long as he kept Tiridates under his influence, he had an instigator and ally that could disrupt Parthia, a pawn being used indirectly. As for the boy, Octavian would hand him over to Phraates on one condition: that Phraates return the prisoners of war from both Crassus and Antony's campaigns, along with the standards. Phraates

---

[71] Ibid., 51.18.
[72] Ibid.

agreed but it would be some time before Octavian's request would be honored.[73]

While Tiridates lived in exile in the province of Roman Syria, he began planning another attack on Parthia. In spring 26 BCE, Tiridates invaded Parthia again with successes and issued coins of himself with the title Arsaces Philoromaeus or "Arsaces Friend of the Romans." However, his claim to the throne did not last long, and he was ousted from power, after which he fled to Spain, where he joined Octavian, now Emperor Augustus. But Tiridates would return in March 25 BCE, when he had coins struck once again in the city of Seleucia. By May of that year, the mint in Seleucia was issuing coins bearing the image of Phraates. This tells us that Phraates was again in full control. As for Tiridates, he simply is mentioned no more. Once Phraates had regained full control of his throne and empire, Octavian also planned a campaign against Parthia. However, Octavian had other issues and another Parthian invasion was mere fantasy at the time: no need to waste more fine men to fulfill a dream.[74]

Dreaming of an empire expanding to the borders of India and possibly beyond is one thing, but to negotiate and to receive the prisoners of war and the standards lost was a reality. When Phraates heard of Augustus' arrival in Syria, he feared another invasion, and quickly met with the Romans to hammer out a deal.[75] On May 12, 20 BCE,[76]

---

[73] Ibid., 51.18; 53.33.
[74] Debevoise, 138.
[75] Dio 54.8.

Antony's War to Avenge Crassus to Fulfill Caesar's Dream

Augustus commissioned Tiberius to receive the prisoners and standards from the Parthians. While gathering Rome's standards was easy, gathering the prisoners of war was not. While some of the prisoners agreed to go, others committed suicide due to shame; others, who decided not to go or commit suicide, disappeared within the Parthian society.[77] Augustus waited eagerly in Syria for Tiberius to return to him. Once Tiberius returned with the souls and the standards, Augustus celebrated. Phraates also had to make another agreement, to cease its claim on Armenia and to give five of his sons over as hostages in an act of good faith. Phraates agreed and there was peace between the two superpowers.[78]

---

[76] Ovid, *Fasti* 5.
[77] Dio 54.8.
[78] Suetonius, *Augustus* 21.3; *Tiberius* 9.1; Just 42.5.

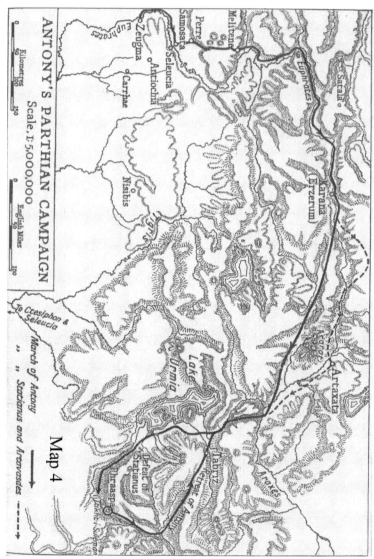

Figure 26 Antony's Parthian Campaign. Map from *Rome's Wars in Parthia*. Courtesy of Rose Mary Sheldon

Antony's War to Avenge Crassus to Fulfill Caesar's Dream

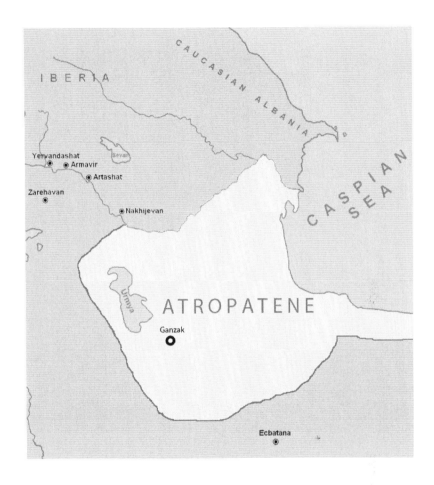

Figure 27 Mark Antony's target.
http://commons.wikimedia.org/wiki/File:AtropateneHistoryofIran.png
Author: Aivazovsky.
(CC BY-SA 3.0)

Figure 28 King Artavazdes II provided additional aid to Antony but once the Parthian and Roman troops were engaged in combat, he turned around and went back to Armenia.
http://commons.wikimedia.org/wiki/File:ArtavasdesII.jpg
Author: Aryamahasattva

6

PROXY ALONG THE EUPHRATES

As both parties returned to their respected capitals, Augustus used propaganda to pretend that he had conquered the Parthians, declaring, "that he had recovered without a struggle what had formerly been lost in battle." Augustus rode into Rome on horseback and was awarded a Triumphal arch. Soon afterwards, he ordered sacrifices and had the standards placed in the temple of Mars Ultor on Capitol Hill. But before Augustus could celebrate and set sail for Rome with the former prisoners and standards in hand, he gave Tiberius another order: accompany Tigranes III to Armenia and place him on the throne. The people of Armenia at this time had no problem with this, for they were tired of Artaxes and opted to be ruled by his brother Tigranes, who happened to be in Rome. By the time the Romans entered Armenia, Artaxes had been slain by his own people.[1] Once Tigranes took his throne with Roman support, he soon fell under the influence of the Parthians, for his coins bear Parthian titles, suggesting a shift in loyalty.[2]

    Even though peace had been established between the two powers, Augustus may have wanted peace for

---

[1] Dio 54.8-9.
[2] Debevoise, 141-142.

another reason and that was trade. Augustus was no fool, being a politically savvy character, and he understood that any further wars between the two powers would drain the coffers of Rome and destroy his political career. In addition, the penetration and conquest of Germany was far more expedient at the time. Furthermore, establishing peace with Parthia and placing a pro-Roman king on the throne of Armenia would allow the east-west market an unimpeded flow. Roman markets from Syria to Spain would flourish with exports of pepper from India, Arabian incense, East African ivory, and even silk from China. Even though many of these goods already were found in Roman markets, peace allowed certainty and abundance of flow.[3] Even though peace allowed commodities to pass freely across borders, for the most part, emperors like Augustus and those following also saw another opportunity: expansion without war.

One example is when the Emperor Tiberius around 18/19 CE gave Germanicus a mission to secure trade relations with Mesene. Germanicus sent a merchant by the name of Alexander the Palmyrene on a diplomatic mission to the kingdom of Mesene, also known as Characene. Alexander's mission was to make contact and establish a commercial relationship. Mesene was economically and politically strategic, for its location is on the Persian Gulf and its harbors connect Mesopotamia with India. Another

---

[3] J. Thorley (1969). The Development of Trade Between the Roman Empire and the East under Augustus. *Greece and Rome* (Second Series), 16, pp 209-223.

reason besides establishing a commercial relationship is one of diplomacy. The kingdom of Mesene was a Parthian vassal state, which, at times, took advantage of the internal conflict that plagued the Arsacid court by declaring independence, only to be subjugated when the conflict subsided. Because of their delicate situation, Germanicus likely felt that it was necessary to extend a hand, an alternative to the Parthians, and expand the Roman sphere of influence. In other words, Rome's grand strategy in the Near East was to build a coalition of friendly nations along the Parthian borders.[1] Trade routes now open to the Roman Empire would provide future emperors the opportunity to expand Rome's sphere of influence along the Euphrates. The cold war instigated a tug of war over the many thrones that dotted the landscape between Rome and Parthia.

A GIFT FOR PHRAATES

Augustus presented Phraates a gift around the same time he received the prisoners and standards. The gift Augustus presented to Phraates was a beautiful concubine by the name of Muse or Thermusa. Phraates accepted the gift. Musa would eventually bear Phraates a son and name him Phraataces. Phraates grew to love Musa

---

[1] Leonardo Gregoratti, The Palmyrenes and the Arsacid Policy. http://www.academia.edu/795802/The_Palmyrenes_and_the_Arsacid_Policy.

so much that he made her his legitimate wife.[2] Musa's influence over Phraates grew stronger, and after a while, she was able to persuade him to send his four sons to Rome as a show of fidelity. Phraates agreed to send them, for Musa convinced him that they could be plotting rebellion, or even worse, to murder their father. Phraates acted quickly and sent a message to Marcus Titius, the Roman governor of Syria, to meet with him; and so he handed over his sons Seraspadanes, Rhodaspes, Phraates, and Bonones, along with two wives and four of their sons. Musa, in fact, wanted the competition removed so that her son Phraataces would be sole ruler once Phraates died.[3]

      There is no doubt that the actions of Phraates upset the Parthian nobility, but evidently, there was still more going on to cause a new political upheaval. Remember, Tiridates had challenged him for the throne a little more than ten years earlier, with some success. Now, he had a new challenger in Mithridates. Unfortunately, there is no information other than his name and the fact that Mithridates challenged Phraates for the throne. However, Mithridates must have had a considerable amount of influence, for he was able to take the throne from Phraates for a brief moment, roughly between 12-9 BCE. Moreover, it seems that the civil war being waged in Parthia went on much longer, since a certain Babylonian Jew, Zamaris, fled the region with five hundred horse archers and one hundred relatives, seeking refuge in Antioch roughly

---

[2] Joseph, *AJ*, 18, 2–4.
[3] Strabo, 16.28.

around 6 BCE. It is evident that Zamaris was no merchant, but rather a powerful landowning noble fleeing for his life, possibly for supporting Mithridates or some other newcomer who challenged Phraates.[4]

As Phraataces grew older and was alone in his father's court, his mother began to persuade her son to take power now by murdering his father. If Phraates died of old age, there would be a family funeral, after which the pursuit of power by way of fratricide would begin. Musa convinced Phraataces to murder his father in 2 BCE. How Phraates died and by what method is unknown, as well as whether Musa was involved directly or behind the scenes. Nevertheless, Phraates, viewed as a tyrant many decades before, was himself killed by a tyrant.

PHRAATACES THE UNWANTED

After the murder of Phraates, Phraataces took the throne as Phraates V. Those who dwelled within the court, such as the nobles and magi, were not ignorant of what had taken place. Word spreads fast and word soon reached all their ears that young Phraates had a weird and wicked love for his mother, not to mention that they were appalled by the murder.[5] The Parthian court was indifferent towards Phraataces, but Augustus likely loved

---

[4] Joseph, *AJ*, 16,8.4; 17,2.1; Debevoise, 144-145.
[5] Ibid., 18, 2–4.

the fact that Phraataces was on the throne. Augustus could play king and policy maker now.

Once Phraataces was firmly rooted, he began to flex his political might towards Rome, first placing a claim on Armenia. King Tigranes III had died, leaving the throne to his son Tigranes IV and daughter Erato in 10 BCE. Both would rule as a married couple. However, Tigranes IV and Erato were crowned without the approval of Rome, and on top of that, they leaned towards Parthia, thus showing their anti-Roman feelings. Augustus would have none of that. Augustus sent an expedition into Armenia around 5 BCE and deposed both Tigranes and Erato, who were replaced by one Artavasdes. But the people of Armenia rejected this king and rose up in revolt to reestablish Tigranes and Erato as the legitimate rulers.[6]

Augustus began to debate the issue and decided to send General Tiberius, who refused to accept the mission and remained retired in Rhodes. Augustus, likely upset over the refusal found a benefit for Tiberius being in Rhodes. The presence of Tiberius so near the region of conflict kept the Parthians at bay for the time being.[7]

As mentioned, Phraataces took the Parthian throne after murdering his father with the help of his mother in 2 BCE. It was also during this time that Phraataces tested the political waters with Rome. He sent an envoy demanding the release of his four brothers as a condition of restoring the peace between the two. However, Phraataces was still

---

[6] Dio 55:10/ Sheldon, 86-87.
[7] Sheldon, 87.

seeking to destroy the competition. Augustus responded to "Phraataces," without the appellation of "king" in his letter. Augustus demanded that Phraataces drop his claim on Armenia and his use of the title of king. Phraataces responded to Augustus, calling himself "king of kings" and demeaning Augustus by calling him "Caesar." Acknowledging Phraataces as just "Phraataces" was, in fact, Augustus' way of reminding Phraataces that he has the four brothers of Phraataces in Rome, each equally capable of being the next king of Parthia.[8]

While Phraataces and Augustus exchanged insults, Augustus had another surprise for Phraataces. Augustus had placed his grandson Gaius Caesar in command of the Roman forces in the east. His duty was to intimidate the Parthians, restore Roman authority in Armenia, and collect intelligence on the east, which Rome lacked, with the possible help of Isidore of Charax.[9] When Phraataces received word of Gaius' arrival in Syria, his attitude changed, for the possibility of war seemed inevitable. Phraataces' ally Tigranes, who at one point acknowledged Roman suzerainty, was killed fighting barbarians. This left his sister Erato in control of the throne, although she would abdicate shortly after.[10]

Phraataces, in hope of avoiding war with Rome, met with Gaius on an island on the Euphrates. The Roman historian Velleius Paterculus was present when the

---

[8] Dio 55:10.
[9] Dio 55:10/ Debevoise, 147.
[10] Dio 55:10a.

meeting took place. At the time, Velleius was serving in the Roman army as a tribune. He makes no negative comment about the meeting. Instead, he mentions that Phraataces was a "young man of distinguished presence." Velleius also had hope that the two powers, with both armies present, could forge a deal and avoid war.[11] Phraataces agreed to relinquish Parthia's claim on Armenia and the return of his brothers who reside in Rome. Afterwards, both sides took turns dining on each other's soil to celebrate the new peace established between the two superpowers.[12]

But Phraataces had no choice. He had no allies to call upon, since Tigranes and Erato were deposed and the throne of Armenia later would be given to King Artavasdes of Media Atropatene with the help of Gaius. Also, internal conflict within Parthia was raising its ugly head again and with Rome on the doorstep threatening war, Phraataces decided that war with Rome could cost him not only his throne, but his empire, while peace would allow him to keep Parthia and focus on the power struggle festering within his borders.[13]

Even though Phraataces relinquished control over Armenia by agreeing that Armenia would be in the Roman sphere of influence, he still was seeking to undermine Rome by focusing on other nations allied to Rome. One nation, often overlooked, was Judea.

---

[11] Velleius Paterculus, *Roman History*, 2.101.
[12] Dio 55:10a.
[13] Ibid.

Proxy along the Euphrates

HEROD, JESUS, AND THE MAGI

In chapter 4, it was discussed that the Roman General Ventidius left Herod high and dry around 38 BCE. Ventidius, who besieged Jerusalem, continued to make threats towards Antigonus that if he didn't pay up, he would attack Jerusalem and place it in the hands of Herod. Antigonus paid up, of course, and when Ventidius felt his coffers were abundant enough, he left with the bulk of his forces to deal with the Parthians in the north, leaving Silo in charge to await the arrival of Herod.[14] When Herod landed in Judea, his forces were minute, but as the days passed, his ranks began to swell with supporters. Herod now had enough troops, and with the aid of Silo, he had to make a decision: where to attack first. Herod decided on Joppa. When Silo heard the news, he broke the siege at Jerusalem to aid Herod. While Silo was on his way, the Jews decided to attack. However, Herod caught wind of the attack and sent a small force to aid the Romans. Together they defeated the supporters of Antigonus. Once Joppa had been captured, Herod went straight for Masada and captured it as well. With no enemy behind him, he could now focus on Jerusalem. While Herod prepared for the capture of Jerusalem, Antony sent Ventidius' replacement to assist him: Gaius Sosius, the governor of Syria and Cilicia. Herod and Sosius would capture Jerusalem and Antigonus would surrender to Sosius, who

---

[14] Joseph, *BJ*, 1.15.2-3.

then sent him to Rome to Antony to take part in a triumphal procession. Herod feared that once Antigonus was in Rome, he might be able to obtain the ear of the senate to hear his cause, which could shift the balance of power back to Antigonus. In order to prevent Antigonus' possible return, Herod paid Antony a great deal of money to have him executed. Antony accepted the money and Antigonus was beheaded in Antioch.[15]

Even though Herod was placed on the throne for being anti-Parthian and thus useful to Rome, he still feared that the Parthians would return and place Hyrcanus on the throne. Herod showed his pro-Parthian sympathies when Orodes II had died. Once Phraates IV took the throne, he decided to reopen diplomatic relations with the Parthians. Herod therefore wrote a letter, handed it to Saramallas, his ambassador, and sent him to the court of Phraates roughly around 36 BCE. Once at the Parthian court, Saramallas handed Phraates the letter, along with many presents, in hope of freeing Hyrcanus and bringing him back to Jerusalem. Phraates agreed and Hyrcanus was sent back to Judea. Herod now had two insurance policies he could rely on in case one or the other found him unfavorable.

When Antony died in 30 BCE, Herod became concerned. Herod was Antony's ally, and with Antony dead, he was left naked. Herod had no clue if Octavian would accept him or dispose of him. His position among the Romans remained uncertain. Therefore, Herod broke his ties with the Parthians and limited Octavian's possible

---

[15] Joseph, *AJ*, 14.16.1-4; 15.1-2; *BJ*, 15.3-6.

choice of replacing Herod with Hyrcanus, the last surviving Hasmonean heir, by executing Hyrcanus on the grounds that he was plotting against him.[16]

Herod was able to keep his throne by showing his loyalty to Rome. As the decades passed, the Parthians decided to intervene politically into the Jews' affairs, thus causing a bit of political upheaval within Judea. However, it started with "wise men from the east."

Sometime around 3 or 2 BCE Jesus was born to the Joseph and Mary. Back in the Parthian capital of Ctesiphon, the Parthian priests, known as Magi, noticed a star in the sky and saw it as a sign that a king was born.

> Where is He who has been born King of the Jews? For we have seen His star in the East and have come to worship Him." When Herod the king heard these things, he was troubled, and all Jerusalem with him....[17]

The above passage is familiar as it comes from the New Testament, Matthew 2:1-2. So what brought the Magi to Jesus, was it really a star? Whatever the star was is not of importance, but it is true that Magi were professional astrologers. However, one has to wonder if the star

---

[16] Ibid., *AJ*, 15.2.3; *BJ*, 1.22.1; Jason M. Schlude, "Herod the Great: Friend of the Romans and Parthians?" 03 29, 2013, http://www.biblicalarchaeology.org/daily/people-cultures-in-the-bible/people-in-the-bible/herod-the-great-friend-of-the-romans-and-parthians/.
[17] Matthew 2:1-2 (KJV).

passage was later added into the book of Matthew because Numbers 24:17 states, "I shall see him, but not now: I shall behold him, but not nigh: there shall come a Star out of Jacob, and a Sceptre shall rise out of Israel." This verse is said to be a prophecy pointing to the birth of Jesus.[18] The question now is, did the Magi recognize the verse of Numbers 24:17 and understand it? It is possible that they did since a large Jewish community still resided in Babylon at the time and I am sure both Jewish and Magi priests did interact and share ideas. However, I doubt that verse brought the Magi to Jesus. Rather, it may have come down to Jesus' genealogy instead.

    The Magi asked, "Where is He who has been born King of the Jews?" Joseph's genealogy is documented in both the books of Matthew and Luke. His line does show a connection to the kings of Judah and Israel. Mary's genealogy is not mentioned in the New Testament. Yes, some will say you can find it in Luke, but when you begin to read the list, it reads like Joseph's genealogy, with some exceptions. It is possible that Mary and Joseph both are related to the same line of people. But the fact that her line is not documented does raise an eyebrow. Therefore, how did the Magi know Jesus was truly a king and how did they determine that? The answer might lay in Mary's undocumented genealogy.

    According to the book of Luke, Elizabeth, the cousin of Mary, was Kohen. If Elizabeth comes from the Kohen line, then so does Mary. Both are descendants of

---

[18] Numbers 24:17

Moses' brother Aaron. Therefore, both women come from the priestly tribe of Levi. In Mary's supposed genealogy according to Luke, a name of interest pops up: Matthat. Is it possible that this Matthat is none other than Antigonus II Mattathias, the same man the Parthians placed on the throne of Judah back in 40 BCE? Another name in Mary's line of interest is Jannai. This could be none other than King Alexander Jannaeus. Therefore, and with speculation, Antigonus II Mattathias would have been Mary's grandfather and Alexander Jannaeus her 3rd great-grandfather. Now, it is true, confirmed by the Jewish historian Josephus, that Herod executed the family of Antigonus II Mattathias. However, Josephus mentions 33 years later that Herod's son Antipater married a daughter of Antigonus. Therefore, what likely happened was that Herod killed all the males leaving the females alive.[19]

Another interesting aspect from the passage of Matthew 2:1-2 is when Herod became concerned when the Magi asked about where they could find this king, for "When Herod the king heard these things, he was troubled, and all Jerusalem with him..." If there were just three Magi, what concern or threat could they have caused? It's just three men, right? The answer is no. The Bible does not state that there were three wise men. No number is mentioned. How many Magi came to visit the

---

[19] Joseph Raymond, *Herodian Messiah: Case for Jesus As Grandson of Herod* (St. Louis, MO: Tower Grove, Publishing 2010), 31-34; Joseph, *AJ*, 16.5.2.

child is unknown, but what is known is that they did not come alone.

The Magi who traveled to Jerusalem were high officials, for according to Strabo, "the council of the Parthians is composed of two classes, one of relatives (of the royal family) and another of wise men and magi, by both of which kings are chosen."[20] The Magi seeking Jesus were loaded down with riches and escorted by an armed entourage, like Surena, who travelled with an entourage of 10,000.[21] Depending on the Magi's status, the higher ranking Magi likely travelled with such numbers. Why else would Herod tremble in fear along with the citizens of Jerusalem? It must have looked as if the Parthians were invading, that war between Rome and Parthia were about to get underway again, with Judah being ground zero.

According to Matthew, when the Magi found Jesus, he was a "young child" in a house, possibly two years old.[22] They did not visit Jesus when he was a baby lying in a manger. Luke's gospel makes no mention of the Magi being present when Jesus was born.[23] Once it was confirmed that the boy was in fact Jesus, they "fell down, and worshipped him: and when they had opened their treasures, they presented unto him gifts; gold, and frankincense and myrrh."[24] Gifts and expensive commodities in the ancient world fit for a king, and the

---

[20] Strab, 11.9.3.
[21] Plut, *Crassus*, 21.
[22] Matt 2:11.
[23] Luke 2:8-20.
[24] Matt 2:11.

first people to worship Jesus were not the Jews, but the Parthians.

Therefore, a question remains. Why did the Magi pick Jesus and what is the significance? The Magi likely picked Jesus because he was a direct descendent of Antigonus II Mattathias. The significant part for his coronation was that his second great-grandfather Antigonus was pro-Parthian. Therefore it's obvious from a political perspective that King Phraataces of Parthia wanted to undermine the Romans regarding the treaty that was established around the same time of Jesus birth, wherein Phraataces agreed to relinquish control over Armenia. Because of this, Phraataces likely wanted some payback and sought out the Jews for information on the whereabouts of Antigonus' descendants. But why would the Jewish scribes agree to such a search? The reason could be that they disliked Herod in Babylon as much as they did in Judea. Therefore, if they could replace Herod or any of his future line with someone who was anti-Roman, they would be free from the influential Roman yoke, thus allowing them a greater degree of autonomy, not only politically, but also culturally.

However, this is all mere speculation, for the answer is uncertain. But given the fact that the Magi visited Jesus, one wonders, why? What are the connections and what is the reason for the interaction? The answer will remain doubtful at best, but it should not be ignored.

PARTHIA'S STRUGGLE

Phraataces' reign did not last long. After the treaty between Rome and Parthia concluded, internal upheaval was at an all time high. It didn't help that he married his mother Musa and minted coins that depicted her with the title of "queen and goddess of the heavens."[25] Nevertheless, Phraataces and Musa's reign didn't last long, as both were killed around 4 CE. It could be said that the Parthian court disposed of them due to their incestuous marriage. This is partially correct; however, another aspect to consider is that Musa was Italian. The Parthian court likely saw Musa as a "Trojan horse" delivered by Augustus in hope of weakening Parthia internally. Of course, whether this was Augustus' intention is unknown. However, the birth of Phraataces and Musa's ability to persuade her husband to send his sons to Rome in order to place the empire in Phraataces' hands, makes one wonder if Musa controlled the throne.

Once Phraataces and his mother Musa were removed, the nobles and magi got together and discussed a possible king. Eventually they settled and awarded the crown to Orodes III in 4 CE. However, they soon found out that Orodes had a violent temper and was extremely unstable. Because of his instability, the nobles plotted his

---

[25] John Richardson, *Augustan Rome 44 BC to AD 14: The Restoration of the Republic and the Establishment of the Empire* (Edinburgh: Edinburgh University Press, 2012), 161.

death. Orodes was killed either at a festival or on a hunting expedition in 6 CE.[26]

With Orodes out of the way, the Parthian nobility sent ambassadors to Rome seeking permission to bring back the eldest son of Phraates IV. Augustus agreed and the ambassadors informed Vonones that he was to be the new king of Parthia. Augustus, delighted by the news, gave Vonones a considerable amount of wealth for his return home. Once Vonones crossed the Euphrates River and ascended the throne, the Parthians cheered and rejoiced that they had a king. Soon cheers were silent as they began to despise him.

When rejoicing ceased, realization and questioning set in among the Parthian nobles. Soon they began to look upon Vonones not as a Parthian, but as a slave, a man who acted more Roman than Parthian. What brought about this disdain for their new king was that Vonones did not enjoy hunting, he lacked interest in horses, and he disliked the national festivals. Not only that, the nobles ridiculed his Greek attendants and his keeping common articles under seal from the public. However, Vonones was rather courteous to all; his manners were very western, which divided the Parthians somewhat; but no matter how nice or courteous Vonones seemed, to their eyes, he was an alien, a Roman sitting on the throne of Arsaces.[27]

The nobles grew disgusted with having to shop for their kings in Rome. That is, if Vonones were to die, they

---

[26] Joseph, *AJ*, 18, 4.
[27] Tacitus, *Annales*, 2.2; Joseph, *AJ*, 18, 2.4.

would have to go back to Rome and select another who would be no different than the current king. If they had to shop for their kings in Rome, how were they truly independent from Roman rule? Was Vonones acting as a puppet for Augustus, thus making Parthia a client state?

The nobles got together and invited King Artabanus of Media Atropatene to a private meeting. The nobles informed Artabanus that they desired him to be their king, for he was also of Arsacid blood and culturally like them, for he grew to manhood among the Dahae. Artabanus accepted their request.[28]

Artabanus assembled his forces along with the Parthians who were loyal to him and advanced on Vonones. Vonones received word that some of the nobles had gone behind his back and selected a king more to their liking and that Artabanus was advancing with an army. Vonones mustered his forces, and when both armies met face to face, Vonones was victorious, for the majority of Parthians were on his side. Artabanus fled back to the mountains of Media Atropatene. Vonones quickly withdrew back to his capital where he gave the order for victory coins to be minted. However, Vonones' victory would be short lived. Artabanus gathered a much larger force and challenged Vonones for the throne again. This time Artabanus was victorious. Vonones fled on horseback with few accompanying him to the city of Seleucia. From Seleucia, Vonones fled to Armenia. Artabanus returned to

---

[28] Tac, *Ann*, 2.3.

the Parthian capital of Ctesiphon and was proclaimed king in 12 CE.[29]

Once Vonones arrived in Armenia, he was crowned king, for Armenia had no king at the time. The throne was vacant due to the Armenians ousting the previous king Tigranes IV, the grandson of King Herod whom Augustus appointed to rule Armenia after the murder of King Artavasdes III. While Vonones ruled Armenia under the protection of Rome, it would be a short reign.[30]

Once Emperor Augustus died in August 14 CE, the security Vonones had enjoyed was now in question. Artabanus decided to place pressure on Vonones while Rome was becoming acquainted with its new emperor, Tiberius. Eventually Artabanus made threats of war, a concern to Rome as they wished to avoid conflict with Parthia. Rome agreed to Artabanus' accession and Governor Creticus Silanus of Syria informed Vonones he must abdicate his throne and come to Syria. Vonones removed to Syria around 15 or 16 CE, keeping his regal titles.[31]

With the Armenian throne vacant, Emperor Tiberius decided to intervene. Tiberius gave his adopted son Germanicus a mission: go to Armenia and place Zeno of Pontus on the throne. The senate agreed and placed all the provinces beyond the sea in the hands of Germanicus.

---

[29] Joseph, *AJ*, 18, 2.4.
[30] Tac, *Ann*, 2.4; Joseph, *AJ*, 18.5.4.
[31] Tac, *Ann*, 2.4.

Zeno was the son of Polemon, king of Pontus. Zeno was popular among the native Armenians and friendly to Rome. Since the time he was a toddler, he had been raised in Armenian manners and customs. He liked to hunt and eat heartily, things barbarians loved to do, according to the Romans. Germanicus marched into Armenia, went straight to Artaxata, the capital, and with the permission of the nobility, placed the royal diadem on his head before the multitude of people, and proclaimed himself King Artaxias III. Rome was back in control.[32]

The presence of Germanicus in the region rubbed Artabanus the wrong way. Artabanus must have feared a possible Roman invasion since Germanicus' authority trumped the Roman governors of their respected provinces in the region. In other words, all legions beyond the sea were under the command of Germanicus. Artabanus, who wishes to avoid conflict, sent envoys to Germanicus, asking him if he would meet with him at the Euphrates River to discuss friendship and alliance. Furthermore, Artabanus requested the removal of Vonones from Syria because Vonones might be able to draw certain chieftains to his cause, creating another unstable situation that could lead to another all-out Parthian civil war. However, Germanicus declined to meet with Artabanus, for reasons still unclear, but Germanicus did honor Artabanus' request that Vonones be removed from Syria. Germanicus relocated Vonones to the province of Cilicia. Vonones, unhappy with the relocation, decided

---

[32] Ibid., 2.43,56.

to make a break for it. He bribed the guards and set forth for Armenia. But when he came to the Pyramus River, he found the natives had destroyed the bridges when they learned of the king's coming. Vonones went up and down the bank, seeking a ford to cross, but there was none. Eventually Vibius Fronto, an officer of cavalry, captured him and placed him in chains. Once Vonones had been secured, Remmius, who was in charge of the king, pretended to be angry, and pierced Vonones with the sword, ending his life.[33]

With Vonones dead and Artaxias established on the throne of Armenia, there was a short peace lasting from 18-35 CE between the two superpowers. Make no mistake, that even though there was peace, there was internal upheaval taking place within both empires.

THE TALE OF TWO BROTHERS

Josephus mentions an event that startled Artabanus, a revolt by two Jewish brothers, Anilaeus and Asinaeus, who rose up in revolt in the Parthian province of Babylonia around 20 CE. The story Josephus provides is a bit romantic, but the political implications of the story are important. Josephus says that the event took place in southern Mesopotamia in the Babylonian city of Neharda, which is located on the Euphrates. The brothers were

---

[33] Ibid., 2.43, 58, 68; Strabo, 16.1.28.

apprenticed in the art of weaving by their mother. However, their master punished them by beating them for being slothful. After being punished, they robbed their master's house of all its weapons. Once they took the weapons, they fled to a place where the river divides. It was from that location they were able to draw the poorest young men to join their cause. They established ranks among the men, built a citadel, and forced the local herdsmen to pay tribute under threat of violence if they did not comply. Many did comply and also joined them, which gave them the confidence to march on other nearby villages, subjugating all they confronted.

  The satrap of Babylonia had to act quickly, for the two brothers' power and influence was expanding. The satrap gathered his forces, consisting of Parthian and Babylonian troops, and marched forth towards the Jewish mini-state. The Babylonian satrap expected the soon-coming engagement to be easy, since he would attack on the Sabbath, a day holy to the Jews, when he expected them not to resist. Of course, they did resist and defeated the satrap's forces.

  Word eventually reached Artabanus of the defeat. Artabanus, startled by the news, sent a message requesting that both brothers meet with him; he was impressed with their courage. He offered only his hand and not the sword. Eventually the two brothers would meet with Artabanus. Artabanus, according to Josephus, allowed the brothers to retain the land of Babylonia so long as they did not pillage the land or treat the people unfairly. Both brothers are said to have reigned in the province for fifteen years.

The remainder of the story sounds like a romance gone bad. Anilaeus fell in love with a Parthian general's wife; he killed the general, thus declaring war on Parthia; then he kidnapped the general's wife. Great misfortune came to his people due to her worship of idols. Since the brothers were now in a state of war against Parthia, they began to raid the lands of Mithridates, the son-in-law of Artabanus, with great success. Mithridates prepared to counter them, but was quickly overcome by a night raid.

The brothers captured Mithridates during this raid. Instead of holding him hostage, they decided to release him and allow him to go back home in fashionable style: stripped naked and placed on an ass. Once he returned home naked and bound, his wife is embarrassed, so much so that she makes it very clear that if he does not avenge this insult, she will divorce him. Mithridates gathers a large force and defeats Anilaeus, who escapes and soon assembles another army. Anilaeus has caused so much commotion in the region that the Babylonians get involved by going to the Jews of Neharda. The Jews at first refused to cooperate, but they realized that as long as the war goes on, they will never be safe. Therefore, they teamed up with the Babylonians and fell upon Anilaeus while he was asleep, killing him and destroying his forces, in 35 CE.[34]

While the story seems a bit novelistic, there is likely some truth to the overall events, particularly the reaction

---

[34] Joseph, *AJ*, 18.9.1-7.

of Artabanus. Artabanus could have killed the brothers who defeated his Babylonian satrap, but decided not to. The reason is obvious: Anilaeus and Asinaeus have collected a considerable amount of power and influence, and not only that, they are on the border shared between Parthia and Rome. Had Artabanus declared war on the two Jewish brothers, the brothers could have easily sent a message to the Romans asking for aid while the Parthians mobilized their forces. However, this is conjecture. There is no guarantee that Rome would come to the aid of Anilaeus and Asinaeus. But Artabanus was smart enough not to react in a hostile manner. The likely reason he did not quash the rebellion is that it could have invited other nearby provinces to rebel against him. If this were to happen, it could gather enough strength and notability to make it lucrative for Rome to get involved and further extend its hand, claiming more areas under its sphere of influence. Artabanus therefore avoided the domino effect that could have destabilized his empire and cost him his throne.

  Even though there was a final showdown between the Parthians and the Jewish brothers, they seem to have burned their bridges not only with the subjects under the jurisdiction of Mithridates, but other nearby Parthian provinces. If they had wished to gain the trust of other provinces indifferent to Parthian rule, it was not going to happen, for their raids nullified any possible unity among the provinces dissatisfied with Artabanus' rule.

ROME'S PROXY WAR IN ARMENIA

In 35 CE, King Artaxias of Armenia died. Artaxias evidently never married nor produced any offspring to continue the line. Evidently, Artabanus paid close attention to the situation in Rome over the events taking place in Armenia. Artabanus quickly mobilized his forces, marched into Armenia, and placed his eldest son Arsaces on the throne. Tiberius objected to this takeover. The actions taken by Artabanus to place his son on the throne of Armenia tells us that Artabanus was extremely powerful, compared with his early reign, when he was strong but cautious.[35]

The reason Artabanus chose to violate the past treaty agreed between Phraataces and Augustus may have been due to reports that Emperor Tiberius was less interested in the affairs of the empire and had removed himself from the spotlight. His disappearance from the day-to-day affairs was due to political turmoil, which damaged his image. Because of his absence, the Roman bureaucracy took charge of the empire. With Rome in a state of uncertainty, which affected foreign policy, Artabanus took advantage of the delicate situation.[36]

Besides claiming Armenia as Parthian property by placing his son on the throne, Artabanus demanded much more. He sent envoys to Rome, demanding that Tiberius hand over the property (treasures) that Vonones left in

---

[35] Tacitus, *The Annals*, 6.31.
[36] Suetonius, *Tiberius*, 41, 60, 62, 63, 64

Syria and Cilicia. But Artabanus went even farther, demanding the boundaries of Parthia should be that of the ancient empires of Persia and Macedonia. But his demand soon became a threat to extend his borders to that which was once held by Cyrus and Alexander. Of course, all this saber rattling is just that, rattling. There is no doubt that Artabanus has a strong military force; however, even a strong military does not necessarily indicate loyalty to the king.[37]

The actions taken by Artabanus to invade Armenia upset not only those in Rome, but also his own people, particularly the nobles. Some of the nobles, if not many, were tired of Artabanus' abuse of power and now reckless foreign policy. Parthia was on good terms with Rome, at least on the surface, until Artabanus decided to reclaim Armenia, placing the country under its sphere of influence without the consent of the nobles. It was at this point that some, if not many, of the nobles decided to take action against their king.[38]

The Parthian nobles secretly selected two men who likely could persuade Tiberius to help them. These two men were Sinnaces and Abdus. Sinnaces came from a wealthy distinguished family; he was likely a merchant and noble. Abdus was a eunuch holding a considerable amount of power in the Parthian court. Both men ventured to Rome and met with Tiberius.

---

[37] Tac, *Ann*, 6.31.
[38] Ibid.

Proxy along the Euphrates

The envoys delivered a simple message: help us. Tiberius understood that the nobles wanted to be rid of Artabanus, but Tiberius likely asked about other Arsacid princes who could be elevated to the throne. The envoys explained to Tiberius that there was none of age because Artabanus had murdered them all. Therefore, they pleaded to Tiberius to allow one of Phraates IV's sons to return to Parthia, they promised Tiberius that if a Parthian prince were to have the support of the Roman army and was at the banks of the Euphrates, Parthia would rise up in rebellion and support that prince's bid to become king. Tiberius agreed to their request and chose the youngest son of Phraates IV, who also happened to be named Phraates.[39]

After Sinnaces and Abdus arranged for the arrival of Phraates, they hurried back home. However, Artabanus caught wind of the plan and decided to meet with both of them separately. Artabanus met with the eunuch, Abdus, first, inviting him to dinner. Artabanus ordered that Abdus' food be poisoned. Soon afterwards, Abdus became ill and disabled from the poison's effect. Sinnaces was spared, likely because of his wealth and status. Artabanus gave Sinnaces many new missions to deal with, thus keeping him occupied and away from court politics.

While Artabanus deals with treasonous men and prepares for Phraates arrival, Tiberius' decision to allow Phraates to return to Parthia seems to be a win-win situation for both Parthia and Rome, tipped in Rome's

---

[39] Ibid., 31-32.

favor. Not only do both empires refrain from direct engagement, but Rome gains some influence over Parthia because the man they sent to be crowned king of Parthia was more Roman than Parthian. Once Phraates was in Syria, he had to exchange his Roman attire for Parthian and let go of his Roman habits and embrace those of the Parthians. Phraates was not happy about the sudden change. However, as fate would have it, Phraates, being very old, since he had been living in Rome for many decades, abruptly died in Syria.[40]

    Artabanus likely rejoiced after hearing the news, for now his throne and empire were safe from civil war. However, once the news reaches Tiberius that Phraates has died in Syria, he looks at his inventory of Arsacid princes and decides on Tiridates III, the grandson of Phraates IV.

    Tiberius knows he cannot just send Tiridates to Parthia. Because Tiberius fears Artabanus and understands that any direct confrontation could be disastrous, he seeks out those who are semi-friendly to Rome and despise Parthia. One such country was the Kingdom of Iberia, located in the South Caucasus. Tiberius sends a message of reconciliation to King Pharasmanes I of Iberia and offers an opportunity. Tiberius' message is clear: help me rid Armenia of the Parthians, and in doing so place your brother Mithridates on the throne. Pharasmanes likely smirked at first, knowing that if he were to invade Armenia, half the Parthian army would be there to toss his forces out and likely invade his kingdom shortly after. It

---

[40] Ibid., 32.

was further explained to Pharasmanes that while his forces were in Armenia, Rome would smuggle in a Parthian prince by the name of Tiridates through the newly appointed governor of Syria, Lucius Vitellius, in an attempt to take the throne while Artabanus was away assisting his son Arsaces in the defense of Armenia. Pharasmanes, likely shaky over the idea, agreed to the deal, after being bribed, of course.[41]

Before Pharasmanes invaded Armenia, he sent agents into the country whose mission was to collect intelligence and make contact with the servants of Arsaces. Once in contact, the servants of Arsaces were offered a considerable amount of gold to murder their king. The deal was made and the Iberians began to assemble their forces and move towards the border. Once word reached the Iberian king that Arsaces had been murdered, the Iberians, likely led by the brother of the king, Mithridates, led the army as they burst through the Armenia border, captured Artaxata, the capital, and confiscated the rest of country with ease.[42]

Messengers arrived quickly at the court of Artabanus, informing him that his son had been murdered and Armenia lost to the Iberians. Artabanus grieved over his son; this soon turned to rage and the need for revenge. Artabanus wanted payback and gave the order for local provincial mobilization nearest to Armenia. The general to lead this army was his son Orodes. While Orodes led a

---

[41] Ibid.
[42] Ibid., 33.

small force to the north, Artabanus gave the order for full mobilization. Full mobilization would have taken months to materialize. Of course, this depends on the size required for the campaign. Even though it is said that Artabanus "marched with the whole strength of his kingdom," how true that statement is, coming from Tacitus, is debatable. This is why Artabanus dispatched agents to hire mercenaries in the north to aid Orodes in the recovery of Armenia. However, Pharasmanes was clever, knowing that Parthia could mobilize only so many men in such a short time and they would resort to hiring mercenaries. Pharasmanes countered this by allying himself with the Caucasian Albanians, creating a barrier from the Black Sea to the Caspian, which prevented Parthian agents from acquiring mercenaries. This gave Pharasmanes a monopoly on the recruitment of mercenaries who lived in the Caucasus. One such group he was able to hire to aid in the invasion of Armenia was the Sarmatians. Once word reached pro-Parthian mercenaries that Iberia had confiscated the throne of Armenia and that the son of Artabanus had been murdered and replaced, they began their journey south to meet up with the Parthian army, knowing they would eventually meet Parthian agents along the way seeking to hire them for their services. However, the Iberian and Caucasian Albanians blocked all routes leading to Parthia, thus their advance came to a standstill.[43]

---

[43] Ibid.

Proxy along the Euphrates

Once the agents returned, they informed Orodes that the routes had been closed and were under military supervision. Orodes gave the order to bivouac, knowing that the main Parthian force led by his father would arrive at some point. While Orodes waited, Pharasmanes got word that a small force of Parthians had encamped, so he gathered his forces and Sarmatian mercenaries and headed towards Orodes' encampment. Once Pharasmanes arrived outside the Parthian camp, he challenged Orodes to battle. Orodes refused to take part in the banter or battle. Pharasmanes continued to taunt the Parthians and harassed those foraging for food. The "strategy that broke the camel's back" was not verbal taunting. Pharasmanes began placing piquets in the fashion of a blockade around Orodes' camp. The Parthians grew tired of this and went to Orodes, demanding battle.[44]

Orodes understood the concern of his men, for if they were to stay in place, they would be slaughtered. The blockade placed around their camp prevented them from utilizing their cavalry to its full effect. Orodes sent a messenger to Pharasmanes' camp, informing him that Orodes accepts his challenge to battle.

The Parthians arrayed their horse archers and cataphracts in battle formation. The Iberians, along with the Albanians, were primarily infantry aided by Sarmatian cavalry. While both commanders gave inspirational speeches before their armies as to why they are better than the other side, the Sarmatian cavalry commander ordered

---

[44] Ibid., 34.

his cavalry to toss their bows aside and charge into battle with lance and sword. The attitude of the Sarmatians set the tone of battle.

The Sarmatians charged first into battle, leading by example before the Iberians and Albanians. The Parthian horse archers likely began to pelt the Sarmatian cavalry as they drew closer. Soon after the Iberian and Albanians poured into battle, the Parthian horse archers could do little, with the odds being against them. The Parthian cataphracts likely smashed into the infantry and pulled away the best that they could in order to reorganize and charge again. Many others were likely snared in the melee and pulled from their horses. Pharasmanes got what he wanted, a battle that was hand-to-hand, rather than playing a game of cat and mouse with the Parthians. Eventually, both Pharasmanes and Orodes would face off against one another. When both men clashed in combat, Pharasmanes got the upper hand with a single blow to the head of Orodes. Pharasmanes could not continue the engagement with Orodes for his horse continued onwards. Orodes, likely discombobulated by the blow, was still alive due to his helmet. However, his body language, not to mention that his guard came to his rescue, caused quite a commotion, for many of his men feared him to be dead, and believing this, they yielded to Pharasmanes.[45]

However, Josephus gives us a different ending. While it may be true that Orodes and his men yielded, according to Tacitus, Josephus writes that Orodes, along

---

[45] Ibid., 35.

with tens of thousands of his men, perished in the battle. Orodes is mentioned no more after his surrender in Tacitus. It seems very plausible that he was executed shortly after his surrender. But when it comes to the many tens of thousands of deaths, Josephus mentions, this is likely false, for Orodes likely led ten thousand troops and likely lost a significant amount during battle. Whatever the case may be, it is obvious and without dispute that the Parthians lost the battle.[46]

Vitellius was likely keeping a close eye on the situation and receiving reports daily on the Parthian whereabouts. He also may have had agents working in the Caucasus as well. In 36 CE, Shortly after the defeat of Orodes, Artabanus assembled a mighty army and headed north towards Armenia. Vitellius knew that Artabanus would invade Armenia if the initial invasion led by his son Orodes had failed. Because of this, Vitellius began to formulate his next strategy, which I am sure he had readily available for the current circumstances. Vitellius understood that Pharasmanes and his allies could not defeat the massive juggernaut heading towards Armenia. Therefore, Vitellius came up with a two-pronged strategy. He would first gave large amounts of currency to the various nomadic tribes living within the Caucasus, particularly the Sarmatians, with instructions not to attack the Iberians or Albanians, but allow them to pass peacefully through and into Parthian territory, where they

---

[46] Joseph, *AJ*, 18.4.4.

would raid the nearby provinces. Vitellius' strategy is simple. The Sarmatian tribes (Alani) will raid the nearby provinces and engage in hit-and-run attacks on Artabanus, thus causing his forces to stutter-step. With the Parthian advancement being hindered, but not stopped, Vitellius takes advantage of the situation by taking his legions to the Euphrates River, making it well known that he intends to cross the river and invade Parthia. While Artabanus was slowly making his way towards Armenia, word reaches him that Vitellius, with his legions, are preparing to invade Parthia–but it was a ruse. This ruse saved Armenia, for Artabanus, disgusted with the situation, believed the report and called off the attack. To fight a two-front war was not worth it, especially one involving Rome. Besides, Artabanus had not the resources or support to fight a war with Rome when his own country despised him for the most part.[47]

ROME'S POLITICAL PROXY WAR IN PARTHIA

While Artabanus went on the defensive to ward off the Sarmatian raiders, Vitellius had another plan. With Artabanus preoccupied with the Sarmatian incursion, Vitellius went on a political campaign to bribe Parthian officials and nobles to reject Artabanus and accept a

---

[47] Tac, *Ann*, 6.36; Joseph, *AJ*, 18.4.4.

Parthian prince who had been held hostage in Rome. He offered Tiridates III, the grandson of Phraates IV, to be the new king of Parthia. It is obvious that this plan had been in play for some time. The Romans knew that many Parthians were disgruntled with Artabanus' rule and looked for a change. Fortunately for the Romans, many of the Parthian officials agreed and swore allegiance to Tiridates, who may have been with Vitellius during the conflict and likely had been left in Syria. Change was not far away.

Once the bribes were accepted and the people found Tiridates favorable to be their king, the nobles kept their part and drove Artabanus to the east. Vitellius understood while Artabanus was away, it gave him enough time to establish Tiridates on the throne of Parthia. Even though the nobles for the most part accepted Tiridates as their king, this guaranteed little, for Vitellius knew that even though Artabanus had fled with a small company of loyal supporters and mercenaries, he soon would be back at the head of another army; and if Tiridates were not found fit to rule, Artabanus would reign again. There was no time to waste; it was best to be quick and place Tiridates on the throne while the nobles still favored him.[48]

Vitellius arranged for a meeting with the Parthian nobles on the banks of the Euphrates. Vitellius would show up at the head of his main legion along with Tiridates and their allies. With both Roman and Parthian

---

[48] Tac, *Ann*, 6.36.

officials on site, Vitellius ordered sacrifices. According to Roman custom, an offering of swine, ram, and a bull was made to the gods. Tiridates would be accustomed to such sacrifices, since he grew up in Rome. Once Rome finished making offerings to the gods, it was Parthia's turn. Tiridates, more Roman than Parthia, witnessed what likely was told to him by his family back in Rome, for a horse was brought forth before him and sacrificed to please the river god. Tiridates went from hearing tales of his homeland to knowing the culture within his homeland. Once the ceremonies ceased, the Romans got to work constructing a temporary bridge of boats across the Euphrates. Afterwards, the Roman army crossed into Parthian territory and set up camp.

  Ornospades, a Parthian who also held Roman citizenship for helping Tiberius in the Dalmatic war, arrived at the Roman camp at the head of several thousand cavalry to swear loyalty to his new king. Afterwards, Sinnaces, the same man who traveled to Rome seeking a replacement for Artabanus many years ago, also arrived with reinforcements. He was likely accompanying Abdageses, who brought the royal treasury to the camp. Once the festivities were over, Vitellius had one last word with Tiridates to "remember his grandfather Phraates, and his foster-father Caesar, and all that was glorious in both of them." Vitellius also made it clear that the nobles must show obedience to Tiridates and respect for Rome. Once all was said, Vitellius led his legions back across the Euphrates and into Syria.[49]

One can only wonder what the conversation was like between the nobles and Tiridates as they ventured towards the capital, and the same can be said of Vitellius among his officers travelling in Syria. Of course, they all hoped for the best. Parthia hopes for peace and stability, Rome hopes to establish an obedient puppet. However, neither would happen.

News spread quickly of Tiridates' arrival and support, especially from the cities who were primarily Greco-Macedonian. The city of Seleucia opened its gates to him with enthusiasm, from which his supporters quickly ousted the aristocrats who supported Artabanus. The cities of Nicephorium, Anthemusias, and a great many others located in Mesopotamia and founded by the Greco-Macedonians during or after Alexander the Great's conquest and confiscation tour, favored Tiridates for his Greco-Roman ways. He was cultured like them. Even Parthian-inhabited cities or cities mixed with various cultures side by side welcomed him with favor. There is no doubt that Tiridates was welcomed by the many inhabitants of Parthia, particularly those living in the western and central portions of the empire, for they were more accepting of western ways. Farther to the east and north, the attitude changes a bit, since most of the inhabitants in those regions are nomadic.[50]

---

[49] Ibid., 37.
[50] Ibid., 41-42.

Once Tiridates reached Ctesiphon, immediate preparations were under way for his coronation. After Tiridates set a date for his crowning, letters were sent inviting the nobles, food was ordered, and entertainment hired, along with increased security. It was to be a new beginning. As the days passed, two nobles, Phraates, possible satrap of Susiana, and Hiero, both of whom were very powerful nobles in control of very influential provinces, decided that they must postpone their arrival at festivities. Tiridates was fine with their delay and decided to push back the coronation, for both men held a considerable amount of power and Tiridates wished not to offend them or his guests. Once a new date was set, the two men again would send their apologies, for they could not make it. A possibility as to why both Phraates and Hiero continuously put off the event is that they may have been in negotiations with Artabanus. Nevertheless, this went on for some time. Eventually Tiridates grew tired and understood that it was best to go ahead and have the coronation, for it would be better to offend two rather than his empire. On the day of his coronation, a member of the Surena family in front of a lively audience crowned Tiridates.[51]

After Tiridates was proclaimed king, his first order of business was to rid Parthia of Artabanus, who was hiding out in the eastern portion of the empire. However, Tiridates had little money to work with. Because of his monetary dilemma, he could do little against Artabanus.

---

[51] Ibid., 42; Debevoise, 161.

Proxy along the Euphrates

Then information arrived that Artabanus left his treasury and harem at a fortress. Tiridates quickly took advantage of the opportunity, besieging the fortress and seizing Artabanus' possessions.[52]

While Tiridates was enjoying his small victory, both Phraates and Hiero, along with other nobles who chose not to celebrate and acknowledged in secret that Tiridates was not their king, sought to find the one whom many despised in Parthia, perhaps themselves at one point. They went searching for Artabanus and found the exiled king in the province of Hyrcania. Artabanus was anything but kingly; he was covered in filth and carried his bow, eking out a living, and likely had few supporters. He had stayed out of sight and out of mind. Artabanus was likely cautious when approached by the men who sought to restore him to the throne, at least until they pledged their allegiance to him. Artabanus was likely curious as to why he was so desired again, and the reason they gave him was that the current king was more Roman than Parthian. They feared that Tiridates was a mere puppet of Rome.[53]

Artabanus, excited by the news, accepted their support and tribute. After collecting a substantial amount of money, he sent agents into Scythia, seeking to recruit Scythian auxiliaries. Artabanus did nothing at first, at least militarily; he was still weak. He had the support, but not the army to back him, at least not at the moment. While

---

[52] Tac, *Ann*, 6.43.
[53] Ibid.

Scythians were being recruited and the nobles prepared their own forces to back the ousted king, Artabanus went on a political campaign. In order to gain further support from the populace, Artabanus kept his nomadic rag-tag attire on in order to gain sympathy. He's one of the people, he's not Roman, he's a simple, hard-charging nomad. Of course, this did win over many in the public. However, there is another reason he continued with his poor, unsightly appearance and that reason was security. Had Artabanus thrust off the robes of a pauper and slipped into royal attire, he would have exposed himself to the enemy. Regardless as to how many supported him, there was always the possibility of assassination by an enemy agent.[54]

Scythian mercenaries, particularly from the Dahae tribe, and perhaps a slew of Parthian nobles with their respected forces, began to arrive at Artabanus' camp. With forces assembled, Artabanus rode off in haste, no time to spare, for he knows little about the king he wanted to oust, and he knows from the intelligence reports he receives that Tiridates is unaware of his movement. While Tiridates enjoyed the luxuries of his court, he received word that Artabanus was approaching the city of Seleucia with a large force. Tiridates was stunned, shocked, and dismayed by the news. He didn't know whether to march and engage Artabanus or stay put and wait for further developments. His military advisors sought to engage Artabanus soon, but were not confident in the men they

---

[54] Ibid., 44.

would be leading. The men that could be mustered for battle were primarily levies with little, if any, experience in combat. To make matters worse, the Parthian military advisors understood that the men forced into this conflict would lack discipline and obedience, thus their value as a loyal fighting force was mere fantasy. Many of the inhabitants acted as traitors and enemies. Their wavering loyalty would not only endanger the nobles leading them but also expose the throne to the contender, Artabanus.[55]

While the idea of mustering levies to war was scrapped, abandoning the throne was not. Abdageses, Tiridates' chief advisor, had another strategy: retreat into Mesopotamia. Abdageses saw Mesopotamia as a strategic location from where they could conduct defensive and offensive war. The Tigris River in front of them provided a natural defensive barrier, which would buy them time to send a message seeking military aid from their allies, such as the Armenians, Elymaeans, and yes, the Romans. Tiridates agreed to the proposal and the king, his court, and a small force crossed the Tigris River and headed for the Euphrates River near the Roman-Parthian border. All went well until the very army accompanying Tiridates decided to trickle away. Evidently, no one told the forces about the plan, which could explain that their moving into Mesopotamia felt more like an exodus than preparing for a defensive war. They did not trust Tiridates, and instead of fighting for the puppet of Rome, they went back to their homes or defected to the camp of Artabanus. As for

---

[55] Ibid.

Tiridates and those loyal to him, they crossed the Euphrates River into Syria. He was back under Roman protection where he was safe. Tiridates was relieved that his embarrassing nightmare was over and that he would be able to live another day.[56]

Once news reached Tiberius that Tiridates had been ousted from power and was safely in Syria, he sent a letter to Vitellius, instructing him to befriend Artabanus. Tiberius, terrified of Artabanus, was terrified at the prospect of a Parthian invasion of Roman provinces west of the Euphrates. What Tiberius did know was that Artabanus could not conduct a massive invasion and, in many respects, he feared a war with Rome; this is why Artabanus was likely happy to receive a letter from Tiberius that sought peace rather than war. In order to cement the deal, Artabanus and Vitellius met at the Euphrates roughly around 37 CE, where a large bridge was constructed over the river. Once the bridge was constructed, Vitellius and his guards, likely on foot, came from west, while Artabanus and his guards, likely on horseback, came from the east, meeting in the middle. Vitellius and Artabanus likely welcomed each other in their own fashion. After greetings and small talk, King Herod of Judea ordered a large tent to be erected at the midst of the bridge and a meal prepared. While both men feasted and drank that evening, likely well into the night, it was during this party that the terms of agreement were established. However, no one really knows what was

---

[56] Ibid.

agreed upon. What we do know is that Artabanus and Vitellius exchanged many presents. What Artabanus received is unclear. What Vitellius received was Artabanus' son Darius; he was to be held hostage in Rome and educated. Another gift mentioned was a rather tall Jewish man by the name of Eleazar, who was seven cubits tall. While we don't know the rest of the details, what could be said with certainty is that there was no war, the Euphrates still remains the border, and Armenia is still under the Roman sphere of influence. After all was said and exchanged, Vitellius went to Antioch and Artabanus to Babylon.[57] The two great civilizations now seemed at peace, but this only lasted for a short time.

---

[57] Joseph, *AJ*, 18.17.5.

Figure 29 Phraates IV. Classical Numismatic Group.
http://www.cngcoins.com/Coin.aspx?CoinID=153426# CC BY-SA 3.0

Proxy along the Euphrates

Figure 30 Map of Characene. Author: NordNordWest.
http://commons.wikimedia.org/wiki/File:Karte_Charakene.png
(CC BY-SA 3.0)

http://www.cngcoins.com/Coin.aspx?CoinID=153426

Figure 31 Coin of the Parthian king Phraataces and of Musa. http://commons.wikimedia.org/wiki/File:Musa.jpg Author: Classical Numismatic Group (CC BY-SA 3.0)

Figure 32 Augustus of Prima Porta. Retrieval of Crassus' standards captured by the Parthians depicted on the cuirass. Author: Sailko.
http://commons.wikimedia.org/wiki/File:Augusto_di_Prima_Porta,_inv._2290,_03.jpg(CC BY-SA 3.0)

Figure 33 Coin of Artabanus III of Parthia.
Author: Classical Numismatic Group.
http://www.cngcoins.com/Coin.aspx?CoinID=96852
(CC BY-SA 3.0)

Figure 34 Lucius Vitellius
(CC0 1.0)

Figure 35 Emperor Tiberius

7

THE WAR FOR ARMENIA

With peace reestablished between Rome and Parthia in 37 CE, all looked well on the surface. Artabanus returned and reclaimed his throne, only to be deposed shortly after by the nobles and replaced by what seems to be his foster son, Cinnamus. The reason Artabanus was deposed is unclear, but when looking back on events dealing with the Romans during and before the reign of Artabanus, it is evident that the Parthian nobles desired an iron king who would not bend or be dictated to when confronted by another nation's foreign policy. Parthia, from the outside, looks divided, but inside, the nobles desire stability, something the Parthian kings have been unable to provide for some time now. Even though Artabanus was again banished from his kingdom, he fled to the Parthian client state of Adiabene, ruled by Izates bar Monobaz, where he planned his triumphal return once again with Izates' help. But before Artabanus could win back the nobles, Cinnamus, according to Josephus, wrote to Artabanus, requesting him to come back and retake the throne. Cinnamus is described as having a "good and gentle" nature. Artabanus agreed and returned to Ctesiphon, where Cinnamus "worshipped him, and saluted him as a king, and took the diadem off his own head, and put it on the head of Artabanus."

Whether the story is true or not, one thing is certain, once Artabanus had retaken his throne, he died.[1]

With Artabanus dead, his sons Vardanes I and Gotarzes II squabbled for the throne, resulting in seven years of civil war between the two, ending with the murder of Vardanes in 47 CE. Four years later, the despotic Gotarzes suffered the same fate, likely having been poisoned.[2] Parthia, after suffering many decades of civil war, got a new king, Vonones II. It seemed there was hope, after all. He had no brothers or kin challenging him for the throne, thus he could focus on the empire itself. However, he did not last long, dying unexpectedly in 51 CE, probably from old age. He was the brother of Artabanus, and during his brother's reign, Vonones II had served as the King of Media Atropatene until 51 CE, when he traded in his Median kingship for Parthian.[3] When Vonones died, the throne passed to his son Vologases I. Vologases, like his father, was placed in a stable political environment with no contests or squabbling, which allowed him to focus on Parthia, rather than on a political challenger for the throne.

Vologases' first order of business was to stabilize the empire culturally by reviving the ancient Iranian

---

[1] Josephus, *AJ*, 20.3.2. Quoted by Marie Louise Chaumont, "Cinnamus," *Encyclopædia Iranica*, Volume V, CARPETS – COFFEE, 1992. http://www.iranicaonline.org/articles/cinnamus-gk

[2] Joseph, *AJ*, 20.3.4/ Tac, *Ann*, 12.14.

[3] Tac, *Ann*, 12.14.

traditions. Parthian coins inscribed with Greek were replaced with Aramaic script, but not just coins. Aramaic became the de facto language of the Parthian Empire. Not only was Greek being pushed out, but also the culture. An example of this is the completely new appearance of many Parthian cities. Babylon, long known for its Hellenic culture, was expanded to incorporate Iranian peoples. The cities of Merv and Susa replaced their Greek designations with Iranian.[1] Vologases also founded a city called Vologesocerta, which was not only to rival the city of Seleucia for cultural interest, but also would become a commercial center that would encompass the Seleucia-Ctesiphon complex by forcing trade from Charax, that semi-independent kingdom to the south, to pass through territory under Parthian control. This proved a successful entrepôt for trade with the West, according to Palmyrene inscriptions.[2]

But what does this have to do with the coming war with Armenia? The answer is Persian revival. Vologases' goal was not to eradicate Hellenism from the Parthian Empire, but to put forward Iranian traditions. Not only was there a desire to change Parthian cultural internally, but Vologases desired to reinstate the borders of the former Achaemenid Empire. He likely saw himself as the heir and the Parthian Empire an extension of that former

---

[1] Farrokh, 148.
[2] Peter Christensen, *The Decline of Iranshahr: Irrigation and Environments in the History of the Middle East, 500 B.C. to A.D. 1500.* (Copenhagen: Museum Tusculanum Press, 1993). 64/ Pliny, 6.122.

glory. Therefore, the province of Armenia must be brought back within the Iranian fold.

THE ROAD TO WAR

In 52 CE, word reached Rome that the Iberians had invaded Armenia under the leadership of Prince Rhadamistus, who ousted and murdered his uncle, King Mithridates, for the throne. Rome reacted with displeasure, but decided against intervening, except for Julius Pelignus, governor of Cappadocia. Pelignus took it upon himself to invade Armenia with the intention of restoring order, then decided to go on a plundering campaign. Eventually Pelignus found himself in trouble, as the auxiliaries he raised to accompany him began slowly to desert him, thus exposing him to the very people he was plundering. Because of the situation he put himself in, he quickly ran to Rhadamistus for protection, which was given. But while Rhadamistus had the Roman governor of Cappadocia in his presence, knowing that Pelignus sought riches, he showered him with gifts. He hoped that Pelignus would support his being crowned king. Pelignus agreed and assisted at the ceremony. However Pelignus' actions were frowned upon by Rome. Ummidius Quadratus, the governor of Syria, placed a legion under the command of Helvidius Priscus to regulate and pacify Armenia. However, even though

Priscus was successful, he was ordered to pull out for fear that their presence might provoke Parthia into war.[3]

Vologases likely received reports concerning the Iberian invasion of Armenia that replaced King Mithridates with Rhadamistus. Upon hearing the news, he was likely excited, yet cautious. Vologases waited for further reports to trickle in concerning Armenia's regime change. Vologases likely wanted to know whether this was a Roman-sponsored changing of the throne. Of course, as time went on, he likely realized that this was an individual incident, and before getting involved, he waited to see how Rome would react. Rome's reaction and intervention in Armenia likely caused Vologases to look the other way, at least until word reached him that the Romans continued no further for fear of war with the Parthians. The news was encouraging. Vologases was not ignorant of Rome's strength, but their political concern suggested watchful waiting to see how Rome would react.

Vologases mustered his forces and set forth for Armenia. Once in Armenia, the Parthians encountered little, if any, resistance, as they were able to march in and take the cities of Artaxata and Tigranocerta without contest. All seemed to be in Vologases' favor until winter came. With supplies dwindling and sickness spreading, Vologases gave the order to pull out. Even though Vologases had to retreat due to the season, his gains were encouraging and he expected to return to finish the job.

---

[3] Tac, *Ann*, 12.44-49.

With the Parthians gone, Armenia was open and without a king. Rhadamistus, after fleeing the Parthian advancement, returned to Armenia and began his second reign rather cruelly by punishing those cities that had submitted without a fight. Before he could do any more harm, the people of Armenia rose up, revolted, and marched on the palace. Rhadamistus was able to escape the mob and return to Iberia. With Rhadamistus out of the picture, Vologases was able to place his brother Tiridates on the throne of Armenia, with approval of the people, around 54 CE. Of course, his act of placing his brother on the throne violated the treaty agreed between the Emperor Augustus and King Phraates IV. However, "that treaty was between them," may have been the thinking of Vologases.[4]

While Tiridates was settling in as the new pro-Parthian king of Armenia, Emperor Claudius fell dead, possibly due to poisoning. Soon after his stepson Nero ascended the throne, news reached Rome concerning of the event around December 54 CE of the Parthians breaking the treaty, devastating the country, and placing a king of their own on the throne. The Roman Senate was now at odds over what to do. Their new emperor, Nero, was just 16 years of age, with no experience. Some argued that much of the war could be conducted as long as Nero had tutors directing and advising him. Others argued that Nero could handle the war, for past leaders like Gnaeus

---

[4] Tac, *Ann*, 12.50-51.

The War for Armenia

Pompeius and Gaius Octavius were aged 18 and 19 during the civil wars.[5]

The real issue plaguing Rome at this critical moment was not so much the age of the emperor but finding an able commander, moving legions, supplying them, and training them, all in preparation for dealing with the physical environment, and the method by which their enemy fights. Nero likely would have not prepared for war unless there was division within Parthia. Yes, division once again plagued Parthia.

While Rome debated on what actions to take, if any, the nobles of Adiabene, a client state of Parthia, approached Vologases and expressed displeasure in their king, Izates, for "abrogating the laws of their forefathers, and embracing foreign customs." Vologases was displeased with the news and revoked Izates' special status of certain kingly honors awarded to him by Artabanus III; if he refused, Vologases would declare war on him. Izates refused to back down and prepared for war. Vologases assembled his forces and made his way towards Adiabene. No sooner had Vologases entered the province and made camp than he received disturbing news that various Dahae and Saka nomads had invaded Parthia. Vologases pulled his forces out of Adiabene and prepared for civil war.[6]

Yes, civil war had engulfed Parthia once again. This nomadic invasion was not some hit and run raid; rather it

---

[5] Tac, *Ann*, 13.6.
[6] Josephus, *AJ*, 20.4.

was led by Vologases' son Vardanes II. Details of the situation are unknown. Vologases likely had a falling out with his son at some point before his invasion of Adiabene. What is certain is that from 55-58 CE, Vologases was busy putting down the revolt.[7]

The Romans undoubtedly monitored the civil strife in Parthia and took advantage of the situation. While Parthia was distracted, Nero agreed that war with Parthia was the best option, even though Rome had been at war with Parthia all along once the treaty had been violated. With war now an obvious reality, it was time to determine the best strategy to take and who was going to lead Rome into Armenia and possibly beyond.

Nero, being young, needed guidance in these tough decisions, and the two men who advised him on political and military affairs were Lucius Annaeus Seneca (Seneca the Younger) and Sextus Afranius Burrus.[8]
Before the recruitment of levies, moving troops, and acquisition of supplies, politics came first. Nero decided that the best option in engaging the Parthians was through political circumvention. Since Rome was not prepared for military intervention, he could at least prepare the way by replacing the governors of Lesser Armenia and Sophene, provinces adjacent to Armenia. Nero was likely advised that the governors of the two provinces were likely pro-Parthian or harbored sympathies for them, and if neither is true, it was best not to take a chance. Therefore, Nero

---

[7] Tac, *Ann*, 13.7.
[8] Ibid., 13.2.

ordered the replacement of the outgoing governors with pro-Roman ones. In doing so, Nero secured future troop movements and effectively secured his borders north of Syria, thus establishing a stable base of operations from which his legions could launch their attack. With questionable provinces secured, a potential suitor to lead the legions was next on Nero's plate.[9]

CORBULO

Nero would eventually settle on a man by the name of Gnaeus Domitius Corbulo. Corbulo was selected for his ability to command and led men into war. He was a hard charger and a disciplinarian with no time for idleness, but the constant need to keep men on their toes and out of trouble. He gained this reputation while commanding the Roman forces in Germania Inferior, located on the west bank of the Rhine, for seven years. While Corbulo toiled in Germania Inferior, he received a message that he was being relieved of his command and appointed governor of Cappadocia-Galatia in Asia Minor around 54-55 CE. His duty was to recover Armenia.[10]

Once Corbulo accepted his new assignment, Nero sent orders to Syria instructing provinces nearby to recruit levies that would support the legions of the East. This

---

[9] Ibid., 13.7.
[10] Miriam T. Griffin, *Nero: The End of a Dynasty* (New Haven: Yale University Press, 1985), 226/Tac, *Ann*, 11.20.

would allow half of the Eastern legions in Syria to move towards the Armenian frontier. The X Fretensis and the XII Fulminata, along with the auxiliaries, would remain in Syria under the command of Ummidius Quadratus, governor of Syria. Once Corbulo arrived in Cappadocia-Galatia, the remaining legions in Syria, the III Gallica and VI Ferrata were placed under his command. Besides the two legions under the command of Corbulo, he also had the cohorts stationed in Cappadocia along with auxiliaries, consisting of both infantry and cavalry at his disposal. To further strengthen Corbulo's forces, Nero sent orders to the kings Agrippa of Chalcis and Antiochus of Commagene to muster their armies and prepare for an invasion of Parthia.[11]

    Before Corbulo entered Armenia, he met Quadratus at Cilicia. What was discussed between the two is not known, but what is certain is that Quadratus was afraid that Corbulo would reap all the rewards once the war started. Nevertheless, both men agreed to send emissaries to Vologases. Their message was simple, choose peace or prepare for war, and if you choose peace, show that you mean it and give over some of your family members as hostages as an act of good will. Of course, Vologases was willing to give up some of his family members, for giving up family members creates a diversion and at the same time rid Vologases of some of the more rebellious elements within his family that could have potentially challenged him for his throne, like his son

---

[11] Debevoise, 179-180/Tac, *Ann*, 13.7.

Vardanes II. Moreover, Corbulo and Quadratus make no mention of Parthia pulling out of Armenia to secure the deal in order to avoid war. This tells us that there were no Parthian forces in Armenia, which was likely due to the civil war taking place in Parthia between Vologases and Vardanes II.[12]

It was also during this time that Corbulo arrived in Cappadocia, where he inspected the III Gallica and VI Ferrata and found them lacking. What Corbulo encountered was a ragtag and undisciplined fighting force, if one can call them a fighting force. Many of the men were without armor, such as breastplates and helmets. Others were not used to picket or night guard duty. Another issue plaguing the Roman ranks was a number of older veterans and those with ill health, which were relieved of their duty and replaced. In order to strengthen the Roman legions assigned to him, he had to retrain, equip, and supply them. In other words, Corbulo literally was in the process of raising two new legions. While the year 55 CE was indeed a rebuilding year, in 56 CE, Corbulo brought in another legion along with its light infantry and cavalry auxiliary attachment, the IV Scythica from Moesia. The IV Scythica not only strengthened his forces, but likely were used to train and be an example of what a real legion is to the other two legions.[13]

---

[12] Tac, *Ann*, 13.7/ A.D.H. Bivar, "The Political History of Iran under the Arsacids", in CHI, vol. 3: *The Seleucid, Parthian and Sasanian Period*, ed. E. Yarshater (Cambridge: Cambridge University Press, 1983), p. 81.

[13] Debevoise, 180/ Tac, *Ann*, 13.35.

Leviathan Vs. Behemoth

CORBULO'S CAMPAIGN

It was not until the end of 57 CE that Corbulo felt comfortable enough to move his legions into Armenia. However, Corbulo's march into Armenia would be short. His troops were forced to bivouac near Erzerum, which was 6,000 feet above sea level, due to a harsh winter that set in. It was also at Erzerum he likely gave the order to build bridges and place them across the Euphrates, since the Euphrates flows though the plain of Erzerum. The weather was so bad, as one would expect at 6,000 feet, that the frozen ground, covered in ice, made it difficult to pitch a tent. Not only was it difficult to temporarily homestead on a piece of land, surviving in the elements was just as difficult. Many soldiers suffered from frostbite and there is no doubt limbs were lost. If losing limbs was not bad enough, consider that some of the men placed on guard duty died in the bitter cold. Even though the men suffered, Corbulo did his best to keep their spirits high by working with and comforting them. Even though Corbulo led by example, some thought otherwise and deserted the camp. Those caught were immediately executed, which led to a great decline in desertion.[14]

Once the bitter cold of winter had subsided and spring arrived in 58 CE, Corbulo prepared to push forward and further into Armenia. He wanted to keep it clean and

---

[14] Freya Stark, *Rome on the Euphrates: The Study of a Frontier* (New York: Harcourt, Brace & World, INC., 1967), 179/ Tac, *Ann*, 13.7,35/ Encyclopaedia Britannica (1911) vol 9, page 894.

in stride. However, things were about to change. When the territory thawed, small enemy units arrived, presumably a mix of Parthian and loyal Armenians. There is no doubt that the king of Armenia, Tiridates, likely collected intelligence on Corbulo's troop movements and knew when the Romans entered Armenia. Rome's presence evidently caused some Armenians to celebrate, so much so that Tiridates had to take action before widespread revolt ensued. However, Tiridates could do little at first, until the winter set in and bogged down the Romans. While Roman forces were bogged down at the high altitude, Tiridates sought the aid of his brother Vologases and went on a campaign to squash and plunder all those whom he thought were loyal Roman supporters. It was during this purge that the Parthians encountered Corbulo's camp.[15]

Ahead of the legions' encampment, Corbulo established a series of defensive positions garrisoned with auxiliary infantry under the command of a first-rank centurion by the name of Paccius Orfitus. Eventually a band of enemy forces would stumble upon Orfitus' perimeter. Orfitus sent word back to Corbulo that they had encountered a small band of the enemy who were acting reckless and that he had an opportunity to engage them. Corbulo quickly sent a message back denying Orfitus' request to engage the enemy until stronger forces arrived. Unfortunately, Orfitus disobeyed orders and engaged the enemy, only to be defeated.[16]

---

[15] Tac, *Ann*, 13.36-37.
[16] Tac, *Ann*, 13.36.

As mentioned, the enemy unit that Orfitus engaged was likely a scouting party attached to a much bigger group, which at the time was ravaging the areas of Armenia that were loyal to Rome. Tiridates, with the aid of his brother Vologases, was responsible for the carnage and plunder sweeping the disloyal portions of Armenia.

Corbulo gave the order to pack up and move out. However, he was in for much more than he bargained. Corbulo attempted to engage the enemy, but the enemy refused. Corbulo grew frustrated with the situation, having expected direct engagement. It tells us that he knew little about his enemy's tactics. However, Corbulo was a quick learner. He therefore decided that in order to engage the enemy, he would have to divide his forces like that of the enemy, pursue each enemy unit, and conduct guerilla warfare on their level. Corbulo hated the very idea and rightfully so, since to divide his forces exposed him. Corbulo understood that he needed additional forces to invade and fight the enemy by conventional means if necessary. Therefore, Corbulo conducted guerrilla warfare while having the protection and support of the allies until the time was right to gather his men. In order to execute this properly, Corbulo sent orders to King Antiochus of Commagene to move his forces immediately to the provinces on his frontier and invade Armenia from the southwest. King Pharasmanes of Iberia at the time took advantage of the situation to show his Roman support and reignited the old feud by harassing the districts of north-east Armenia. Corbulo got further support when the nation of Moschi, located in the Moschian Mountains of the Caucasus, between Iberia, Armenia, and Colchis invaded Armenia and took control of the "wilds."[17]

Even though Tiridates had troops of his own and the aid of his brother, who helped in plundering those Armenians loyal to Rome, it did not last long. Once the Romans entered Armenia along with their allies, Tiridates refrained from engaging, deciding it was best to hit and run while they fled Armenia entirely. One would think that the aid Vologases provided to Tiridates would have been sufficient, if not more, in defending Armenia from outside attackers. The truth of the matter is Vologases did support his brother, but likely sent a small to medium sized force to aid him in putting down potential rebellions. The reason is that Vologases, after defeating his son, could now help his brother in Armenia, but while he was preparing to move a much larger force into Armenia to counter Rome's advance, another rebellion had broken out in the Parthian province of Hyrcania, thus bogging down Vologases once again.[18]

Tiridates, surprised by Rome's invasion, wanted to know why Rome had ventured into Armenian lands and sent envoys with a message to Corbulo. The envoys made it clear that Tiridates thought that placing family members into Rome's hands for political reasons was sufficient to keep the peace. Tiridates spoke for his brother and made it clear that "Vologases had not bestirred himself, simply

---

[17] Tac, *Ann*, 13.37.
[18] Ibid.

because they preferred negotiation to violence. Should war be persisted in, however, the Arsacids would not want the courage and good fortune which had already been proved more than once by disaster to Rome." Corbulo's response was clear, and reminded Tiridates that even though he is the king of Armenia, Armenia belongs to Rome, and if he wishes to hold his power and title, he must submit to his master, Nero.[19]

Neither side was going to budge and soon the negotiations began to fall apart. In the end, it was decided that they would meet at a fixed time and place to hammer out a deal. Tiridates made it clear that he would meet with Corbulo while being escorted by "a thousand troopers." Tiridates also insisted that Corbulo and his escort come without breastplates or helmets, as a sign of good faith. However, Corbulo was no fool. He saw through the ruse and acted as if he did not understand the message. Corbulo understood that to show up without armor before a cavalry force well known for its horsemanship and archery abilities would be suicide. Therefore, Corbulo requested that both sides negotiate before their entire armies, at a place where the hill slopes with a spreading plain below. Such a place would be fashionable for both infantry and cavalry; such a place would be good for battle. The day arrived on which both men were to meet. Corbulo arrived first with his army and arrayed them in battle formations. Tiridates appeared at a distance and in silence, not attempting to approach Corbulo. Tiridates did

---

[19] Ibid.

not trust Corbulo anymore than Corbulo trusted Tiridates. It was a standoff, more or less, with Tiridates hoping Corbulo would make the first move, break formation and expose his men to a cavalry attack. However, Corbulo was no fool and stood his ground. Tiridates, seeing that Corbulo would not budge, decided to turn back, while Corbulo ordered his troops to retire to their camps.[20]

With negotiations going nowhere, Tiridates resorted to guerrilla warfare. Instead of hitting the Roman armies, he decided to attack their lifeline. Tiridates received information that the armies of Corbulo were receiving supplies from the city of Trapezus, from which they must travel over mountains to get to their intended destinations. When Tiridates learned of this, he ordered his forces to disrupt the supply and communication lines, but soon realized that both had escort protection and it was far too risky to engage. While Tiridates tried to find ways to disrupt Corbulo's momentum, Corbulo pushed forward, deciding that the best method to defeat Tiridates was to attack him where it hurts most, his forts.[21]

Corbulo understood that in order to defeat Tiridates, he must attack him where he is weak. The forts that dot the Armenian landscape serve as Tiridates' weak points. Forts are a commanding site, which houses a garrison that looks over the land and at the same time serves as a treasury. Corbulo understood if he were to take

---

[20] Ibid, 38/Sheldon, 107.
[21] Tac, *Ann*, 13.39/Pat Southern, *The Roman Army: A Social and Institutional History* (Santa Barbara, Calif: Oxford University Press, 2007), 301.

these forts, he would not only gain the revenue, but it would cause Tiridates to lose credibility in defending his own people, thus turning them against him.[22]

In order to make a psychological impact on Tiridates, Corbulo chose the biggest fort to attack: Volandum. Corbulo understood that it was not wise to concentrate all his troops on one fort because to do so would leave him wide open for attack. Therefore, Corbulo instructed his general Cornelius Flaccus and a camp prefect by the name of Insteius Capito to take some forces and capture the weaker forts.

While Flaccus and Capito were fanning out across the landscape, Corbulo marched towards Volandum. Once outside the walls, Corbulo studied the fortification making his calculations and finally picked a point of attack. He divided his forces into four divisions, himself leading one in a tightly packed testudo formation. As his forces approached the walls, Corbulo ordered his siege engines, slingers, and artillerymen to commence firing, laying down a volley of firebrands, javelins, and leaden sling-bullets. The firepower was so intense that before the day was over, the walls were stripped of defenders and the barriers and gates crumbled, which allowed Corbulo's men to scale the walls with ease. Once inside Volandum, the Romans plundered and mercilessly massacred all the adult inhabitants of the city, while those still alive, primarily children, were sold into slavery. No Roman

---

[22] Tac, *Ann*, 13.39/ Adrian Goldsworthy, *In the Name of Rome: The Men Who Won the Roman Empire* (London: Phoenix, 2004), 315.

soldier died and only a few received wounds. While Corbulo enjoyed his victory at Volandum, both Flaccus and Capito enjoyed their victories as they subdued and plundered three forts that same day. Word was spreading fast of Rome's unstoppable momentum, which caused a panic to spread in the nearby areas, causing many to capitulate without a fight. With the area cleared of hostiles, Corbulo was now confident that he could take the Armenian capital of Artaxata.[23]

After the sacking of Volandum, Corbulo quickly collected all the intelligence they had gathered on Artaxata. Corbulo decided that in order to take the city, the route least traveled was the best option. If they chose to take the nearest route, they would have to cross the Araxes River, and the closest crossing by bridge was far too close to the city walls, which would place them within firing range.[24]

Before moving out, Corbulo ordered his forces to assemble into a square formation. On the right flank was the III Gallica with the VI Ferrata on the left flank. Protecting the rear was 1,000 cavalry while some men from the X Fretensis were placed in the center to protect the baggage. Corbulo understood that marching in this fashion would provide protection on all fronts. He knew the enemy would attack in a hit and run fashion, but the square formation would avert the full effect. Tiridates knew that attacking the Romans head on while in a square

---

[23] Tac, *Ann*, 13.39.
[24] Ibid.

formation would be suicide, but hit and run attacks were his only option unless he could get Corbulo to terrain that was more open. Tiridates' forces made repeated feigned attacks, but would quickly gallop away, hoping that some of the Romans would break rank and pursue. Corbulo would not fall for this ruse and continued to push on until nightfall. Corbulo ordered his men to bivouac and sent out a scouting party. Tiridates, seeing that he was in a no-win situation, pulled out. Reports reached Corbulo that the enemy is possibly heading either to Media or Albania. Given that the northern kingdoms, like Albania, were hostile to Parthia, Tiridates likely headed towards Media Atropatene. Once Corbulo was in sight of Artaxata, the citizens peacefully surrendered the city, opened the gates, and the Romans marched in. Corbulo likely stayed in the city for the winter before moving out again in 59 CE. Once spring arrived, the Roman forces were on the move again, but before they left, Corbulo gave one last order. He ordered the citizens of Artaxata to evacuate the city. Corbulo did not have enough men to garrison the city; since he could not provide the city with a garrison, the city itself became a threat, for if the city is left alone, it could be re-garrisoned by the enemy. Therefore, the city must be burned and the walls leveled.[25] Once Artaxata was obliterated, Corbulo pushed on to Armenian's second capital, Tigranocerta.

---

[25] Ibid, 40-41/J.G.C. Anderson, *The Eastern Frontier under Augustus*, in CAH, Cambridge, 1934, vol. X, pp. 239-83.

The War for Armenia

Corbulo hoped that news of the destruction of Artaxata would spread like fire throughout Armenia. His goal was to intimidate the inhabitants of the city of Tigranocerta. While his forces marched south towards Tigranocerta, word reached many of the inhabitants in the way, causing some to hide or take up arms. Those who hid or resisted the Romans were punished or killed.

While the Romans were able to fight back any attack on their march, they were running low on supplies. The troops slowly became exhausted due to the long hot marches under the sun. With water and food running low, their bodies began to slow down and pain crept in. Corbulo kept their spirits high by showing patience. Hunger and exhaustion would diminish once they came upon a field of crops. After the men had their fill, they proceeded onward and came across two Armenian fortresses that refused to surrender. The Romans took one of the forts by storm, and the other, being a bit more difficult, was taken by siege.

Corbulo's momentum was growing stronger by the day, causing many to flee or find alternative methods in dealing with the Romans. One alternative in hopes of stopping the Romans was to assassinate Corbulo. While Corbulo was in his tent, a barbarian was discovered with a dagger. After being tortured, the man admitted that it was a plot designed by him and his associates. These associates happened to be high ranking Armenians in the service of Corbulo, and because of their sedition, they were punished. Not long after, an envoy of Corbulo's returned from Tigranocerta, reporting that the city was open to the Romans. Moreover, to prove their surrender, the citizens of the city presented Corbulo with a golden crown.[26]

Once Corbulo arrived outside the city, he was refused entry. The Romans soon besieged the city. To make the inhabitants think before they go any further, Corbulo took one of the men, who conspired to assassinate him, an Armenian noble by the name of Vadandus, and executed him. Afterwards, Vadandus' severed head served as a projectile, which was shot out of a ballista, and is said to have fallen "in the midst of a council which the barbarians were holding at that very moment." The sight caused the council to change their minds and they quickly surrendered the city to Corbulo.[27] Soon after the capture of Tigranocerta, Corbulo captured another fort called Legerda.[28]

It's obvious that Corbulo was now in charge of Armenia. It's also obvious that with the lack of a Parthian presence, due to a rebellion taking place in Hyrcania, to counter the Romans, allowed Corbulo to subjugate Armenia easily and at a steady pace. Once the winter subsided, Tiridates in the spring of 60 CE collected his forces, pulled out of Media Atropatene, and invaded Armenia. However, it seems word had reached the Romans of his coming beforehand, which could be by the Hyrcanian envoys who were just at Rome and made a deal

---

[26] Tac, *Ann*, 14.23-24.
[27] Front, *Strat*, 2.9.5.
[28] Tac, *Ann*, 14.25.

to ally themselves with the Romans. Therefore, it's likely that both Roman and Hyrcanian forces worked together when it came to collecting intelligence and providing that information to one another on the whereabouts of the Parthians in the regions that border Armenia. Once Tiridates had crossed into Armenian territory, Corbulo immediately sent his lieutenant-general Verulanus with the legions along with some auxiliaries to counter the advancement, which resulted in victory. Not long after Tiridates' expulsion from Armenia, Tigranes, Rome's newly selected client king to take the throne of Armenia, arrived.[29]

Tigranes, who was the great-great-grandson of Herod the Great, was described as being "servile submissiveness." His arrival in Armenia was anything but exciting. While many Armenians preferred a king from Rome, many others placed their faith in the Arsacids. There was great division within Armenia and to help Tigranes rule effectively, four other client-kings were selected to govern over parts of Armenia close to their borders.[30] Once all was established and secured, Corbulo would leave Tigranes with 1,000 legionaries, along with 3,000 to 4,000 cavalry and infantry auxiliaries.[31] Afterwards, Corbulo returned to Syria to take on his new duty as governor there due to the death of Quadratus.[32]

---

[29] Ibid., 14.26.
[30] Ibid.
[31] Sheldon, 107.
[32] Tac, *Ann*, 14.26.

COUNTERATTACK

Rome was fully aware that Armenia was far from secure. While there was some security, it would only last as long as Vologases was distracted by the rebellion in Hyrcania. However, that distraction was about to end abruptly.

In 61 CE, Tigranes made a big mistake. Thinking that the Parthians would be too weak to attack, decided to attack and ravage the Parthian satrap of Adiabene on its border, and why not, he had Rome backing him if the situation got out of hand. King Monobaz II of Adiabene seriously considered surrendering to Rome but decided against it. Instead, he requested Vologases' aid. Vologases must oblige or risk losing much more. In some ways, one could say this is what Vologases has been waiting for, but in reality, he wants to avoid any conflict with Rome and rightfully so. Vologases had to act quickly and come up with a plan of attack. He first must take care of business in Hyrcania, which he did, begrudgingly offering peace, which the Hyrcanians happily accepted. Vologases understood that he could deal with the Hyrcanians later. The stability of his kingdom was far more important, especially when an extension of Rome is attacking his borders. The best way to resolve this was to invade Armenia and take Rome head on.

During the upheaval, Vologases called for his council. Nobles from all over met with Vologases. With Tiridates by his side, he made it clear before the council that Tiridates was king of Armenia and "encircled Tiridates' brow with a diadem." The act, this symbol, before the council, showed that Vologases would go to any extent to place Armenia back under the Parthian sphere of influence, and if possible, recover territory that once belonged to the former Achaemenid Empire that Vologases dreamed of restoring. With that said, Vologases placed his cavalry along with the auxiliaries from Adiabene under the command of a noble named Moneses. Moneses mission was to drive Tigranes out of Armenia. While Moneses pushed into Armenia, Vologases was preparing to lead the main Parthian forces into Syria. Vologases' strategy was to stretch the Romans thin.[33]

Once the orders were executed, news of their movement reached Corbulo. He quickly assembled his forces and sent two legions under the command of Verulanus Severus and Vettius Bolanus to aid Tigranes. In the meantime, Corbulo sent a letter to Nero requesting him to send a separate general to defend Armenia. While Verulanus and Bolanus were heading to Armenia, Corbulo would remain in Syria. Corbulo sent his remaining legions to the banks of the Euphrates, while quickly assembling and arming the provincials. Corbulo also stationed guards at specific wells and instructed his men to cover up some of the streams with sand, so that the enemy would have nothing to quench their or the thirst of their animals once in the desert.[34]

---

[33] Ibid., 15.1-2.
[34] Ibid., 3.

Corbulo was concerned more for Syria then Armenia. He instructed Verulanus and Bolanus to "conduct all their operations with deliberation rather than dispatch, as he would prefer to sustain rather than to make war."[35] If the Parthian forces in Armenia were insignificant and the Parthian forces invading Syria overbearing, he would need them to return to the defense of Syria quickly, a smart move.

Tigranes, on hearing of Moneses' entry into Armenia, was ready for action. He had a substantial mix of Roman and Armenian troops along with enough supplies to defend Tigranocerta. Once Moneses arrived, the siege began, but resulted in utter failure. The Parthian horse archers could do little to the defenders on the walls, and the Adiabene infantry who attempted to scale the walls were slaughtered. Even though Tacitus mentions that siege engines were present at Tigranocerta, it is obvious that they abandoned them since they were unskilled in using the devices. In the end, the defenders of Tigranocerta sallied forth and defeated the remaining Parthian and Adiabene forces.[36]

With the siege ending in failure, Corbulo sent a message to Vologases who was encamped at Nisibis, just 37 miles away from Tigranocerta. A centurion named Casperius would deliver the message to Vologases. Corbulo made it clear that "He had better give up the

---

[35] Ibid.
[36] Ibid., 15.4/ Adrian Goldsworthy, *In the name of Rome: The men who won the Roman Empire* (London: Phoenix, 2004), 319.

siege, or he, Corbulo too would encamp in his territory, as on hostile ground." Vologases deeply wanted to continue but the message proved that he could not. Vologases knew that they could not take Tigranocerta; he knew that Roman legions were now in Armenia, and, to make matters worse, locusts had devoured every blade of grass and leaf in his area. Vologases was in a no-win situation. Therefore, Vologases replied, making a truce with Corbulo, making it known that he had ordered Moneses to pull out, and requesting that he send an envoy to Nero to negotiate for the control over Armenia. Vologases gave the order and his forces moved back into Parthia where he would retire for the time being. While the Parthians pulled out of Armenia, Corbulo also pulled his legions out, sending them to the Cappadocia frontier for the winter of 61/62 CE.[37] While many found this to be a victory back in Rome, others were suspicious, suggesting the possibility that Corbulo and Vologases had made a secret pact. While it is possible there was a secret pact, the pact likely was Cobulo's doing. In other words, Corbulo feared Nero; too much glory placed his career in harm's way. Therefore, it was best to return to Armenia and work on a contingency plan with Nero in dealing with Parthia.[38]

---

[37] Tac, *Ann*, 15.5-6.
[38] Tac, *Ann*, 15.6; Sheldon, 108.

Leviathan Vs. Behemoth

THE BATTLE OF RHANDEIA

As if things could not get any worse, enter Lucius Caesennius Paetus, Nero's selection to provide security over Armenia and to deter any future Parthian attacks. However, Paetus was anything but a general; he had no military experience and despised Corbulo's fame, but it could have been worse. Paetus was consul in 61 CE before receiving his new duty as governor and general of Cappadocia.[39]

Once Paetus arrived at his new duty post, Corbulo was ordered to divide the six legions under his command, placing three of them to Paetus. Corbulo would retain the III Gallica, VI Ferrata, and X Fretensis, who were the more experienced, while Paetus received the XII Fulminata, IV Scythica, and the newly arrived V Macedonica, who were not as experienced--much like Paetus. In addition, Paetus was granted auxiliaries from Pontus, Galatia, and Cappadocia.[40]

While Roman legions rested in quarters, the envoys Vologases sent to Rome came back empty handed. There is no doubt that the envoys, while in Rome, likely had overheard many things; one such thing to stir the pot may have been Paetus. Now there is no way of knowing if Paetus and Parthian envoys ever met while he was consul

---

[39] Simon Hornblower, Antony Spawforth, and Esther Eidinow, *The Oxford Classical Dictionary* (Oxford: Oxford University Press, 2012), 262; Tac, *Ann*, 15.6.
[40] Tac, *Ann*, 15.6.

in Rome. But Paetus was quite open about the prospect of direct Roman rule over Armenia, and it's possible that the envoys caught wind of it and informed Vologases of this man in whom Nero has placed faith to look over the security of Armenia. In other words, even though the envoys came back empty-handed, Paetus' political views towards Armenia amounted to Nero's answer to Vologases.[41]

In 62 CE, Paetus took the offensive with the XII Fulminata and IV Scythica, leaving the V Macedonica in Pontus, and entered Armenia. Paetus entry into Armenia effectively renewed the war, but he welcomed the challenge. Paetus hastily entered Armenia without sufficiently preparing his winter camp or providing enough supplies to his legions as they stormed through the portions of Armenia left untouched by Corbulo. Paetus took many forts but he had not the men to provide security in the newly taken districts. To make up for a lack of supplies, Paetus resorted to plundering to make up for the difference. However, the supplies he captured soon spoiled and, with winter setting in, he had to return home. Once back in quarters, Paetus wrote a letter to Nero, using "pompous language" to cover up the facts of the offensive.[42]

While Paetus acted as if he won a major victory, Corbulo was more of a realist. There is no doubt that when Corbulo heard of the news of Paetus' invasion, it was an

---

[41] Ibid., 15.6-7.
[42] Ibid., 15.8.

extension of Nero's answer, war. Corbulo, knowing Nero, and likely knowing Paetus' feelings towards him, knew that an immediate continuation of war was at hand and therefore kept near the Euphrates River. As Corbulo continued his work in fortifying the bridge crossings, Parthian horsemen in great numbers were in the vicinity scouting out the area. This was a cause for concern. Corbulo took immediate action by launching a flotilla of great size, equipped with ballistae and catapults, which was able to drive off the reconnaissance party. Once the area was clear of enemy forces, Corbulo quickly stationed auxiliary infantry in the hills while his legions built an entrenchment camp. Establishing a foothold on the Parthian shore startled the Parthians, causing them to give up on any plans that they had on Syria and focus their strength on Armenia instead.[43]

With Syria out of the question, Vologases moved his forces into Armenia. Paetus, who was unaware of Vologases' advancement, especially with winter approaching, did not expect an attack. Paetus had one legion, the V Macedonica in Pontus, while the rest he dispersed and granted furloughs to many of his officers. Once news reached Paetus that Vologases was now in Armenia, he immediately slapped together what men were still nearby and set out to meet Vologases. Once on the move, Paetus sent ahead a scouting detachment ahead of him. However, they would find the Parthians, which resulted in the deaths of a centurion and a few soldiers.

---

[43] Ibid., 15.9.

When the remainder came back to inform Paetus of what had happened, he panicked and returned to his camp. Paetus quickly issued orders, dividing his forces and placing 3,000 men at Taurus, some cavalry in part of a plain. His main force was across the river some 25 miles away. Moreover, he sent his wife and son to the fortress of Arsamosata, with a cohort for their defense.

While his winter quarters were at Rhandeia, located on the Arsanias River, a tributary of the Euphrates, his camp was some 40 to 50 miles away from the Isoghli crossing on the northern bank of the river. Had he made camp at the south bank of the Murad Su River, he would have secured his communication lines. By staying on the north bank, he risked being bottled in by the enemy, with no outreach. Parthian scouting parties likely picked up on this and relayed the information back to Vologases. Once Vologases received the news that the Romans were spread thin--a legion protecting a road here, a cavalry unit there, he committed to a full-scale attack on Armenia during the dead of winter; it was worth the gamble.[44]

However, Vologases should have taken advantage of the situation much earlier. Vologases defeated the legions stationed at Taurus and the Cavalry on the plain while hindering the main army of Paetus and severing communications to that force. Eventually, Paetus found himself besieged at Rhandeia. Fearing for his life, he sent a message to Corbulo demanding assistance. Corbulo was

---

[44] Tac, *Ann*, 15.10; Sheldon, 109-110.

already a step ahead, having taken a thousand men from each legion along with 800 cavalry and an equal number of auxiliaries just for this moment, if it were to arise. However, it would take a second messenger to break through the lines to inform Corbulo of the situation at hand. Corbulo left half his men to staff the forts along the Euphrates and chose the nearest route. Corbulo would move through the province of Commagene, through Cappadocia, and finally into Armenia. Unlike Paetus, Corbulo had plenty of supplies for this long, tough journey to rescue the man who ridiculed him for being too "soft." Paetus, surrounded by Parthian forces, could do little. Vologases pressed on harder during the siege, engaging the Roman entrenchments and even advancing closer, hoping to lure the Romans out into open. Many of the Roman soldiers fearfully stayed in their tents and would only fight if their lives depended on it, others had to be contained by the general's order, while the reminders were held back by cowardice. They were all praying for Corbulo, the savior.[45]

While Paetus knew not when Corbulo would arrive to save them, he began the negotiation process with Vologases. Paetus wrote a letter of protest to the king, denouncing him for his actions against the people of Armenia, saying that the Armenian people had always been under Roman dominion. Paetus seems to have forgotten that Armenia had been claimed by Parthia long before Rome's arrival. Nevertheless, Paetus offered peace,

---

[45] Tac, *Ann*, 15.12-13.

to stop looking at the present and to embrace each other as equals rather than enemies.[46]

Vologases ignored Paetus' protest and made it clear that he must wait for his brother Pacorus and Tiridates, and then together they would decide the fate of Armenia. However, Vologases was no fool. He was kept up to date on the whereabouts of Corbulo. Knowing that Corbulo was days away, he decided to send his cavalry commander, Vasaces, to Paetus, and forced him into negotiations. Paetus dwelt on the past, making the argument that such men as "Luculli and Pompeii, and of all that the Caesars had done in the way of holding or giving away Armenia." Vasaces, after listening to Paetus, responded "that we had the mere shadow of possession and of bestowing, but the Parthians, the reality of power."[47] After much arguing over the terms of agreement, both sides stopped for the day. The next day Monobaz II of Adiabene was brought into to be a witness to the proceedings. After much deliberation, Paetus had no choice but to accept the terms. Paetus swore before the standards and witnesses brought forth by Vologases, that the Romans would pull out of Armenia, and that all the forts and supplies now would be officially Parthian. Vologases had one last request, that he should be able to freely send envoys once again to Nero. Once all was agreed to, the looting began. Not only did the Parthians take their share, but the Armenians soon followed, looting

---

[46] Ibid., 15.13.
[47] Ibid., 15.14.

the Roman soldiers of clothing and weapons. The Roman men had no other option but to look ahead, take the abuse, and ignore the theft. In addition, the Romans were to bridge the Arsanias River in front of their camp as a symbol of their defeat. To make matters worse, they marched past the bodies and weapons of their comrades that Vologases had ordered to be piled up. It was over, for now.[48]

  Once Paetus, along with his tattered men, crossed the bridge, he quickly made his way to Corbulo, leaving the wounded behind. When Paetus met Corbulo, being mixed with emotions, he tried to persuade him to invade Armenia, that their combined forces could get the job done. Corbulo would not budge; he had not received any instructions from Nero to advance into Armenia. Paetus likely made the argument that his men were on their way to Armenia anyway, but Corbulo reminded him that he was on his way to save the legions from certain doom, not to invade Armenia. Corbulo made it clear to Paetus that his negligence caused him to move part of his forces, which endangered Syria, for he knew not the designs of the Parthians. Corbulo further reminded Paetus that the march back to Syria was uncertain, since his men were tired, the Parthian horsemen never tire, and to keep pace with them in order to avoid being slaughtered on the plains was now his mission. Seeing that Corbulo would not budge, Paetus retired to Cappadocia. Corbulo turned around and began his speedy march back to Syria.

---

[48] Ibid., 15.14-16; Dio, 21.

Corbulo was in luck though. Vologases sent a messenger by the name of Monaeses to arrange a meeting between the two men, instructing him to remove his fortresses and forces from Parthian territory. It was obvious that this meeting would take place on the bridge that spanned the Euphrates. Corbulo, taking no chances, quickly removed his forces and also removed the center of the bridge before the Parthians arrived, a precautionary measure no doubt. Afterwards, both sides held an arms-length conference that lasted for some time; eventually both sides made agreements. Corbulo would stay out of Parthian territory so long as Vologases would keep his word and stay out of Armenia until his envoys that he sent to Nero arrived with further information. The Euphrates would serve once again as the established boundary between the two powers.[49]

THE AFTERMATH

Meanwhile, at Rome, victory arches were erected at Capitoline hill, authorized by the Senate, which had no inkling of what was taking place back east in Armenia. But appearance is everything, a sign that all was well, Rome was in charge and victorious, even though rumors likely swirled in the Senate that spoke otherwise, but had not been confirmed by the men who were there. Even Nero grew anxious about the situation, wondering what was

---

[49] Ibid., 15.16-17.

true, what was not.⁵⁰ The only shred of evidence that Nero and the Senate had was the dispatches from Paetus, which proclaimed victory. However, that was about to change.⁵¹

In the spring of 63 CE, a Parthian envoy arrived in Rome, bearing a letter from Vologases, which indicated that the gods favored Parthia and thus placed Armenia in their hands, that he had besieged Tigranes and allowed Paetus and his legions to depart safely. The letter also made it clear that Tiridates could not journey to Rome, for his duties as king prevented him from doing so, but he would not refuse the journey to Rome if Nero summoned him to be recognized and inaugurated as king of Armenia before the Senate and legions.⁵² Vologases' letter and the dispatches by Paetus contradicted one other. In order to solve this dilemma, the centurion who had arrived with the envoys was asked about Armenia, in which he replied, "that all the Romans had quitted it." Nero, likely distraught over this new bit of information, went to his advisors, asked what was best, "dangerous war or a disgraceful peace." Without hesitation, his advisors advocated war. As for Paetus, when he returned to Rome Nero did not punish him, but pardoned him instead. The Parthian envoys left without an answer once again, but did not come back to Vologases empty handed; they had some presents for the king.⁵³

---

⁵⁰ Ibid., 15.18.
⁵¹ Ibid., 15.8.
⁵² Ibid., 15.24.
⁵³ Ibid., 15.25.

The War for Armenia

Nero was fine with war and why not. He had Corbulo in Syria who knew his men and understood the methods by which the enemy fights. Therefore, Nero increased Corbulo's power. Gaius Cestius Gallus would take charge of the Syrian administration, while Corbulo would receive the XV Apollinaris from Pannonia under the leadership of Marius Celsus. In addition, Corbulo would receive the broken spirits of the IV Scythica and XIII Fulminata, which were stationed in Syria. Before Corbulo set off for war, he picked the best men to fight alongside him from the III Gallica, and VI Ferrata of Syria, the V Macedonica of Pontus, and those from the newly arrived XV Apollinaris. Moreover, Nero gave direct and specific orders to the client-kings and governors of nearby provinces to obey the commands of Corbulo, giving him more auxiliaries to utilize and initially giving him more power, power which has not been seen since the time of Pompey under the Lex Manilia (Law of Manilius). Corbulo had supreme command in the war against Vologases.[54]

Once assembled, Corbulo gave the order and the legions marched off to war once again. Corbulo would take the route that Lucius Lucullus took a century ago, clearing all obstacles that hindered their progress. Parthian scouts likely saw the advancement and quickly sent a message to Tiridates and Vologases that the Romans under Corbulo had invaded. Hearing this, Tiridates and Vologases sent envoys with a message of peace. Corbulo, hearing the pleas of kings, responded by ordering some

---

[54] Ibid.

centurions to go with the Parthian envoys. Corbulo's message was a warning of what he was going to do and what he is capable of doing to Armenia if matters do not change. If Tiridates wants a kingdom intact and as a gift, he must submit part of himself to Rome; if Vologases cares about the welfare of his people, he must ally himself with Rome to avoid his people's further injury, whether by Romans or internal upheaval festering in Parthia, or perhaps both. Corbulo didn't disappoint, he lived up to his threat and attacked and drove many of the Armenian nobles who were opposed to Tigranes from their establishments. It caused a widespread panic throughout the land.[55]

Vologases knew that he could not win, he had neither the troops nor the resources to conduct a long protracted war and sued for peace, while Tiridates demanded the time and place to conduct peace negotiations. Vologases decided that the place should be where Paetus surrendered at Rhandeia. Corbulo agreed to the place and to the time. Corbulo wanted the grounds of Rhandeia cleaned up. He gave the mission to Paetus' own son, who served as a tribune, to take some men and "cover up the relics of that ill-starred battlefield." On the day of the meeting, Corbulo sent Tiberius Alexander and Vinianus Annius, Corbulo's son-in-law, to the camp of Tiridates as pledges against ambush. Each leader took with him 20 horsemen and agreed that the only way Tiridates could secure his kingship of Armenia was from the hands

---

[55] Ibid., 15.27.

The War for Armenia

of Nero. Tiridates agreed, and days later, before the Roman and Parthian armies, he removed the crown from his head and placed it at the feet of a statue of Nero. Corbulo made it clear that in order to receive this crown, you must receive it now from the hand of Nero. In addition, Tiridates also had to hand over his daughter as a hostage to Rome until he arrived to reclaim both kingdom and daughter. This agreement took place in late 63 CE.[56]

Tiridates would eventually journey to Rome to receive his crown, but it would be in 66 CE. Tiridates went on a grand tour, making stops to visit his mother, brothers like King Pacorus of Atropatene, and, of course, Vologases at Ecbatana. Afterwards, Tiridates went to Rome, taking with him his wife, who wore a golden helmet in place of a veil, his sons, and the sons of Vologases, Pacorus, and Monobaz. Besides family, a huge entourage of servants, 3,000 Parthian cavalry and numerous Romans escorted him once he passed over the Euphrates. Nero made sure the cities he passed through were decorated, pleasing to the eye, and that shouts coming from the citizens were compliments to make the journey all the more pleasant. Not only was it pleasant, it was also costly. Of course, free of charge, unless you're a Roman taxpayer. Nero used the state treasury to fund Tiridates long journey, costing Rome a staggering 800,000 sesterces daily for nine months. Tiridates was carful in every aspect not to offend Rome or to offend his priestly office, as he would stop on his journey to observe Zoroastrian traditions. Once he arrived

---

[56] Ibid., 15.28-30; Sheldon 114.

in Italy, Nero sent Tiridates a two-horse carriage. The two would meet at Neapolis. Once the two were in sight of each other, Tiridates was asked to remove his dagger, but he refused. To make Nero feel safe, he nailed it down in its scabbard. Once in Nero's presence, he knelt down, crossing his arms across his chest, and called Nero master.[57]

    Nero was pleased and admired him so much, that that he ordered for a gladiatorial exhibition in the nearby city of Puteoli. The party did not end there. It soon made its way to Rome. Once the feasting and partying was over, it was time to get down to business. Rome became overcrowded. Many citizens began to climb the rooftops around the center to get a glimpse of the procession and ceremony about to take place. Nero, wearing his imperial triumphal garb, entered the forum, accompanied by Praetorians and the senate. Nero ascended the rostra, seating himself in his imperial chair. Tiridates proceeded to walk towards Nero with his suite. He passed between lines of heavily-armed troops, and once he made his way to Nero, the crowd roared. Tiridates was alarmed by this, but humbled himself before Nero and reaffirmed his allegiance. Nero accepted Tiridates' submission and declared Tiridates king of Armenia, placing the crown upon his head. After the pomp and ceremony had ended, Tiridates returned home a very rich man. Nero had given him 200,000,000 sesterces to help rebuild Artaxata. Tiridates also picked up many Roman artisans in his

---

[57] Dio 63.1-2.

The War for Armenia

journey back home, some given to him by Nero, others attracted by high wages offered if they would accompany him. However, all good things must end. Corbulo would not allow Tiridates to take with him any of the artisans whom Nero did not give him, which caused Tiridates to despise the emperor more than ever.[58]

In summary, the war between the two powers resulted in compromise. Had there not been compromise, war would have continued, and Rome would likely have beaten Parthia in the end, given the fact that Vologases, who ascended the throne quite peacefully, had many enemies within his own court. Vologases knew that it would be better to make peace with Rome, for any further continuation risked much, which even Corbulo himself noted. Vologases and Corbulo were not ignorant of each other's position and what could be gained and what could have been lost. However, Corbulo had the upper hand in this affair. Therefore, both won when it comes to compromise, but Rome would gradually lose its political influence in Armenia. With an Arsacid dynasty now firmly rooted, it was only natural for that king to lean towards Parthia.

Proxy

One of two situations that stressed their relations was when Paetus (the same Pactus who lost to the

---
[58] Ibid., 63.3-7.

Parthians), now governor of Syria, replacing Corbulo in 72 CE, collected intelligence that indicated that Antiochus of Commagene had made a pact with Vologases against Rome. Paetus sent this critical information to Emperor Vespasian, for the capital of Commagene, Samosata, is one of the best crossings on the Euphrates River, giving the Parthians a tremendous foothold to conduct operations in Syria and Cilicia. Vespasian gave Paetus the authority to take action. Moving against Antiochus, he took him by surprise. Antiochus fled with his wife and children and took refuge in the court of Vologases. Eventually, Vologases handed them over to the Roman authorities. Antiochus would live well and spend the remainder of his days in Sparta. Afterwards we find that Commagene, Lesser Armenia, and Cilicia were brought under direct Roman rule in 72 CE.[59]

If Roman-Parthian relations were not strained enough, consider that in 75 CE, Vologases sends a request for Roman aid against the Alani, but Vespasian ignored his request. These same Alani Nero is said to have considered seeking an alliance with against Parthia during the Jewish-Roman War 66-70 CE, in order to prevent them from sending possible aid, which never materialized, for he committed suicide 68 CE. However, there was one Roman force in the area of the Caucasus at the time. It was during this time that Vespasian was aiding Mithridates of Iberia in fortifying his capital, Metsheta. While it is possible that the effort being made to beef up the security of this city was to

---

[59] Debevoise, 198-199.

ward off an Alani threat, it may very well have been to ward off the Parthians in case war resumed.

The reason for this is that Marcus Ulpius Traianus (senior), the father of the future emperor to come, returned to Rome and received a triumphal insignia for a diplomatic victory against the Parthians. This diplomatic victory over the Parthians may indicate that Vespasian went forward with Nero's plans and allied with and instigated the Alani in 72 CE to make an alliance with the independent kingdom of Hyrcania. Afterwards, the Alani passed through the Iron Gates of the Caucasus and Hyrcania into Media Atropatene, which was under the rule of Vologases brother, Pacorus, and ravaged the province, before advancing into Armenia, where they defeated Tiridates on his own turf. Of course, the Alani did not stay, but returned home after having their fill of booty.[60] The Romans sought an alliance with the Alani that was both defensive and economical, and that was by securing the Trebizond supply route while using nomadic elements, such as the Alani, to provide protection while at the same time being able to tap into or perhaps create new trade routes.[61]

Vologases likely knew of Rome incorporating the various client states between each other's borders; what he seems not to know is that its very design was a new

---

[60] Ibid., 200-202; Naphtali Lewis and Meyer Reinhold, *Roman Civilization Vol 2: The Empire Selected Readings* (New York: Columbia University Press, 1990), 33.
[61] Freya Stark, *Rome of the Euphrates: The Story of a Frontier* (New York: Harcourt, Brace & World, Inc., 1967), 201.

weapon against Parthia, and the Alani raid on Parthian and Armenian territories was a test run of the new weapon.

A NEW FRONTIER

Rome soon realized that the system put in place by Augustus was no longer feasible; it was time to implement the policy of Tiberius, which was to absorb the client-kingdoms. The absorption of the client-kingdoms was necessary in order to ward off the possibility of switching sides. The danger of a kingdom being in the middle between two powers was that at any moment, for the right amount of money, or if the king leaned more toward Rome than Parthia and vice versa, uncertainty would be created between the powers. Sides can change in an instant. In order to be rid of this thorn in Rome's side, they confiscated kingdoms near or between the Roman-Parthian borders after the Roman-Parthian War over Armenia concluded. Rome gobbled up the client kingdoms of Colchis and Pontus in 64 CE, Commagene, Lesser Armenia, and Cilicia in 72 CE and so forth. Vespasian understood the need for further security, and did reach out to the Alani and made what seems to be a pact.[62] With both social and political tensions in the new areas under direct Roman rule, the need for security was a necessity. The

---

[62] Everett L. Wheeler, *The Army and the Limes in the East*. A Companion to the Roman Army, edited by Paul Erdkamp. Malden, MA: Blackwell, 2007. 242-243; Debevoise, 196-199.

number of legions and garrisons were increased greatly along the Euphrates during the reigns of Nero, Vespasian, Titus (79-81), and Domitian (81-96 CE). But to ensure that further security was present along the frontier, Rome occupied the client states of Albania and Iberia. The strategy was to tighten the Euphrates security forces; find new client-kingdoms or the equivalent thereof, such as nomadic tribes; encircle Armenia; and hug the border shared with Parthia in case war was to resume. This strategy gave Rome the advantage of both military and political flexibility to defend and strike from whatever vantage point deemed necessary to secure and expand the empire.[63] Fifty years of rough peace soon followed before the Romans under the rule of Trajan would unleash this weapon.

---

[63] Ibid., 242-243; Touraj Daryaee, *The Oxford Handbook of Iranian History* (Oxford: Oxford University Press, 2012), 176.

Figure 36 Coin of Vologases I. Author: Classical Numismatic Group. http://commons.wikimedia.org/wiki/File:VologasesICoinHistoryofIran.jpg (CC BY-SA 3.0)

Figure 37 Bust of Nero at the Capitoline Museum, Rome. Author: cjh1452000. http://commons.wikimedia.org/wiki/File:Nero_1.JPG (CC BY-SA 3.0)

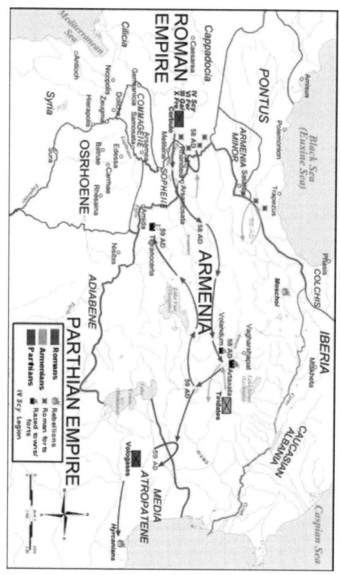

Figure 38 Map of the troop movements during the first two years (58 to 60 CE) (CC BY-SA 3.0)

The War for Armenia

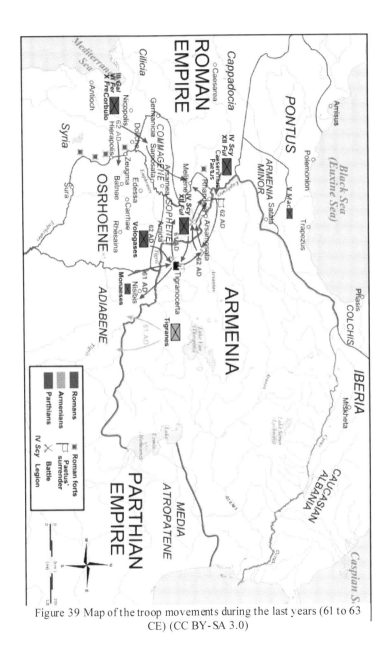

Figure 39 Map of the troop movements during the last years (61 to 63 CE) (CC BY-SA 3.0)

8

TRAJAN'S PARTHIAN WAR

The Emperor Domitian contemplated the idea of invading Parthia, according to the Roman poets at the time, but his plans were postponed when he was assassinated in 96 CE. However, a young officer named Trajan who served under Domitian would fulfill those plans once he became emperor.[1]

After Emperor Nerva died in early 98 CE, Trajan became emperor. A few years after Trajan came to the throne he set off to conquer the people of Dacia; this is known to us as Trajan's Dacian Wars 101–102 and 105–106. The Dacian Wars were profitable to Trajan, half a million pounds in gold and twice the amount of silver[2] flooded the Roman market. Trajan then turned to philanthropy, which gradually dwindled away due to his repeated devaluation of the denarius. It was just becoming too expensive to build, among other things.[3] With the treasury depleted, Trajan set his sights on the Nabataean kingdom and

---

[1] Malcolm A. R. Colledge, *The Parthians* (New York: Praeger, 1967), 52.
[2] B. D. Hoyos, *A Companion to Roman Imperialism* (Boston: Brill, 2013), 8.
[3] H.J. Haskell, *The New Deal in Old Rome: How Government in the Ancient World Tried to Deal with Modern Problems* (Auburn, Alabama: The Ludwig von Mises Institute, 2009), 192-193.

annexed it. Trajan's reason for annexing the kingdom seems not entirely for strategic interest in the military sense when dealing with Parthia, for Nabataea does not share a border with the Parthians.[4] Therefore, its strategic value was trade, for its lucrative trade routes flowed south, deep into the rich lands of Arabia Felix.[5] However, it does have military possibilities, if one considers the network of roads that run through the area on up to northern Mesopotamia.[6]

It was during this time that Parthia fell into political turmoil, both internally and externally, which eventually led to Trajan's invasion of Parthia.

In 78 CE, Vologases I died. Parthia, like times before, fell into a dynastic struggle. Three pretenders ascended and fell from throne starting with Vologases II who was quickly disposed in 80 CE. Vologases II may have been the legitimate heir of Vologases I, but it remains unknown. The same applies to Pacorus II: whether he was legitimate or a pretender is also unknown, since there is a

---

[4] Warwick Ball, *Rome in the East: The Transformation of an Empire* (London: Routledge, 2007), 63-64.

[5] William J. Bernstein, *A Splendid Exchange: How Trade Shaped the World* (New York: Grove Press, 2008), 62-63.

[6] Ferguson, R. James, "Rome and Parthia: Power politics and diplomacy across cultural frontiers" (2005). *CEWCES Research Papers*. Paper 10. http://epublications.bond.edu.au/cewces_papers/10

dearth of sources that mention him. There would be many more claimants to the throne during this short time. It was Pacorus II who was able to secure Parthia for himself for a length of time; but once he died, Parthia was once again deeply divided by claimants to the throne. However, one such claimant to gain a foothold would be King Osroes I of Parthia, 109 CE, but even his rule was shaky at best, leaving Parthia partially unstable and open for foreign invasion.[1]

This civil war taking place in Parthia and the peace that we assume followed relieved Rome of any major threat to come out of Parthia. It allowed Rome to continue building up its military, political, and economic presence in the region. While Rome was building and preparing for the possibility of war, Parthia was still trying to find a way to stabilize their own empire. When that day came, they made one vital mistake that would cause Parthia from here on out to spiral out of control until their downfall: they replaced the king of Armenia without Rome's consent.

In 110 CE, the king of Armenia died. King Osroes I of Parthia decided to invade Armenia and place his nephew Axidares on the throne as the new king without consulting Rome. It was a political jab at Trajan. Instead of responding, Trajan felt that action speaks louder than words. However, Trajan ignored this for a few years before proceeding east.[2]

---

[1] Farrokh, 158.
[2] Dio 68.17.2-3.

Leviathan Vs. Behemoth

TRAJAN'S PREWAR PLANNING AND PREPARATION

It seems evident that Trajan had been planning for the invasion of Parthia for quite some time. Why he desired to invade Parthia is debatable. Cassius Dio says that the real reason was "a desire to win renown."[3] No need of an argument there, but another reason was economic. F.A. Lepper mentions that "Trajan's real objective in going to war with Parthia was the securing of the overland trade-routes through Mesopotamia."[4] Trajan wanted to rewrite the regulations, which in turn would force new requirements or conditions favorable to Rome. In other words, price controls.[5] Nevertheless, both are correct. He may have been planning this invasion long before he invaded Dacia. However, what is known is that after Dacia, there is ample evidence to support his desire to invade Parthia.

In the autumn of 111 CE, Hadrian departs Italy.[6] In April 112 CE, Trajan appoints his officer and future emperor Hadrian as commander of the eastern provinces. Hadrian's mission was likely to prepare the logistics for

---

[3] Ibid., 68.17.1.
[4] F A. Lepper, *Trajan's Parthian War* (London: Oxford University Press, 1948), 158.
[5] Marcus Cornelius Fronto, Marcus Aurelius, Antoninus Pius, Lucius Aurelius Verus, translated by Charles Reginald Haines, *The Correspondence of Marcus Cornelius Fronto with Marcus Aurelius Antoninus, Lucius Verus, Antoninus Pius, and Various Friends, Vol 2* (London: Heinemann, 1919), 215.
[6] Sheldon, 126.

the coming war. However, it remains uncertain.[7] Furthermore, Julius Quadratus Bassus, governor of Cappadocia, is appointed to organize the northern armies and prepare them for the eastern campaign.[8] However, he would be dismissed from his post in 113 CE. His replacement was Marcus Julius Homullus.[9]

Shortly before Trajan set off onto his eastern adventure, he issued coins that do come into question. One coin, for instance, shows the deification of his natural father, Marcus Ulpius Traianus (who defeated the Parthians through shady diplomacy) and his adoptive father Nerva on the same coin facing each other. Another coin that was minted states *"FORT(una) RED(ux)* — 'May Fortuna return you [safely].'" Both coins imply that Trajan has the power to war against Parthia and is preparing for that very war to come. Another important factor was the restoration of the Via Egnatia in 112 CE. This Roman road runs from Italy to the Greco-Balkan peninsula. The road provided for faster transportation to move men, supplies, and official dispatches to the eastern provinces.[10]

In 113 CE, Rome's eastern legions received orders informing them to prepare for a major offensive against

---

[7] Julian Bennett, *Trajan Optimus Princeps* (London: Routledge, 2001), 187; Dio 69.1.1.
[8] Sheldon, 126.
[9] A Chronology of the Governors of Galatia: A.D. 112-285
Robert K. Sherk, *The American Journal of Philology*, Vol. 100, No. 1, Tekmhpion. A Special Issue in Honor of James Henry Oliver (Spring, 1979), pp. 166-175 The Johns Hopkins University Press
Article Stable URL: http://www.jstor.org/stable/294236
[10] Bennett, 187.

Parthia next year. Legions already in the vicinity were the X Fretensis from Jerusalem, Judea; III Gallica from Raphana, Syria'[11] IV Scythica, Zeugma, Syria; XII Fulminata, Melitene, Cappadocia; VI Ferrata, Samosata, Syria; and the XVI Flavia, Satala, Cappadocia.[12] Other legions would receive orders and be dispatched to the area, such as the I Adiutrix from Brigetio, Pannonia; XV Apollinaris from Carnuntum, Pannonia; II Traiana from Egypt; III Cyrenaica from Arabia Petraea.[13] A *Tribunus militum* of the XI Claudia, stationed in the province of Moesia Inferior, guarding the lower Danube in Durostorum, led cavalry detachments during the Parthian campaign.[14] In addition, a large amount of auxiliary units were assigned to assist the 10 legions. In total, Trajan had well over 80,000 men preparing to invade Parthia.[15]

Osroes likely received word of the influx of troops gathering near Armenia. He quickly sent an envoy to meet with Trajan, who left Rome in the autumn of 113 CE, likely on the sixteenth anniversary of his adoption by Nerva. Trajan took Via Appia and jumped to Via Traiana to Brundisium. From Brundisium, he took a ship to Corinth from where he made his way to Athens, where he would meet the Parthian envoy. It was in Athens that the

---

[11] Ibid, 194.
[12] Sheldon, 129.
[13] Stephen Dando-Collins, *Legions of Rome: The Definitive History of Every Imperial Roman Legion* (New York: Thomas Dunne Books, 2010), 412.
[14] Fergus Millar, *The Roman Near East 31 BC-AD 337* (London, England: Harvard University Press, 1993), 103.
[15] Bennett, 196.

Trajan's Parthian War

Parthians began to tremble, for they knew that Trajan was not a man of threats, but a man of action. Trajan looked at the gifts brought to him and listened carefully to the Parthian ambassador who pleaded with him. Osroes had replaced his nephew Axidares with his other nephew, Parthamasiris, in hope of avoiding confrontation. Trajan did not speak and rejected both king and gifts. His mind was made up "that friendship is determined by deeds and not by words, and that accordingly when he should reach Syria he would do all that was proper." War was inevitable.[16]

Trajan would leave Athens, making his way across the Aegean landing in the province of Asia, proceeding south through Lycia until he reached the Mediterranean Sea. From there, he would sail to the city of Seleucia Pieria, Syria. Afterwards, he retired to his base in Antioch for the winter. The Roman troop congestion overcrowded the facilities at Laodicea. Many of them took quarters where the X Fretensis used to live, near Cyrrhus.[17] While troops down for the winter, waiting for the ice to thaw and the passes to clear in the high elevations of Armenia, Trajan arrived at Antioch on January 7, 114 CE.[18]

While in Antioch, an envoy representing King Abgarus of Osrhoene visited Trajan and brought gifts. Abgarus was not present. He feared "both Trajan and the

---

[16] Sheldon, 128; Dio 68:17.2-3.
[17] Dando-Collins, 413; Dio:68.17.2-3.
[18] Sheldon, 128; Dio 68:18.1.

Parthians alike" and decided it was best to stay neutral.[19] However, one has to wonder if Abgarus also sent an envoy bearing gifts to Osroes as well, for Abgarus is said to have bought his kingship from Pacorus II. Pacorus was dead by 105 CE, and Abgarus' kingship did not begin until at least 109 CE.[20] Therefore, Abgarus received his kingship from Osroes, even though coins bearing Pacrous II's likeness were still being minted in 115-116 CE.[21] Other envoys representing their respected kings would make their way to Trajan, such as Mannus, king of the Scenite Arabs, and Sporaces, ruler of the adjacent kingdom of Anthemusia.[22] Overall, each envoy that approached Trajan made the journey in hope of retaining their sovereignty and to keep the diplomatic channels open. However, many of them would soon realize that Trajan was not interested in compromise or negotiation.[23]

THE ARMENIAN CAMPAIGN OF 114 CE

Before Trajan could invade Parthia, he had to conquer Armenia. Armenia was of vital military strategic and economic importance, considering the network of

---

[19] Dio 68:18.1.
[20] Samuel H. Moffett, *A History of Christianity in Asia. 1, 1.* (Maryknoll, N. Y.: Orbis Books, 2009), 83.
[21] Anthony Richard Birley, *Hadrian: The Restless Emperor* (London: Routledge, 2003), 68.
[22] Ibid, 195.
[23] B. Campbell, 'War and Diplomacy: Rome and Parthia, 31 BC – AD 235,' in J. Rich and G. Shipley, *War and Society in the Roman World* (New York and London: Routledge, 1993), 234-35.

trade routes that passed through the territory. Its strategic military value allows Rome to invade Parthia with ease. Understand that if Armenia were to remain under Arsacid control, Rome would run the risk of invasion. It allows the Parthians, if ever united, to run amuck through the Roman provinces of Cappadocia and Syria. With Armenia under Roman control, multiple openings into Parthian territory are available, and Rome has a better advantage to defend Syria and Cappadocia.[24]

Once winter subsided, Trajan began his journey north towards Satala in two stages. First, Trajan would journey from Beroea (Aleppo, Syria) to the headquarters of the IV Scythica, located at the fortress of Zeugma. He continued from there along the right bank of the Euphrates River until he reached the headquarters of the VI Ferrate at Samosata. From Samosata, he pushed north, taking the easiest route by crossing the Malatya Daglari to reach the fortress of the XII Fulminata at Melitene.[25]

While Trajan was making his last preparations before invading Armenia, a messenger presented him with a letter from Parthamasiris, pretender king of Armenia. In the letter, Parthamasiris made it clear that his claim and actions were fait accompli and that Trajan should quit wasting his time, make the journey to him, and place the crown upon his head to make it official. It was signed, yours truly, "King" Parthamasiris of Armenia. Trajan,

---

[24] Edward N. Luttwak, *The Grand Strategy of the Roman Empire: From the First Century A.D. to the Third* (Baltimore and London: The John Hopkins University Press, 1979), 106, Map 2.7.
[25] Sheldon, 129; Bennett, 195.

likely taken by his audacity, ignored the pretender. Parthamasiris knew that he had made a mistake when he received no response. He would send a second letter omitting this title, asking that Homullus, governor of Cappadocia, be the chief negotiator on Trajan's behalf. Trajan did not agree and decided that it would be best if he sent Marcus Julius' son to verify the offer presented by Parthamasiris.[26]

While the son of Marcus Julius made his way to Parthamasiris, Trajan crossed the Euphrates. He then made his way through the Elazig Pass and into enemy territory until he reached the Armenian city of Arsamosata, of "which he took possession without a struggle." Afterwards, he made his way through the Pülümür Pass, crossing the Euphrates again and arriving in late May 114 CE, at Eriza, headquarters of the XVI Flavia Firma stationed there.[27]

With Trajan's presence firmly rooted, many of the local kings and princes understood that a major shift in power over the region was about to take place. Therefore, many of them made their way to him and presented him with gifts and flatteries. While at Satala, it had been agreed to by both parties that Trajan and Parthamasiris would meet 110 miles east at Elegeia, which was 180 miles west of Parthamasiris' capital at Artaxata. Trajan arrived first and evidently waited for some time before Parthamasiris showed up with his entourage. His tardiness was to avoid

---

[26] Dio 68: 19.1; Bennett, 195.
[27] Dio 68: 19.2; Bennett, 195.

potential attacks from Axidares' supporters. Even though his arrival was better late than never, it was not a good move.[28]

Parthamasiris dismounted from his horse, proceeded towards Trajan, who was seated upon a tribunal before his army, saluted him, removed his diadem, and laid it at Trajan's feet. Silence fell over the encampment as Parthamasiris eagerly waited for Trajan to pick up the crown and place it on his head. Instead, an uneasy silent stare-down occurred until the legions shouted and hailed Trajan imperator "as if because of some victory." It was a victory; it was victory without bloodshed. Parthamasiris objected to Trajan's decision; in disbelief, he tried to flee, but could not, for he was surrounded by the legions. Seeking a private audience with Trajan did little. Parthamasiris made it clear that he did not want to speak in front of the crowd; he wanted to talk in private. His wish was granted, his plea was heard, and Trajan granted him nothing he asked. Parthamasiris rushed out in a rage and left the camp. Parthamasiris no doubt was angry about the decision and likely was hoping that Trajan would change his mind and call him back, which Trajan did shortly after. Trajan as before, ascended the tribunal. Parthamasiris, hoping that his actions had changed Trajan's mind, would be disappointed. Trajan asked him to speak before all those watching, tell everyone here what you want. Trajan wanted to make sure that what was said privately to him was now made public so

---

[28] Dio 19.2; Bennett, 196.

no one could say otherwise, not even the nobles who accompanied Parthamasiris. Parthamasiris, likely all anger and nerves, made it clear before all that he came voluntarily, that he had not been defeated or captured, he was here on his own accord as the rightful ruler of Armenia, and wanted Trajan to honor his side of the obligation as Nero had done with Tiridates. But Parthamasiris was about to learn that Trajan was not Nero. Trajan made it clear to him and before all that Armenia was now effectively Roman territory and that L. Catilius Severus was to serve as the first governor of Armenia.[29]

Parthamasiris immediately left with his Parthian companions. They would receive a Roman escort back to Parthia, a means to protect the prince from those who supported Axidares. However, his life ends mysteriously once outside of Elegeia. No one knows what happened, but rumor has it that Trajan was responsible for his assassination. It is said that he brought on his own death by trying to escape the Roman escort. As for the Armenian nobility standing before Trajan, they were to stay. Trajan informed them that they were now his subjects, or better yet, the property of Rome.[30] On that day, Trajan killed two birds with one stone. He abolished the monarchy and Armenia was no longer a sovereign entity, but a Roman province. With that, the Roman Senate granted Trajan the title of Optimus, or "Most Excellent," a title he would

---

[29] Dio 19.3-5; 20.1-4; Bennett, 196.
[30] Bennett, 196.

adopt into his nomenclature, and one he held in highest regard above all other titles he was given.[31]

While Trajan was in Elegeia for the summer, his commanders went about the Armenian countryside, using the same tactics that had worked before in other mountainous areas by making their way through valleys, navigating the rivers, and occupying key points at their heads. In doing so, they methodically isolated the irregular alignments of mountains, which lack the broad linear sweep of a range or chain, by utilizing a network of roads and forts on every side in order to subjugate the remaining holdout cities, forts, and districts. Such commanders and legions assigned to carry out this task was Lusius Quietus, who commanded one division. He moved into the highlands south of Lake Van and was reported to be fighting the Mardi. General C. Bruttius Praesens, commander of the VI Ferrata, was conducting missions in the highlands of Armenia, and due to deep snow, his men adopted the snowshoes worn by the natives. Another legion on the move may have been the III Scythica, which made its way to the Caspian Gates, while a fourth legion may have advanced as far as the Dariel Pass.

While his commanders were busy informing the Armenian people that they were now Roman subjects, minor kings and local satraps came to present gifts and gratitude, such as a horse that was taught to kneel on its forelegs. One can only image the amount of political flattery and treasure brought before Trajan in hope that

---

[31] Dio 68.23.1

they could stay in power. Trajan during this time also appointed new kings for the Caucasus provinces of Apsilae and Albani. Overall, Trajan had a good summer, annexing Armenia, shoring up his northern boundary by showing his support to the minor kingdoms in the Caucasus, and preparing for the invasion of Mesopotamia.[32]

    You would think that the Parthians, with the amount of time it took Trajan to take Armenia, would have been waiting for them once they arrived in Parthian territory in 115 CE. A possibility to consider as to why the Parthians are absent in all this is the civil war. Even though King Osroes I ruled Parthia, he only ruled a portion of the empire, for there was another claimant to the throne who came before Trajan's invasion and that was Vologases III. Overall, the move secured not only the east-west route that runs through Mesopotamia, but also those routes leading northward. Furthermore, Freya Stark makes a great observation stating that: "By pushing out a great promontory (i.e., by the annexation of Armenia), that automatically put the Tigris in place of the Euphrates, he made the conquest of Mesopotamia essential…".[33]

---

[32] Dio 68.18.3; Sheldon, 132-33; Bennett, 196, 198.
[33] Trajan's Parthian War and the Fourth-Century Perspective, C. S. Lightfoot, *The Journal of Roman Studies*, Vol. 80, (1990), pp. 115-126 Society for the Promotion of Roman Studies Article Stable URL: http://www.jstor.org/stable/300283; Stark, 209.

THE INVASION OF MESOPOTAMIA 115 CE

Spring, 115 CE. Trajan left his winter headquarters from either Elegeia or Artaxata and headed south to complete his Mesopotamia campaign on foot with his men. While pushing south, his legions practiced military maneuvers. Trajan does this in order to calm the men's nerves and to prepare them for anything lurking nearby. The route Trajan may have taken is debatable, but possibly was the route Corbulo took.[34] His first mission was to move his army over the central Taurus Mountains to subjugate the territory between the Euphrates and Upper Tigris. In doing so, Trajan installed a series of permanent garrisons at opportune points to safeguard the regions. By mid-summer, he was ready to annex Upper Mesopotamia.

His strategy was to take Mesopotamia by storm utilizing a pincer move. While Trajan pushes south, skirting the borders of Osrhoene, he takes the city of Batnae (Incidere), the capital of Anthemusia, to punish King Sporaces for his lack of fealty to Rome. Afterwards, Trajan pushes on, takes Nisibis, the main strategic center, and uses it as a base. After Lusius Quietus subjugated the Mardi south of Lake Van, he swings toward the southwest and advances into eastern Mesopotamia. When word reached King Mebarsapes of Adiabene that Lusius was on his way, King Mannus of the Scenite Arabs sent an auxiliary force to aid in Mebarsapes in defense against

---

[34] Dio 68.21-1-2; Stark, 209.

Lusius. However, the auxiliary force sent with Mebarsapes was defeated and driven back, thus allowing Lusius to take the fortress of Singara south of Nisibis without a fight.[35] Shortly after, Trajan marched into Adiabene where he would meet with Lusius. Trajan granted Lusius possession of Singara and certain other cities, perhaps including Dura Europos, thus completing the occupation of Mesopotamia.[36]

With King Mebarsapes driven back beyond the Tigris River, King Mannus sent a peace envoy to meet with Trajan. However, Trajan viewed Mannus with suspicion, for he sent the auxiliary force to aid Mebarsapes. Trajan refused to meet the king until he showed himself. Another envoy, representing King Manisarus of Gordyene, possibly a member of the Arsacid dynasty who openly challenged Osroes for the throne, approached Trajan, asking for support, that the two should unite, and that he would return parts of Armenia and Mesopotamia that he had taken from Osroes. Trajan refused the offer, as he did with Mannus, until he showed in person. With Osrhoene surrounded on three sides now, King Abgarus decided it would be best to meet with Trajan before he lost his kingdom, as King Sporaces did for not sending gifts without being present. In the end, Abgarus swore fealty

---

[35] Dio 68.23.1-2; 22.1-2; 21.1; Sheldon, 133; Trajan's Parthian War and the Fourth-Century Perspective, C. S. Lightfoot *The Journal of Roman Studies*, Vol. 80, (1990), pp. 115-126 Society for the Promotion of Roman Studies Article Stable URL: http://www.jstor.org/stable/300283
[36] Bennett, 199; Dio 68.22.2.

and Trajan pardoned him and swore to protect his kingdom.

Once Trajan was back in Antioch, he sent a dispatch towards the end of 115 CE to the Senate, informing them that he had successfully annexed Armenia and Mesopotamia. This letter arrived to the Senate on February 21, 116 CE. The Senate granted Trajan the name *Parthicus* and immediately issued new currency to mark the event. Afterwards, prayers and games would further honor his achievements.[37]

While Trajan relaxed, looking over the objectives for next year, an earthquake struck with such great force that he barely made it out alive with a few slight injuries, while many others were not so lucky. The quake not only severely damaged Antioch, but many of the cities nearby as well. The aftershocks continued for several more days and Trajan took his headquarters to the hippodrome.[38]

THE CAMPAIGN OF 116 CE

Sometime in spring 116 CE, Trajan set out for his final campaign against Parthia. One would think that Trajan would be happy with the current annexation. But men of power desire more, and Trajan decided that to see how much more he could conquer--and why not? It may

---

[37] Ibid; Dio 68.22.1; 23.1-2.
[38] Dio 68.24-25.

seem risky. But up to this point, and considering the limited amount of primary sources concerning Trajan's Parthian War, the Parthians had showed little effort in defending their homeland in pitched battles, which was likely due to internal political strife and civil war. But this does not rule out the possibility that the Parthians did indeed defend their homeland through a scorched-earth policy by methodically destroying all potential resources, such as water and wells as they fled before Trajan. As you will read and notice, it may have forced Trajan to rely primarily on his supply lines, which became more stretched as the Romans pushed further into Mesopotamia. Because of such factors, Trajan decided to conquer on, even though doing so risked much, as overextending your forces and supply lines leaves them dangerously open for attack from both internal and external forces.[39]

During the previous year, Trajan partially subjugated Adiabene. Lusius Quietus would have continued but lacked the resources to construct a bridge to cross the Tigris River and to attack the capital of Adiabene. Trajan was informed of the issue during the winter of the previous year. He therefore ordered the construction of pontoons at Nisibis due to the plentiful forest nearby atop Mount Massius (Tur 'Abdin) north of the city. Once near, he had great difficulty in bridging the stream opposite the Gordyean Mountains, for the Adiabenians were nearby and harassing the Romans as they struggled to piece together this bridge. Trajan solved this issue by utilizing

---

[39] Bennett, 201; Farrokh, 160.

ships, constructed quickly and tied together, and solders to feign attacks on the enemy nearby, appearing as if they were going to cross, only to quickly retreat. Other ships were moored mid-stream, allowing the legionaries and archers to provide covering fire. This allowed the pontoon bridge to be built quickly, efficiently, and with little hindrance. Once finished, the Romans quickly crossed the river, likely near the modern city of Cizre.[40]

The next phase of the campaign gets tricky and somewhat confusing due to accounts provided by Cassius Dio and John Xiphilinu. Not all the place names given are identified. Nevertheless, it seems that Trajan split his army in two. Trajan, however, was not with the first division; instead, he was commemorating an arch in his honor to the north of the town of Dura Europos in early 116 CE. One division swept south along the Euphrates, using the route taken by Alexander to capture Ninus (Nineveh), Arbela, and Gaugamela, where Alexander defeated Darius III in 331 BCE. However, this seems unreasonable, for others have pointed out that no general would take the Euphrates route if he could use the Tigris. This division seems to have taken the Tigris route, for they would capture Adenystrae (modern day Ebril) without a fight. It is said that Sentius, a Roman centurion, escaped with his comrades, killed the commander of the Adenystrae garrison, and opened the gates to the Romans outside. Adiabene was now under Roman control, probably the occasion for Trajan's twelfth imperial salutation.

---

[40] Bennett, 201; Sheldon, 137; Dio 68.26.1-4; 22.3.

Afterwards, Trajan is said to have formed the territory into the province of Assyria. However, even this is debatable, for even though Trajan's forces captured many of the cities in Adiabene, much of the province remained in enemy hands; thus no "Adiabene capta" coins. Trajan was likely with the second division that traveled to Dura Europos, where they would link up with a supply fleet and then proceed down the east bank of the Euphrates until reaching Babylon. Trajan met no resistance along the way because the Parthians were dealing with the usual civil strife that plagued their kingdom.[41] Dio mentions that Trajan visited the asphalt wells at Hit, 150 miles north of Babylon, the place where the materials were obtained to construct Babylon. Ammianus Marcellinus records in the fourth century that people visited Ozogardana, and were "shown a tribunal of the emperor Trajan."[42]

As mentioned, Trajan was accompanied by a fleet of 50 ships, divided into three squadrons of which four vessels were the van carrying the imperial vexilla on the Euphrates. The largest of the vessels was the emperor's flagship, decorated in gold and bearing the emperor's name on the sails, according to Arrian. Trajan's objective was to cross the Tigris using this fleet to attack Ctesiphon. He proposed that a canal be cut between the Euphrates and Tigris at Sippar (Abu Abba) where the two rivers are just 20 miles from each other. After he along with his

---

[41] Bennett, 201; Sheldon, 137; Dio 68. 26.4.
[42] Sheldon, 137; Bennett, 201; Ammianus Marcellinus, *Roman History*, 24.2.3.

advisors inspected the land, they notice that to do so could bring disaster as at this particular point, the Euphrates was at a higher elevation than the Tigris. Therefore a canal might drain the one while flooding the other. The other option considered was using the Naharmalcha (Royal River), but the problem with this is that the canal was further south of Ctesiphon. Therefore, Trajan decided to have his fleet brought overland by means of capstan devices and rollers. Trajan was able to take the city of Seleucia on the west bank and from there he crossed the Tigris without resistance and entered the city of Ctesiphon without a fight.[43]

      Once in Ctesiphon, Trajan marched into royal quarters and found that Osroes and his entourage had fled, leaving behind his daughter and the golden throne to be captured by the emperor. Trajan's army saluted him as imperator and thus established his right to the title of Parthicus. The Senate granted Trajan the privilege of celebrating as many triumphs as he desired. Trajan had not encountered any resistance from Osroes, as the Parthians decided to follow the age-old tradition of fleeing to the other side of the Zagros Mountains when faced by a superior enemy. Trajan ordered coins to mark the event with the legend *PARTHIA CAPTA*. Afterwards, Trajan likely set about reviewing his newly acquired territory, perhaps intending to form a province of Babylonia.[44]

---

[43] Sheldon, 138; Bennett, 202; Dio 68 28.1-2; Arrian, *Parthica* fr 67.
[44] Sheldon, 138; Bennett, 202; Dio 68 28. 2-3.

Once Trajan left Ctesiphon, he boarded his ship and his fleet set sail down the Tigris to the Persian Gulf, making stops along the way to receive homage from Athambelus and the inhabitants of Mesene and Spasinus. After nearly losing his life to a tidal bore, he eventually arrived at Charax (Basra), a town located at the mouth of the river. He arrived just in time to see a merchant ship sailing for India, and publicly lamented concerning his age when compared with Alexander: "I should certainly have crossed over to the India, too, if I were still young."[45]

The war with Parthia, at least during his time, was finished. He sent another laurelled letter to the Senate, announcing all that he accomplished, and erected a statue that marked the limits of his grand advance. He decided to leave his ships behind at Charax, for he intended to use them yet again for a future campaign farther to the east. The Senate once again voted him a glorious triumph over as many nations he wished and with many honors, of course. This included his thirteenth imperial salutation and another round of coins to be issued with the legend *FORT(una) RED(ux)*, wishing the emperor a safe return to Italy.[46]

---

[45] Sheldon, 138; Bennett, 202; Dio 68 28.3-4; 29.1.
[46] Sheldon, 138; Bennett, 202; Dio 68 29.2.

BLOWBACK

Trajan left Charax sometime during the winter of 116/117 CE and headed north for Babylon to pay his respects at the tomb of Semiramis and to visit the house and make a sacrifice where Alexander had died in 323 BCE. While he paid his respects to the past, the present showed up.[47] The capture of Ctesiphon had infuriated the Parthians and united them. Before Trajan knew of it, Osroes' nephew, Sanatruces II, was nominated to replace Parthamasiris as king-in-exile of the Armenians. He was a grand organizer and was able to incite widespread rebellion throughout northern Mesopotamia. Trajan likely was in shock upon hearing that most of the territory he had conquered in the north was now in full rebellion and the garrisons left behind had either been expelled or massacred. Trajan, like Roman leaders in past, had underestimated the Parthians, and had inadequate intelligence services to monitor the districts. The Parthians and their allies were very good at monitoring the enemy and struck when the opportunity presented itself. Rome had become overextended and too comfortable.[48]

Trajan quickly sent three divisions to quash the rebellion. One force, led by Appius Maximus Santra, engaged the enemy. The Romans were defeated and Maximus slain. The second force, led by Lusius Quietus, recovered Nisibis among other cities, including Edessa,

---

[47] Dio 68 30.1; Bennett, 202; Debevoise, 234.
[48] Dio 68 29.4; Bennett, 203; Sheldon 139.

which he sacked and burned to the ground. Why he did this is uncertain. Abgarus either joined the Parthians or the Parthians replaced him with a pro-Parthian candidate. For his actions, Lusius was promised that in the following year, he would receive a consulship. A third force was under the joint command of Erucius Clarus and Julius Alexander. Together they captured Seleucia and burned it.

The situation was so bad that Trajan offered an armistice before the Parthians revolted. Trajan went on the offensive himself, but not in the military sense. Instead, Trajan played politics, and decided that to please the Parthians and end the war, he would install the next king and perhaps assert some authority over the contested areas. This was all for show to buy time, since Trajan knew that the Parthians would not support a Parthian king crowned by a Roman emperor; and he made sure that Parthamaspates was not only the king of the Parthians, but also king of the neighboring tribes who were loyal to Rome. If war broke out over the legitimacy of Parthamaspates' rule, those tribes loyal to him and to Rome would cause a diversion that would give Rome the upper hand if they were to intervene again. Trajan crowned Parthamaspates, a son of Osroes, as the new king of Parthia. Trajan placed the crown on Parthamaspates' head before an assembly in which Parthamaspates paid obeisance to Trajan, thus confirming his subordinate status. At that moment, Parthia was now a Roman client state, at least for a brief moment in time. Trajan defended his decision in a letter he sent to the senate and explained:

> So vast and infinite is this domain, and so immeasurable the distance that separates it from Rome, that we do not have the compass to administer it. Let us then [instead] present the people with a king who is subject to Rome.[49]

After establishing peace in both Parthia and Armenia by establishing client-kings, Trajan hurried to the north to recover what he could of Mesopotamia. His first priority was to take Hatra, which was still in revolt. Hatra had a strategic importance, for it controlled the central route from Nisibis to Ctesiphon, and Trajan needed it to restore Roman rule beyond the Tigris. Trajan laid siege to Hatra, which in itself was a daunting task. In the surrounding area, there was no water, timber, or fodder for an army to utilize during a siege. Because of the hot conditions and lack of resources, the Romans suffered much discomfort. Instead of being plagued by those revolting, the Romans were plagued by flies swarming their food and water, which in turn caused suffering and disease to affect the troops. Even though the Romans came close to taking Hatra, Trajan nearly lost his life during a cavalry charge, and due to the melee, was driven back. Even though the wall had been breached, the Romans failed to capitalize on it; to make matters worse, Mother Nature also unleashed

---

[49] Dio 68 30.3; Scriptores Historiae Augustae, *The Life of Hadrian*, 5.4; Bennett, 203; Sheldon 140.

sudden thunderstorms with hail on the besiegers. Trajan lifted the siege and returned west to Antioch.[50]

AFTERMATH

Besides Rome's conflict with Parthia, the Jews took advantage of the situation and revolted against Rome as well, but that is a different story. Even though Rome and Parthia were now engaged in a semi-peace, Trajan had had enough; he was ill and his illness was getting worse. He placed Hadrian in charge of the Roman armies of the east and returned to Rome where he could enjoy his grand triumph. Trajan boarded his royal yacht at Seleucia Pieria in the summer of 117 CE. Trajan was sixty-three years old and sick. Trajan soon began to believe his illness was due to poison. His suspicion arose when the wine taster, M. Ulpius Phaedimus, who had similar symptoms, died; he was 28. As the royal ship coasted near the shores of Cilicia, Trajan's condition got worse. The ship entered into the nearest harbor, Selinus, where he took to his bed and died.[51]

Overall, the aftermath was not so bad for Rome. Trajan had everything for such an invasion and in many ways was able, due to careful planning, to avoid the pitfall that Crassus and Antony endured. The only thing Trajan

---

[50] Dio 68 31.1-4; Bennett, 203-204; Sheldon 140-141.
[51] Dio 68 33.2; Bennett, 206-207; Sheldon, 142.

lacked was the fact that he overestimated the outcome while underestimating potential insurgency. He soon came to the realization that there was no version of this where he comes out on top, for he began to pull himself from the situation before it was too late by agreeing to peace with Parthia. Even Hadrian understood this when he heard the news that Trajan died, for he quickly abandoned the Eastern Campaign and reasonably resorted to a new frontier policy of passive defense, which could and must be instituted, for it was much cheaper. As Dio states in regard to Mesopotamia "this conquest has been a source of constant wars and great expense to us." When Dio wrote this passage, he was referring Septimius Severus, but the same can be applied to what Trajan was about to face, had he lived and the burden Hadrian did face once he was emperor. Hadrian made clear from both an economic and political point of view the reason for the abandonment by quoting the dictum of Cato, that those who could not be subject should be free. War costs, and any attempt to re-conquer Mesopotamia would be futile.

Trajan's more aggressive officers resented Hadrian's decision to abandon the campaign and were replaced or died under suspicious circumstances. However, even though most of the territory east of the Euphrates was abandoned, the Romans were not as relaxed as it seems. Rome still had influence beyond the Euphrates. The client kingdom of Mesene maintained loyalty to Rome for a short time. Roman officials continued to be present along the river and in the Parthian capital of

Vologesia, a Palmyran merchant built a temple to the Augusti in the city.[52] Parthia was taking no chances and wanted to have a firmer grip on the borderlands. A Greek document from Dura Europus dated 121 CE mentions that a certain Manesos was installed along the southern portion of the Euphrates and given the title of *strategos* of Mesopotamia and Parapotamia ('the district along the river') and was made *arabarkhes* "arab-ruler" under the King of Kings by Osroes I.[53]

However, this was not the end, for more wars loomed in the not too distant future between the two powers.

---

[52] Dio 75 3.2-3; Sheldon, 142-143.
[53] Jan Retso, *The Arabs in Antiquity: Their History from the Assyrians to the Umayyads* (London: RoutledgeCurzon, 2005), 439; Millar, 447.

Trajan's Parthian War

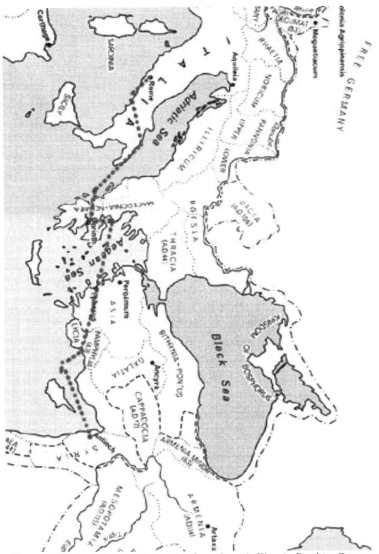

Figure 40 Trajan's Journey East. Map from *Rome's Wars in Parthia*. Courtesy of Rose Mary Sheldon

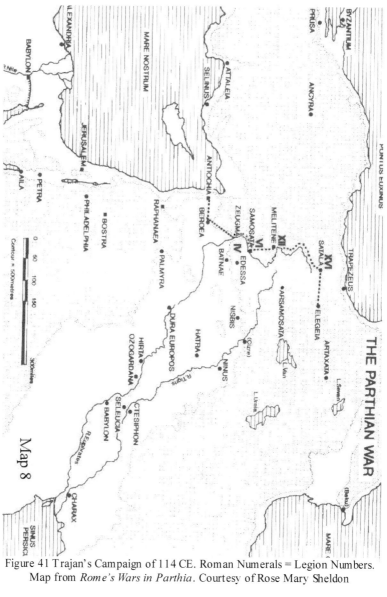

Figure 41 Trajan's Campaign of 114 CE. Roman Numerals = Legion Numbers. Map from *Rome's Wars in Parthia*. Courtesy of Rose Mary Sheldon

Trajan's Parthian War

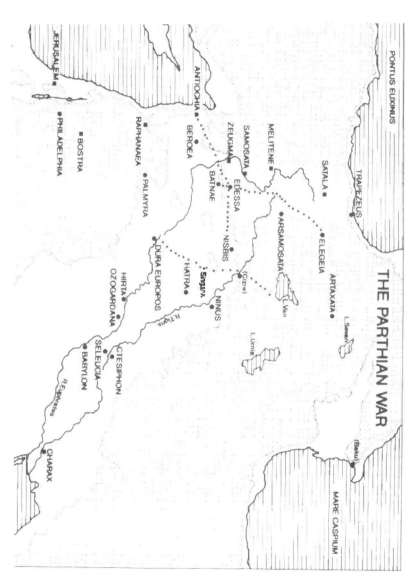

Figure 42 Trajan's Campaign of 115 CE. Map from *Rome's Wars in Parthia*. Courtesy of Rose Mary Sheldon

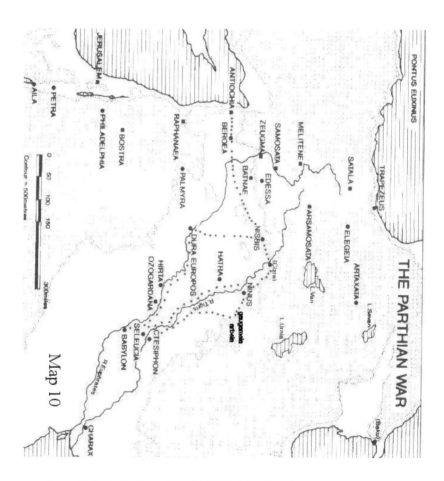

Figure 43 Trajan's Campaign of 116 CE. Map from *Rome's Wars in Parthia*. Courtesy of Rose Mary Sheldon

9

FROM HADRIAN TO THE COLLAPSE OF THE PARTHIAN EMPIRE

To honor Trajan, Hadrian established the Parthian games, which went on for a number of years until the Romans realized that there was nothing worth celebrating, since Trajan's conquests had been abandoned by Hadrian. While Rome mourned and celebrated the death of Trajan, the Parthians were still in a state of civil war and facing pressure on the eastern borders from the expanding Kushan state, which likely affected Vologases III's bid for the throne. The civil war, along with foreign incursions, allowed some districts to challenge Parthian authority. The province of Bactria seems to have broken free from Parthian rule, like Hyrcania before, and sent envoys to meet with Hadrian, seeking friendship.[1]

While Rome was entertaining possible new allies, the Parthians were busy ousting King Parthamaspates. Parthamaspates fled to the Romans, possibly around 122/123 CE. The event caused quite a stir, with the

---

[1] Dio 69 3.2; SHA, *Hadrian*, 21.14; John E. Hill, *Through the Jade Gate to Rome: A Study of the Silk Routes During the Later Han Dynasty 1st to 2nd Centuries CE: An Annotated Translation of the Chronicle on the 'Western Regions' in the Hou Hanshu* (Charleston, South Carolina: BookSurge Publishing, 2009), 29.

possibility that the Romans received reports of an increased Parthian presence along the Euphrates. Hadrian, not taking any chances, journeyed to the eastern frontier to avert a potential conflict due to his backing of Parthamaspates. Hadrian also met with Osroes to assure him that Rome recognized him as the rightful king and Rome only desired peace. As for Parthamaspates, Hadrian would grant him the province of Osrhoene.[2]

A few years later, around 126/127 CE, relations between Rome and the Kingdom of Iberia had become strained. King Pharasmanes of Iberia instigated the Alani to invade and raid the Roman client state of Albania and the Parthian vassal kingdom of Media Atropatene, which appears to be under the control of Vologases III and not Osroes. However, it was during this raid into Media Atropatene that Vologases III approached the Alani and paid them to take their raiding west into Armenia and Roman Cappadocia. The Alani eventually stopped and turned back when they encountered the Roman army led by Flavius Arrianus. Arrianus likely sent a dispatch back to Rome detailing the event and questioning the loyalty of Rome's allies to the north for allowing the Alani to flood into the provinces. Meanwhile, Vologases III sent an envoy to Hadrian to protest and press charges against Pharasmanes. Overall, the situation required Hadrian to travel east yet again to restore the peace. Hadrian would arrive on the eastern frontier around 128/29 CE to meet with kings and to offer gifts. However, some were not

---

[2] Dio 68.33.2; SHA, *Hadrian*, 12.8; Debevoise, 241.

inclined to meet with Hadrian, preferring to stay in their respective capitals, including Pharasmanes, who instigated the Alani to raid Parthian and potentially Roman lands. Pharasmanes scoffed at Hadrian's invitation. While touring the frontier, Hadrian visited Osroes and presented him with a gift of friendship. Hadrian returned Osroes' daughter and promised to return the golden throne that Trajan had captured at Ctesiphon.[1]

Once Hadrian had returned to Rome, Osroes' reign did not last much longer. With Parthia still in a state of civil war, even the secured areas were being contested within by pretenders to the throne. While Vologases III controlled a large portion of Parthian real estate,[2] a pretender rose up and deposed Osroes I: his name was Mithridates IV.[3] Mithridates' reign lasted for roughly 11 years and he controlled a very small amount of territory pertaining primarily to Mesopotamia. How Mithridates died is uncertain, but an unknown king took the throne, issuing coins with no name roughly around 140 CE. Whether this unknown king or Vologases III defeated

---

[1] Dio, 69.15.1-2; SHA, *Hadrian*, 13.8; Arrian and the Alani
A. B. Bosworth, *Harvard Studies in Classical Philology*, Vol. 81, (1977), pp. 217-255 Published by: Department of the Classics, Harvard University Article DOI: 10.2307/311121 Article Stable URL: http://www.jstor.org/stable/311121

[2] Daryaee, 176.

[3] Daniel T. Potts, ed. *Araby the Blest: Studies in Arabian Archaeology* (Copenhagen: Carsten Niebuhr Institute of Ancient Near Eastern Studies, 1988), 164.

Mithridates IV is also unknown. Nevertheless, Vologases III would finally take the throne around 140/141 AD.[4]

Hadrian would die 138 CE and be replaced by Antoninus Pius. Vologases III would die in 147/48 CE and be replaced by Vologases IV, who happened to be the son of Mithridates IV. During the reign of Vologases III and somewhat during the reign of Vologases IV, Roman-Parthian relations were relaxed, but with some tensions. Shortly after Vologases took the throne, he began to prepare for an invasion of Armenia. Rome got word of this potential attack and reinforced its troops in Syria. However, Vologases was persuaded to forgo the war by a letter from Antoninus, to which he agreed, in return requesting the golden throne. Antoninus refused his request. Even though Vologases tried to demonstrate a show of force, his empire suggested otherwise. Parthia seemed united under Vologases, but it was largely fragmented and fragile, as demonstrated by the envoys from the Hyracanians and Bactrians (possibly Kushans) who visited the court of Antoninus, demonstrating the continued independence of their respected kingdoms. Even though Parthia seemed weak, it still had a tendency to show strength, as it did in 150/51 CE when Vologases attacked and conquered Mesene, ousting King Mithridates, son of former Parthian king Pacorus, who was not killed

---

[4] Daryaee, 176; Wayne G. Sayles, *Ancient Coin Collecting VI: Non-Classical Cultures* (Iola, WI: Krause Publications, 1999), 58.

but "driven from the land." He may have fled to Syria to take refuge.[5]

Relations between Rome and Parthia continued to remain at ease. While Rome grew comfortable, the Parthians continued to watch, collect intelligence, and make their plans. On March 7, 161 CE, Antoninus Pius died and was replaced on that day and the next by Emperors Marcus Aurelius and Lucius Verus.[6] With Rome undergoing a change in regime, Vologases launched his attack and caught the Romans off guard.

PARTHIAN WAR OF LUCIUS VERUS

In 161 CE, Vologases received word of Antoninus' death a few months later. The truce was off. Vologases mobilized his forces, entered Armenia, and installed an Arsacid prince, Bakur (Pacorus), on the throne later that year.[7]

---

[5] D. S. Potter, "The Inscriptions on the Bronze Herakles from Mesene: Vologeses IV's War with Rome and the Date of Tacitus' "Annales," *Zeitschrift Fur Papyrologie Und Epigraphik*. 88, (1991): 277-290; The Roman Empire and the Kushans, John Thorley, *Greece & Rome*, Second Series, Vol. 26, No. 2 (Oct., 1979), pp. 181-190 Published by: Cambridge University Press on behalf of The Classical Association Article. Stable URL: http://www.jstor.org/stable/642511

[6] Anthony Richard Birley, *Marcus Aurelius: A Biography* (Abingdon: Routledge, 2006), 114.

[7] David Braund, *Rome and the Friendly King: The Character of the Client Kingship* (London: Croom Helm, 1984), 43.

Rome had been expecting an attack to materialize once word reached Vologases of Antoninus' death. In order to prepare for the worst, L. Attidius Cornelianus, the governor of Syria at the time, who was due for replacement, remained at his post. Changing the guard would be detrimental, for a fresh governor with no experience, particularly experience in the east, would give Parthia the upper hand. Therefore, M. Sedatius Severianus, a Gaul and governor of Cappadocia, was given the duty of monitoring Armenia, and authority to go in and deal with any troublesome situations.

Once word reached Severianus that the Parthians had overrun Armenia, he went to an oracle, Alexander of Abonutichus. Lucian of Samosata mentions that Alexander led Severianus to believe that all would be well and promised him victory, stating, "Under your charging spear shall fall Armenians and Parthi; Then you shall fare to Rome and the glorious waters of Tiber, Wearing upon your brow the chaplet studded with sunbeams." Afterwards, Severianus led his legion into Armenia, likely following Trajan's route northward and likely being watched by the Parthians until the moment was right for attack. The Parthian force, led by Osrhoes (Chosroes), likely launched a surprise attack and forced Severianus into Elegeia where they surrounded him. For three days, Severianus attempted to fight back, but it was of no use. With his legion being decimated before his eyes, he decided to commit suicide. According to Lucian, once news of the disaster reached Alexander, the oracle, he quickly expunged his previous statement from the records and replaced it. "Better for you that your forces against Armenia march not, Lest some man, like a woman bedight, dispatch from his bowstring Grim death, cutting you off from life and enjoyment of sunlight."[8]

While one Parthian force remained in Armenia, another was on the move, possibly led by Vologases himself. This force would go to captured Edessa, where Vologases had placed Wael, son of Sahru, on the throne.[9] Afterwards, the Parthians crossed the Euphrates and into Syria, where they spread terror and destruction throughout the land. To make matters worse, the possibility of rebellion was imminent, since there were many Parthian supporters. Governor Attidius Cornelianus tried to stop the Parthian advance, but was defeated and driven back, making the situation in Syria critical and leaving the east open to further incursions.[10]

News of the Parthian victories reached Rome during the winter of 161-62 CE. Marcus and Lucius decided that in order to prevent rebellion in Syria and to remove the Parthians from Roman territory, one of them must go and lead the legions in person, which had not been done since Trajan some 45 years earlier. Therefore, between the co-emperors, it was decided that Lucius must lead, for he was young and strong.[11] He would not go

---

[8] Birley, 121-122; Lucian, *Alexander the False Prophet*, 27; Lucian, *How to Write History*, 21; Dio 71.2.1; Sheldon, 156.
[9] Debevoise, 246.
[10] Paulus Orosius, *Historiae adversus paganos*, 7.15.2; Sheldon 156.
[11] Dio 71.1.3; Birley, 123.

alone; he would have the best generals to assist him in the war, such as Avidius Cassius, Statius Priscus, G. Julius Severus, and Martius Verus.[12]

The legions gathered for this campaign were the I Minervia, II Adiutrix, V Macedonica, while parts are all the following legions may have served: III Gallica, III Augusta, I Adiutrix, X Gemina, and possibly II Traiana.[13] The number of legions moved to defend the Roman east from further Parthian incursions and to go on the offensive weakened Rome's northern frontier. The governors in the northern provinces along the Rhine and Danube were advised to avoid hostilities and deal with any disturbances in a diplomatic, respectful, manner whenever possible.[14]

In the summer of 162 CE, Lucius set off on his journey to take command of the eastern legions and was accompanied by Marcus as far as Capua. From Capua on Lucius gorged himself at everyone's villa, and because of this, he became very ill. After he recovered, he journeyed on, taking his time. While in the Italian province of Apulia, he decided to hunt before making his way to Brundisium, sailing across the Adriatic Sea, making landfall at Dyrrachium, and traveling along the Via Egnatia before making his way to Athens and Corinth, accompanied by orchestras and singers, and making use of all the pleasure centers throughout the cities that border the coast of Asia. How long it took him to make the journey is unknown.

---

[12] Sheldon, 156.
[13] Debevoise, 247-248.
[14] Sheldon, 156-157.

However, once he arrived in Antioch, he straightened up briefly.[15]

When Lucius met the Syrian troops, he found a miserable body of men. They were demoralized, mutinous, disobedient, undisciplined, and unruly. They were rarely at their assigned posts or with their units. Instead, for the most part, they stayed drunk from noon till the next day. To make matters worse, many of the soldiers were unused to carrying their arms and equipment, and if the Parthians were threatening battle, instead of mobilizing to engage the enemy, they would flee before them.[16] Avidius Cassius, a native Syrian, was brought on board to help with the situation. The task given to Cassius was to strip the legions of the luxurious lifestyle to which they had grown accustomed, such as bathing in hot water, and whip them into shape. While the legions of Syria were stripped of their luxuries, Lucius indulged in them. After establishing his headquarters at Antioch, Lucius preferred to spend his time in the shade, listening to the running waters at Daphne in the summer. Once winter set in, he would travel to Laodicea, leaving the heavy labor of the war to the generals in charge.[17]

Even though Lucius was living the high life, he undoubtedly and understandably was worried about his own life and the condition of the troops in the region. Fearing the worst, he reached out in a personal letter to

---

[15] SHA, *Verus*, 6.7-9; 7.1; Birley, 126.
[16] Fronto, 209.
[17] SHA, *Avidius Cassius* 5; *Verus* 7.3; *Marcus Antoninus* 8.12; Sheldon, 157.

Vologases, asking him to put an end to the war by agreement. Vologases spurned the offer, interpreting it as weakness or cowardice.[18]

Besides his negotiating attempt, there is no record of Lucius taking part in the campaign. There is one instance where his staff demanded that he make a rapid trip to the Euphrates, which he did. The generals obviously could not rely on Lucius for leadership, because the pleasures of life occupied his time. Marcus Aurelius, who likely was aware of Lucius' conduct, took it upon himself, so we are told, to have "planned and executed everything necessary to the prosecution of the war."[19]

COUNTERATTACK 163 CE

Spring, 163 AD. The Roman counterattack was underway. Leading the attack was Statius Priscus, who entered Armenia and seized the capital, Artaxata. Instead of razing the city, he founded a "new city," Kaine Polis (Kainopolis), not far away. With Armenia now secured by Roman forces, Priscus reinstalled the pro-Roman king Sohaemus, who was once a senator and consul. This suggests that he must have been in exile for an extended period. The event was commemorated on coinage of the year and bore the legend REX ARMENIIS DATUS with the

---

[18] Ibid, 213; Sheldon, 157.
[19] Sheldon, 157; SHA, *Verus* 7.6; *Antoninus* 8.14.

image of Lucius sitting on a platform, surrounded by his officers saluting Sohaemus as he stands before him. Afterwards, both emperors received the title Armeniacus. While Priscus was occupied with Armenia, the Parthians invaded the principality of Osarhoene, entered Edessa, and removed the pro-Roman ruler Mannus.

The Romans responded by sending forces, likely under the command of Cassius, along the Roman side of the Euphrates in Syria where they engaged the Parthians at Sura and were victorious. This indicates that the Parthians were still present in Syria 163 CE. Sura was the turning point in the war; the recovery of Sura allowed the Romans to push across the Euphrates and occupy the fortresses of Dausara and Nicephorium located on the northern, Parthian bank of the Euphrates. Roman forces would continue to flood into Osrhoene from Armenia, led by M. Claudius Fronto, occupying Anthemusia, southwest of Edessa.[20]

With Osrhoene partially occupied, since the Romans had yet to advance on Edessa, it secured the border between Syria and Osrhoene and allowed the Romans to concentrate, hem in, and expel any remaining Parthian forces scattered about the Syrian landscape. This gave Rome time to prepare for a large offensive into Parthian territory.

---

[20] Birley, 130-131; Sheldon, 157.

THE CAMPAIGN OF 165-166 CE

A year would pass between Priscus' offensive into Armenia and the stabilization of Syria before Rome advanced into Parthia. The long pause was due to the Romans carefully planning and preparing. Once Cassius had removed the remaining remnants of the Parthians from Syria in 164 CE, Marcus Aurelius made Cassius into a sort of *generalissimo*, thus giving him the ability to act more freely as he chose. Cassius, determined to carry the war deep into Parthia, planned a three-pronged attack on Mesopotamia. Details of Cassius' attack on Mesopotamia are fragmented.[21]

In 165 CE, the Romans began their campaign, possibly led by Martius Verus, who captured Edessa and reinstated the pro-Roman ruler Mannus. Afterwards, the Romans pursued the Parthians eastward to Nisibis and captured the city. They followed the Parthians, led by general Chosroes, who escaped by swimming the Tigris and taking refuge in a cave. Cassius advanced with the second force down the Euphrates, where he engaged the Parthians in a bloody battle at the fortified city of Dura-Europus, thus forcing the Parthians into an armistice.[22]

Towards the end of 165 CE, Cassius had pushed far south, moved into Mesopotamia, and continued on to the narrowest point on the Tigris to attack the twin cities: Seleucia on the right bank and the Parthian capital,

---
[21] Sheldon, 159.
[22] Lucian, *The Way to Write History*, 19; Birley, 140; Sheldon 159.

Ctesiphon, on the left. The 400,000 inhabitants of Seleucia, who retained their Hellenistic characteristics, welcomed the Romans in a friendly manner and opened the gates. Soon turmoil roused its ugly head when someone broke the armistice, causing the Roman legions to storm the city and destroy much of it by fire, a great catastrophe no doubt. Some point the finger at Cassius for not maintaining troop discipline, but this seems unlikely since he was a stern disciplinarian. On the other hand, the Romans blamed the disaster on the Seleuceni for a lack of faith. We will never know who struck first, but that day ended nearly 500 years of one of the major outposts of Greek civilization in the East.

With Seleucia smoldering in ashes, Cassius moved on to Ctesiphon and captured it. Once inside, they destroyed the summer palace of Vologases, plundered temples, and searched for hidden treasure. The Parthians did nothing, for they had nothing, and the Romans quietly left with a large amount of booty. Everything that Parthia had regained after the death of Trajan was now once again in Roman hands. If the Parthians ceased to resist, an invisible army of microbes did not.[23]

While the Romans enjoyed the victory and spoils of war, they contracted something unseen while looting Seleucia: plague. This nemesis would be "The Antonine Plague 165-180 CE," which swept out of Babylonia and raged across the Mideast and Mediterranean, reaching Rome and even Gaul and Germany. The cause of the

---

[23] Dio 71.2.3-4; Sheldon 159-160.

plague was ascribed to Roman soldiers looting temples. The source of the plague "originated in Babylonia, where a pestilential vapor arose in a temple of Apollo from a golden casket that a soldier had accidentally cut open, and that it spread thence over Parthia and the whole world." The reason why plague would come out of a temple is that temples in the ancient world were museums of mythic and historical significance. All sorts of treasures were displayed for public viewing, "look but do not touch." A temple priest or priestess could do little to stop a marauding army from opening a casket, chest, or breaking a vase that might contain biological terror. It was especially true for the priests who served and honored the god Apollo, for these priests were very knowledgeable in poisons. Furthermore, Apollo was the guardian of rodents, and rodents can be vectors of bubonic plague, typhus, and other diseases, thus making the temples of Apollo laboratories for experiments with poisons and primitive vaccines.[24]

Cassius' army returned, but he lost many soldiers through famine and disease.[25] With news of Cassius capturing the cities of Seleucia and Ctesiphon reaching Lucius, laurelled dispatches were sent to Rome announcing the victory. Lucius received the title of

---

[24] SHA, *Verus* 8.1-4; Adrienne Mayor, *Greek Fire, Poison Arrows & Scorpion Bombs: Biological and Chemical Warfare in the Ancient World* (Woodstock, NY: Overlook Press, 2003), 132-135.
[25] Dio 71.2.4.

Parthicus Maximus, "greatest conqueror of Parthia," and so would Marcus; both became Imperator III.[26]

War was over, or so it would seem, but there is always something left to conquer. In 166 CE, Lucius arranged for Fronto to write the official history of the war. Cassius and Martius Verus would draw up memoranda for Lucius, which he promised to send to Fronto. Parthia was not fully conquered yet. Lucius decided that the war must go on, but farther into Parthian territory, a final show of Roman might, you could say. This time, the Roman armies would advance across the Tigris into Media under Cassius and were victorious.[27] How far Cassius penetrated Media is unknown. A possible reason for leading an expedition into Media was to take advantage of trade routes. Earlier in the chapter, it was mentioned that envoys from the Hyrcanians and Bactrians visited Rome. Considering that the Kingdom of Hyrcania bordered Media to the west, but did not quite reach the province of Bactria to the east, which could suggest that the envoys from Bactria were really Kushans and that the Romans sought to link up with them in order to establish a stable trade route linked to China.[28] Because of the victory, Lucius accepted another title, Medicus.

---

[26] Sheldon, 160-161.
[27] Ibid.
[28] The Roman Empire and the Kushans, John Thorley *Greece & Rome*, Second Series, Vol. 26, No. 2 (Oct., 1979), pp. 181-190 Published by: Cambridge University Press on behalf of The Classical Association, Article Stable URL: http://www.jstor.org/stable/642511; The Silk Trade between China and the Roman Empire at Its Height, 'Circa' A. D. 90-130 J. Thorley Greece & Rome, Second Series, Vol. 18, No. 1

The victories of Cassius soon reached many eastern ears, with fanciful rumors circulating that he had crossed the Indus River. Lucian of Samosata was one of many writers who cashed in on mocking the war, and he even wrote about the greatness of Cassius as he led "the third legion, the Celtic contingent, and a small Moorish division, [which] have crossed the Indus in full force under Cassius."[29] However, it was over for Rome. They could advance no further by the spring of 166 AD. Plague had ravaged the military ranks, stopping their forward progress into Media.[30]

The date of Lucius' return is questionable, as there is no record. The Misenum fleet was still at the mouth of the Orontes River at the end of May 166 CE, so it must have been later. Of course, Lucius would not have returned to Rome until peace had been established, but that was not going to happen in his lifetime, as Lucius would die of apoplexy in 169 CE and a formal treaty would not come about until 175 CE.[31]

When Lucius returned to Rome, a triumph was held on October 12, the first since the days of Trajan some 50 years earlier. A grand spectacle of pomp and nostalgia marched past the citizens of Rome, displaying all the trophies of war both past and present. Those generals and

---

(Apr., 1971), pp. 71-80 Published by: Cambridge University Press on behalf of The Classical Association, Article Stable URL: http://www.jstor.org/stable/642389.

[29] Lucian, *History,* 31; Sheldon 160-161.

[30] Daryaee, 177.

[31] Sheldon, 161; Orosius, *Book* 7.15; Daryaee, 177.

others who participated in the campaign were decorated according to their success after four years of expensive bloodshed.

To keep the Parthians at peace, Cassius, who had the most victories, was made governor of Syria, while Martius Verus was made governor of Cappadocia. Both men remained at their assigned posts for a number of years.[32] Rome could have annexed Mesopotamia for a second time, had plague not decimated their ranks. Even if there were no plague, it is doubtful Rome could have held Mesopotamia. Instead, they annexed a portion of northern Mesopotamia by enlarging Syria to include Dura Europus and left garrisons at several strong points beyond the frontier, including Kinopolis in Armenia and Nisibis.[33]

The treaty between Parthia and Rome of 176 CE was brought about by the possibility of Roman civil war. Governor Cassius of Syria declared himself emperor after receiving a false report that Marcus Aurelius was dead, without waiting for confirmation. Cassius proclaimed himself emperor at the request of Marcus Aurelius' wife, Faustine, for she did not want the empire to fall into the hands of Commodus, who was too young and naive to handle such responsibilities. Cassius quickly became public enemy number one in the Senate. Vologases threatened war to take advantage of the fragile Roman situation, but soon backed down once he learned that Marcus was not dead after all. Vologases would later send

---

[32] Birley, 145-147.
[33] Sheldon, 161.

envoys to assure the emperor that all was well between the two.[34]

Lucius' Parthian War was really Cassius' war. Cassius was the real victor. Besides, Cassius' expedition was the first invasion of Parthia in which the Romans came out on top, unlike Trajan's campaign in which he did take Mesopotamia, but lost it soon afterwards and did not deprive Parthia of any actual possessions. Rome now absorbed Western Mesopotamia, but never turned it into a province. Therefore, Lucius' Parthian War was anything but decisive and ended in compromise.

Even though Parthia had been beaten and had lost territory, war continued; Vologases would live for another 25 years, and did try to recover lost territory, but quickly backed down. It was becoming all too clear to the Parthians that their empire was slowly declining and they had no idea how to stop Rome, the sporadic internal rebellions, and loss of territory.[35]

By 191 CE, the aged Vologases had a challenger. Coins bearing the image of a new contender by the name of Vologases V emerged. The last minting of coins bearing Vologases IV's image was in 192 CE.[36] This was not the end of Parthia, nor of the war between the two powers, as another Roman emperor was on his way and his name was Septimius Severus.

---

[34] SHA, *Marcus Aurelius* 22.1; 26.1; Sheldon, 162-163.
[35] Sheldon, 162.
[36] Debevoise, 255.

From Hadrian to the Collapse of the Parthian Empire

SEPTIMIUS SEVERUS CAMPAIGNS IN MESOPOTAMIA

While Vologases V was securing his throne in 192 CE, Rome had five claimants in what is known as the "Year of the Five Emperors" contending for the throne the following year in 193 CE. All contenders for the Roman throne were mostly eliminated, except for Septimius Severus and Pescennius Niger of Syria. Severus occupied Rome and was awarded the title of emperor by the Senate. Severus marched out of Illyricum with the full support of the army and navy. When Niger received the startling news, he ordered that all governors of the eastern provinces guard closely all the passes and harbors. But he realized he was going to need more help and sent letters to the kings of Armenia, Hatrenians, and Parthia, seeking aid. The king of Armenia declined the invitation but did make it clear that he would defend his own lands if Severus were to attack him. King Barsemius of the Hatrenians sent some native archers to aid him. Abgarus IX of Osrhoene and the ruler of Adiabene actually sent troops. Vologases agreed and requested his satraps to collect troops to aid Niger, but seems not to have committed any troops after all.[37] His lack of commitment may have been a claimant to the Parthian throne in 190 CE, Osroes II. Osroes II came to power shortly before the death of Vologases IV and had

---

[37] Herodian, *History of the Empire since the Death of Marcus Aurelius*, 3.1.1-3; 9.1; Debevoise, 255.

coins bearing his image minted in Ecbatana.[38] How long Osroes II was able to stay independent in Media is unknown. It seems plausible that he was still alive during Severus' war against Niger, thus keeping Vologases' forces busy dealing with him and rebellions taking place in Persia.[39] Severus had far more legions than Niger.[40] Once defeated, Niger attempted to escape to Parthia, but likely was denied entry. Giving Niger asylum would have brought the war to Parthia. Instead, Vologases allowed some of his followers entry into Parthia, where they acted as military advisers.[41]

While Vologases was hindered from taking direct action, he played an indirect role, using monetary funds to support the Hatrenians and Adiabene, who were his vassals. By taking this approach, he could disclaim any involvement. Vologases likely instigated Osrhoene to rebel and likely ordered Adiabene and Osrhoene to besiege Nisibis when word of Niger's death was confirmed in 194 CE. Both Osrhoene and Adiabene sent embassies soon after to Severus. They were not seeking a pardon, but making the case that they were fighting on Severus' behalf. They also sent gifts and promised to return the captives and spoils that were still left. But what they would not

---

[38] E. Yarshater, *The Cambridge History of Iran Volume 3.1* (Cambridge: Cambridge University Press, 1983), 297.
[39] _____, Baija Natha Puri, and G.F. Etemadi, *History of Civilizations of Central Asia Vol. II* (Paris: UNESCO Publishing, 1994), 132.
[40] Graham Webster, *The Roman Imperial Army of the First and Second Centuries A.D.* (Norman: University of Oklahoma Press, 1998), 88.
[41] Herodian, 3.4.7.

hand over were the captured forts, nor receive Roman garrisons. Instead, they demanded that Rome remove themselves and their remaining garrisons; they wanted independence.

Severus considered their complaints and decided to wage war against them. Vologases was obviously playing both hands. If Niger were victorious in his war with Severus, he would have a western ally; if Severus were to win, he had never allied himself with Niger and his vassals acted on their own behalf.[42]

Late in the spring of 195 CE, Severus, at the head of his troops, crossed the Euphrates, advanced into Osrhoene, and paid a visit to Edessa. Abgarus IX, seeing Severus, capitulated, quickly handed over his sons as hostages, and adopted the Roman names of Lucius Aelius Aurelius Septimus.[43] Severus' next journey was to Nisibis, a long march in which his men suffered greatly because of the lack and quality of water. Once at Nisibis, he established his headquarters there and possibly received envoys from "the Arabians," likely from Hatra, who came to present a more reasonable offer than previously made. Severus refused the offer, which he might have considered if the ruler had showed up in person. Severus advanced no farther from Nisibis. He separated his army and formed different divisions commanded by three separate generals to attack different enemies. The generals chosen were

---

[42] Dio 75.1.2; Sheldon, 164; Kevin Butcher, *Roman Syria and the Near East* (London: British Museum Press, 2003), 48.

[43] Sheldon, 164; Judah Benzion Segal, *Edessa: The Blessed City* (Piscataway, N.J.: Gorgias Press, 2005), 14.

Claudius Candidus, Julius Laetus, and T. Sextius Lateranus. He would later divide his army again, but changed the commanders. The second group consisted of three divisions led by Anullinus, Probus, and Laetus, who marched to a district of Arche (unidentified) in Mesopotamia and subdued it. Afterwards, Nisibis was made into a Roman colony under Syria. Afterwards, Severus' troops poured into Adiabene and took it.[44]

Because of the victories, Severus received three imperial salutations and took the titles of "Parthicus Arabicus" and "Parthicus Adiabenicus." He declined the title Parthicus Maximus, since he had not conquered Parthia. With Niger's forces beaten and reabsorbed, he was able to establish a loyal bond with his legions. However, despite all the success, Severus had to put off conquering Parthia and return west to deal with a rival, Clodius Albinus.[45]

While Severus was away, Vologases declared war on Rome. Vologases knew that if he would ever have a window of opportunity to take advantage of the Romans while they were in a state of civil war, it was now. He would sweep rapidly northward through Mesopotamia, and, according to one writer, cross the Euphrates and enter Syria. Vologases tried to take Nisibis, but failed to do so, as the defense set up by Laetus was able to repel the

---

[44] Dio, 75.3; Sheldon, 164-165.
[45] Sheldon, 165.

attackers. Had Nisibis been captured, the Parthians very well could have moved on into Armenia.[46]

Even allies of the Parthians were now reconsidering their pact with Vologases. Narses, king of Adiabene, refused to join him in his sweep across Mesopotamia and instead favored Rome. Vologases took back control over Adiabene after looting several cities and drowning its pro-Roman monarch, Narses in the Greater Zab. Vologases' push westward would end as fighting in the east reignited. Vologases advanced towards Khorasan with a large army to quash the revolt. Once his forces crossed a small river, they found themselves surrounded and taken by surprise. The situation was so bad that they were forced to abandon their horses and retreat. While on the run from their attackers, they were cornered in the mountains. They made a stand and lost many men in the melee. The loyal Parthian troops were able to reorganize, counterattack, and pursue the enemy to the sea (the Caspian?). After the battle, Vologases' army began their march home, but on the way, they encountered a contingent that had been separated from the main body. After two days of bloody fighting, the enemy force slipped away during the night. Vologases returned home in triumph.[47]

While Vologases enjoyed his victory, back in Rome Severus was "seized with a desire to win glory for victories, not only over fellow countrymen and Roman

---

[46] SHA, *Severus* 15; *Herodian* 3.9; Sheldon, 165.
[47] Debevoise, 258-259; Sheldon 165-166.

armies, but also barbarians."[48] This brings up a question. Was Severus seeking glory or good money?

When Severus took power, he reformed the military. He replaced the old Praetorian Guard with a new Praetorian Guard and increased its ranks with troops loyal to him. He increased their numbers. The Urban cohorts became *milliariae* (i.e., each c. 1,000 strong); the firefighters and police in Rome known as the *Vigiles* (watchmen of the city), were increased to 7,000, and do not forget the creation of three new legions for his coming campaign against Parthia, which consisted of the I, II, and III Parthicae.[49] On top of that, he increased the soldiers' pay from 300 denarii to 500 denarii, and other subsidies were added.[50]

In order to pay for all this and his various expeditions, especially the one to conquer Parthia, he had to debase the currency to coin more specie. Roman currency was on a steady decline before Severus took power, but once he did, Severus debased the currency for financial gain to pay for his troops and all their needs at the expense of the taxpayers, causing inflation and reducing the purchasing power of Roman citizens. Thus, Gresham's law takes effect, which is, "Bad money drives

---

[48] Herodian, 3.9.1.
[49] Graham Webster, *The Roman Imperial Army of the First and Second Centuries A.D.* (Norman: University of Oklahoma Press, 1998), 93-94.
[50] David L. Vagi, *Coinage and History of the Roman Empire, C. 82 B.C.--A.D. 480.* (Chicago: Fitzroy Dearborn Publishers, 2000), 268.

out good."⁵¹ The silver currency content dropped gradually under Severus. From 193-194 CE, the silver content was 78.5%; from 194-196 CE, 64.5%; and from 196-211 CE, the silver content dropped to 56.5%.⁵² Therefore, Severus was seized with a desire to win, because to lose was far more costly, and the empire that could provide Rome with a fresh, more valuable currency to circulate was Parthia. Parthian coins during the reign of Vologases contained a silver content of 77.9%, 25% more than Roman coinage.⁵³

SEPTIMIUS SEVERUS' SECOND CAMPAIGN TO MESOPOTAMIA

In early 197 CE, Severus sent the bulk of his legions ahead while he, along with the I and III Parthica, left in the latter part of 197 CE. The II Parthica would stay behind in Italy. Severus would leave from Brundisium. He sailed directly to Asia Minor, probably landing at the Cilician port of Aegeae, and completed his journey to Syria by road. His first task was to stabilize Syria by expelling any remaining Parthian forces still wandering about the

---

⁵¹ Murray N. Rothbard, *What Has Government Done to Our Money?* (Auburn, Alabama: Ludwig von Mises Institute, 2005), 24-25.
⁵² Tulane University, "Roman Currency of the Principate" http://www.tulane.edu/~august/handouts/601cprin.htm#_ftnref1 (accessed 13 March, 2014); Vagi, 272.
⁵³ Forum Ancient Coins "Silver Content of Parthian Drachms https://www.forumancientcoins.com/numiswiki/view.asp?key=Silver%20Content%20of%20Parthian%20Drachms (accessed 13 March, 2014).

territory causing trouble.⁵⁴ With Syria secured, Severus began planning his Parthian campaign. Possibly in the summer of 197 CE, Severus dispatched a force against the Armenians. But why would Severus approach Armenia in a hostile manner, given the fact that Armenia refused to join Niger in his bid for the Roman throne?⁵⁵ Cassius Dio says that King Vologases of Armenia heard of the approaching Romans and arrayed his forces before them, but was able to secure an armistice, which allowed him to send "money, gifts, and hostages to support his plea for peace and by promising pacts and good will."⁵⁶ It was not Vologases of whom Dio speaks, rather, it was King Khosrov I.⁵⁷ Vologases had been the Roman client king of Armenia before he confiscated the throne of Parthia in roughly in 192 CE.⁵⁸ From then on, he was king of both Armenia and Parthia. When news arrived of Severus coming, roughly in 197/98 CE, Vologases quickly relinquished his throne to Khosrov, who may have been his son⁵⁹ or perhaps his brother.⁶⁰

While Armenia and Rome make good, Severus began the preparation for the invasion of Parthia via the Euphrates. Meantime, he sent detachments under other

---

⁵⁴ Birley, 129; Sheldon 166-167.
⁵⁵ Herodian 3.1.2; Sheldon, 166.
⁵⁶ Dio 75.9; Herodian 3.9.2.
⁵⁷ Richard G. Hovannisian, *The Armenian People from Ancient to Modern Times: From Antiquity to the Fourteenth Century Vol. 1* (New York: St. Martin's Press, 1997), 71.
⁵⁸ Debevoise, 255.
⁵⁹ Hovannisian, 71.
⁶⁰ Dio 76.9.

leaders to ravage Eastern Mesopotamia and Adiabene, which evidently had been reoccupied by the Parthians, and to relieve the Roman garrison at Nisibis; but the Parthians had already withdrawn before their arrival.[61]

To keep the supplies flowing, Severus followed Trajan's lead and built a fleet of ships in Upper Mesopotamia where timber was plentiful. Severus and his forces marched down the left bank of the Euphrates into Babylonia, while his fleet loaded with supplies followed close by on the river. Accompanying Severus was the brother of Vologases, possibly Khosrov I. The Parthians did not await his arrival, but retired homeward and likely conducted a scorched earth policy, for by the fall of 198 CE, Severus reached the abandoned, dilapidated cities of Babylon and Seleucia. Supplies were likely running low at this point.[62] He then proceeded to Ctesiphon using either one of the canals uniting the Tigris and the Euphrates, or else (like Trajan) he conveyed the ships on rollers across the narrow neck of land that separates the two rivers. By the time they accomplished their objective, it was the beginning of winter. The Romans disembarked on Parthian beaches, assembled, and marched down the road to the capital.[63]

While the Romans were on the move, they plundered the region and burned villages. This is usually the norm for an invading army, but the Romans may have

---

[61] Sheldon, 166-167.
[62] Dio 76.9; Sheldon, 167.
[63] SHA, *Severus* 16; Herodian 3.9.9; Sheldon, 167.

been desperately searching for adequate food and water to alleviate their suffering from diseases and various ills like diarrhea from eating unfamiliar plants and roots. It is said that Vologases was taken by surprise, thinking that Severus was too busy dealing with the Hatrenians and therefore not a concern. While it is possible, it seems unlikely. The Parthians likely kept track of Roman troop movements and harassed them during their slow march towards the capital by conducting hit and run attacks. Another source mentions that he took the field against the Romans, only to be defeated, and fled to Ctesiphon, where he shut the gates, which was a bad idea given the Romans were excellent at engineering warfare. While many dates are suggested for when Ctesiphon was captured, it may have taken place in the winter of 198 CE or on January 28, 199 CE, instead of January 28, 198 CE. The evidence is not as straightforward as the precision of the date might suggest.[64] Nevertheless, the Romans had no issue punching holes through the city walls, then pouring through the openings with little or no resistance. Vologases, his entourage, and the garrison fled. Severus refrained from chasing him, as there were other matters of importance at hand, like money, but also his men were too weak to follow, and to do so would have been suicide.[65]

Once inside the city, the Romans stripped it of wealth and people. One source mentions the capture of

---

[64] A. D. Lee, *Information and Frontiers: Roman Foreign Relations in Late Antiquity* (Cambridge: Cambridge University Press, 1993), 93; Birley, 130-131.
[65] Herodian 3.9.10; Dio 76.9; SHA, *Severus* 16; Sheldon, 167.

only women and children, thus suggesting the slaughter of the male population.⁶⁶ Other sources suggest that all found in the city were taken captive. Regardless of who was taken, a number of the inhabitants were killed, and as many as 100,000 were taken captive, along with the treasuries, ornaments, and jewels.⁶⁷

With the rape of Ctesiphon over, Severus took the title of Parthicus Maximus and the date chosen was on the exact centenary of Trajan's accession.⁶⁸ With a new title, Severus abandoned Ctesiphon. Dio mentions that the "sole purpose of his [Severus] campaign had been to plunder this place, he was off again, owing partly to lack of acquaintance with the country and partly to the dearth of provisions."⁶⁹ While it is true that before his army took the city they lacked supplies, once inside, the new supplies to replenish the men would soon dwindle. In addition, they had inadequate military intelligence. Therefore, he must leave or face destruction. The reason Severus left by the Tigris route likely was due to the Parthians having destroyed just enough along the Euphrates to starve the Romans, while at the same time the Romans had exhausted the remaining resources available. By taking the Tigris, Severus could find supplies and also make a stop at an age-old target that not even Trajan could capture, Hatra.⁷⁰ Severus wanted to capture the city in revenge for

---

[66] Herodian 3.9.11.
[67] Dio 76.9; SHA, *Severus* 16; Herodian 3.9.11.
[68] SHA, *Severus* 16; Sheldon, 169.
[69] Dio 76.9.
[70] Dio 76.9; SHA, *Severus* 16; Sheldon, 169-170.

the support they gave to Niger. Moreover, if Severus could take the city, he'll look better then Trajan. However, the odds were against Severus as he tried to besiege Hatra twice, only to fail and leave empty-handed.[71]

Besides Severus' failure to capture Hatra on separate occasions, the Parthians were absent. Roman forces were suffering a great deal while focusing all their attention on Hatra. Vologases could have ordered hit and run attacks on the Roman supply line, followed by a counterattack on the Roman forces at Hatra and in nearby provinces. Instead, the Parthians were silent. The only reason for the Parthians making no attempt to attack the Romans and to relieve Hatra was that Vologases had not the men, money, or materiel to do so. In a sense, it was a victory for the Parthians. Severus' failed sieges at Hatra bought the Parthians time to rethink their strategy.

Vologases would continue to reign as king until his death in 208 CE. However, information about Parthia after the war is blank. Roman historians only write when war between the two powers is taking place. Severus would die shortly after on February 4, 211 CE, at York. He gained little in his Parthian campaign. According to Dio, Severus "used to declare that he had added a vast territory to the empire and had made it a bulwark of Syria."[72] The argument that it was defensive is most certainly a façade. Severus knew that he could not hold Ctesiphon or any of the regions in the vicinity. While it is true that after the

---

[71] Dio 76.10-11; Herodian 3.9.3-8.
[72] Dio 75.3.1-3; Sheldon 171.

war, Roman Syria did have a buffer between them and the barbarians, Severus gained little territory, but a whole lot of glory; more importantly, he got a fresh flow of new money.

THE PARTHIAN WAR OF CARACALLA

When Severus died in 211 CE, his son Marcus Aurelius Severus Antoninus Augustus, better known as Caracalla, became emperor. He shared power briefly with his brother Geta until he murdered him later that year, which placed him solely in charge of the empire.[73] Once he was sole emperor, Caracalla could emulate his hero, Alexander the Great. Caracalla was a passionate admirer of Alexander and wished to conquer the east as Alexander had.[74] In order to do so, he had to win over his legions, starting with the Praetorian Guard. Caracalla quickly subdued them and then the legions, stating, "I am one of you." He said, "it is because of you alone that I care to live, in order that I may confer upon you many favors; for all the treasuries are yours."[75] The Praetorians were given 2,500 denarii and their ration allowance was increased by one-half, while the legionaries' pay was increased by 50% more than Severus had paid his men. However, it is hard

---

[73] Herodian 4.1; 4.4; Dio 78.2.
[74] Dio 78.7-9; SHA, *Caracalla* 2.
[75] Dio 78.3.2.

to say what this increase meant in numerical terms. The amount paid to his men ranged from 600, 675, and 750 denarii yearly.[76] Of course, all the treasuries are yours, starting with the public. The increase in military pay vastly increased the state's need for revenue. In order to pay for his military, Caracalla declared in his *Constitutio Antoniniana* (Edict of Caracalla 212 CE) that all free men in the Roman Empire are now Roman citizens and will pay taxes. Dio takes a hostile approach to the edict, stating, "This was the reason why he made all the people in his empire Roman citizens; nominally he was honoring them, but his real purpose was to increase his revenues by this means, inasmuch as aliens did not have to pay most of these taxes."[77] Another method to increase revenue was the debasement of coin. Caracalla's motive, like emperors before him, was to debase currency to increase short-term gains to pay his military and to conduct war. The new coin introduced to the Roman market was the Antoninianus. The coin was supposedly equal to two denarii, but it was only worth 1.5 denarii and contained only 50% silver, causing an increase in inflation.[78] And if looting the public through excessive government spending and debasing specie were not enough, he made it clear that there was no end to the flow of money. "There is no longer any source of revenue, just or unjust, left to us," he replied, exhibiting his

---

[76] Yann Le. Bohec, *The Imperial Roman Army* (London: Routledge, 2001), 210.
[77] Dio 78.9.
[78] Vagi, 272; Walter Scheidel, *The Cambridge Companion to the Roman Economy* (Cambridge: Cambridge University Press, 2012), 271.

sword. "Be of good cheer, mother: for as long as we have this, we shall not run short of money."[79] In other words, the health of the state depends on making war, and it begins with Caracalla. The revenue he needs lies in Parthia.

TROJAN HORSE DIPLOMACY

As mentioned, Vologases died in 208 CE. His son by the same name, Vologases VI, would become king of Parthia, only find himself at war with his brother Artabanus V, who also claimed the throne. Caracalla even said that he started the conflict in order to enhance his position by playing the brothers against one another in order to weaken Parthia. If true, his plan worked. While the Parthians waged war against one another, Caracalla began his consolidation of the eastern provinces loyal to Rome and adjoining Parthia, and it started with King Abgarus IX of Osrhoene.[80]

King Abgarus began to expand his control over kindred tribes. Caracalla got news of this and decided to take advantage of the situation by inviting him to a meeting, then he had Abgarus arrested and imprisoned. As for Osrhoene, he subdued it. Armenia was next on Caracalla's list when news arrived that the Armenian king,

---

[79] Dio 78.10.4.
[80] Dio 78 (77.12.2-3; 13.3).

Khosrov I, was quarrelling with his sons. Caracalla, as he did with Abgarus, invited Khosrov to a meeting in a friendly letter. Caracalla made it clear that he wanted to make peace between them. Instead, he did the same as he did to Abgarus. However unlike Osrhoene, Armenia revolted and took up arms.[81]

When Caracalla's bid to subdue Armenia failed, he prepared for the worst. Knowing that Armenia and Parthia had close ties and that his attempt to take Armenia had failed, Caracalla assembled his forces at his winter quarters in Nicomedia (Izmit), built two large siege engines, and prepared for a possible Parthian attack. But Caracalla had been preparing for this all along. Remember, he styled himself after Alexander the Great and saw Parthia as his Persian Empire. Therefore, to get things started, he demanded that the Parthians hand over a Cilician philosopher by the name of Antiochus and likely the prince of Armenia, Tiridates. Artabanus, who could not resist his demands, since he was at war with his brother Vologases, agreed and handed over the men. Caracalla called off the attack for the time being.

With war between Rome and Parthia averted, Caracalla felt confident enough to send the troops into Armenia, given that Parthia was too weak to be a threat. In 215 CE, Caracalla sent a Roman army under Theocritus to quash the rebellion. Instead, Theocritus and his forces were defeated. Even though Caracalla lost trust, it didn't

---

[81] Dio 78. (77.12.1-2).

stop him from continuing his deceitful foreign policy. His next trick was aimed at Parthia.[82]

Back in Parthia, the war between Vologases VI and his brother Artabanus V waged on, with Artabanus clearly winning the war on territory. He seems to have extended his sway over Mesopotamia, although coins of Vologases were still minted in the city of Seleucia. While war raged in Parthia, Caracalla moved his headquarters to Antioch in the summer of 215 CE.

Caracalla, desirous of the title Parthicus, devised a plan in 216 CE. He decided that the best way to win over the Parthians was to write Artabanus a letter. Once the last scribbles were written, he gave it to his embassy along with expensive gifts of fine workmanship. Artabanus likely enjoyed the gifts, and when he opened the letter, Caracalla made it very clear that he wished to marry one of his daughters. Caracalla's objective was to unit two empires under one great power, which would benefit both men, since not only would a much stronger army emerge from this union, but the trade restrictions could be lifted. Artabanus at first did not approve of the request, saying, "that it was not proper for a barbarian to marry a Roman" and "it was not fitting that either race be bastardized."[83]

Therefore, Artabanus declined the offer. Artabanus was no fool; at least at first, he likely knew of Caracalla's deceitfulness when dealing with other nations. But this was not the end. Caracalla persisted and offered even

---

[82] Ibid., 78.21.1.
[83] Herodian 4.10.1-5.

more gifts and showed enthusiasm for the marriage and for the union between the two powers. Artabanus finally believed that Caracalla was telling the truth. Artabanus publicly announced the wedding and felt that permanent peace had finally been established.[84]

Caracalla crossed the rivers and was welcomed by sacrifices, decorated altars, incense scattered in his path, and likely all sorts of entertainment. Once he was near the palace at Ctesiphon, Artabanus came out to meet his future son-in-law in the plain before the city, with his daughter nearby. With an entire city jubilant over the event, crowned with flowers in their hair and wearing the finest robes, the populace danced to the music of flutes and drums. The men left their horses and their bows to partake in the drinking. Nothing out of the ordinary was suspected. When the Parthians were good and drunk, especially the men, the decisive moment would be unveiled.[85]

Caracalla gave the signal and the happy party, celebrating what they thought was to be a peaceful end to many centuries of bloodshed, was slaughtered. Artabanus nearly died, but was helped onto a horse and escaped with a few men. The Roman troops took much booty and many prisoners. Caracalla then gave the order to pull out and marched away unopposed. However, this was not to be the end, for Caracalla gave his men permission to loot and burn all the towns and villages they came across and to

---

[84] Ibid., 4.11.1.
[85] Ibid., 4.11.2-4.

carry as much as they could, for it was all theirs for the taking.⁸⁶ How far they went into Parthian territory remains unknown. Caracalla is said to have taken the Tigris route, made his way into Media, sacking many of the fortresses, and even took the city of Arbela, where his men dug open the royal Parthian tombs, scattering the bones.⁸⁷

Once the looting, burning, and slaughtering were finished, Caracalla went off into Mesopotamia, where he sent the Senate a dispatch announcing to the Roman people that the entire east was subdued in 217 CE. The Senate was well aware of Caracalla's actions before he committed to them, and due to fear and the desire to stay on his good side, through flattery, awarded Caracalla the titles he wished to bestow and issued coins bearing the legend *Victoria Parthica* to commemorate the victory. Afterwards, Caracalla would stay in Mesopotamia for some time, engaging in chariot races and hunting wild animals.⁸⁸

In the spring of 217 CE, Artabanus came down from the mountains with forces he had gathered the previous year and neared Roman territory. While Artabanus was preparing his counterattack, Caracalla was heading back towards Edessa. On April 8, 217 CE, outside of Carrhae, he decided that he needed to relieve himself before he visited the Temple of the Moon. He ordered his escort to move along, as he wanted some privacy, and his

---

⁸⁶ Ibid., 4.11.5-7.
⁸⁷ Dio 79.1; Sheldon, 173.
⁸⁸ Herodian 4.11.8-9; Sheldon, 173.

guards respected his wishes, except for one. Julius Martialis ran towards him as if the emperor had called him and stabbed Caracalla in the back, killing him.[89]

BATTLE OF NISIBIS 217 CE

For roughly three days, the Romans were without an emperor until they chose a Praetorian Prefect, Macrinus, who was not a soldier by any means.[90] There was no time for mourning Caracalla's death or rejoicing in Macrinus' ascension, for the Parthians were fast approaching. Artabanus was seeking retribution, and once he entered Roman territory, he burned several cities in Mesopotamia.[91] Word eventually reached Macrinus of the coming Parthians, who were great in number, "including a strong cavalry contingent and a powerful unit of archers and those mail-clad soldiers who hurl spears from dromedaries."

Macrinus assembled his forces and moved out. Macrinus understood the severity of the situation and took to diplomacy in the hope it could avert battle and restore peace in the region. Macrinus sent the captives and a friendly message to Artabanus, urging him to accept peace, urging that he was not to be blamed for Caracalla's

---

[89] Dio 79.5; Herodian 4.13.
[90] Herodian 4.14.2-3.
[91] Debevoise, 266.

actions. Artabanus looked over the letter and rejected it immediately. He responded to Macrinus that if peace were to exist between the two, Rome must "rebuild the forts and the demolished cities, abandon Mesopotamia entirely, and make reparation for the injury done to the royal tombs as well as for other damage." Before any further deliberation could be established, the Parthian army had arrived outside the Roman headquarters at Nisibis.[92]

While normally the opposing armies lined up for battle, the first engagement was a skirmish over a waterhole. Some of the Parthians nearby rushed out to help their comrades, but were taken by surprise when the armor-bearers and baggage-carriers rushed out of the camp to counter them. Had it not been for their numbers and ferocity, Macrinus would have lost his camp.[93]

Early the next morning, right before sunrise in the dim light of dawn, both armies began to assemble into battle formations. Macrinus placed his legions in the center with lanes left open to allow light infantry to deploy at the front or rear as dictated by the needs of the battlefield. Roman cavalry, Arabian light cavalry, Moorish javelin men, and presumably slingers, were stationed on the left and right flanks to counter and prevent the Parthian cataphract or horse archers from outflanking or encircling them.

Artabanus' forces consisted of horse archers, cataphract cavalry, and the newly introduced cataphract

---

[92] Dio 79.26.
[93] Ibid.

camels, who were possibly ridden by Arabs rather than Parthians. Parthian tactics do not appear to be any different than what had been demonstrated at Carrhae in 53 BCE, in which the battle would begin with cataphract charges, with horse archers following closely to shoot into the Roman ranks after each cataphract assault.[94]

At sunrise, the vast Parthian army appeared. Artabanus, along with his men, saluted the sun, as was their custom, and with loud cheers, the cataphract charged while the horse archers fired over their heads. The cataphract horsemen and dromedary riders inflicted considerable damage to the Roman ranks along with the relentless shower of arrows from above. But even the Parthians suffered considerable losses since the Romans were at their best in close combat. After a while, the Romans began to feel the pressure and had to make a quick decision while the Parthians were regrouping. The Romans pretended to retreat and as they did, they threw down caltrops and other pointed devices, which the sand concealed, making them nearly invisible. The Parthians, thinking that the Romans were fleeing the battlefield, gave chase, and when the horses and the soft-footed camels stepped on the sharp devices, they suffered great injury and would throw the rider. The rider was now vulnerable to be captured or killed since his armor weighed him down. Or, if he were to get up, he could not run far, for his robe would trip him.

---

[94] Herodian 4.15.1; Farrokh, 168.

For two days, the armies would fight in this manner, with disastrous results from morning until night, both celebrating in their camps as if they had won. On the third day, the Parthians tried to encircle the Romans, but the Romans had given their divisions and extended their front line to avoid being this. The Romans were being worn down by the relentless attacks of the Parthians, who had numerical superiority. But they could extend their lines to avoid being outflanked for only so long. The consistent Parthian onslaught eventually wore down and demoralized the Romans, causing their lines to collapse and Macrinus to flee, but it was the arrival of nighttime that likely saved them. With nothing else left to be gained, especially with the piled-up dead bodies creating barriers, the Romans acknowledged defeat and retired to their camp.

The slaughter of both men and animals was so great that the entire plain was covered. Bodies were piled in huge mounds, camels lay in heaps. The numbers of corpses that littered the battlefield hampered any further attacks, for not only could you not gain a foothold without stumbling, but even finding the enemy was a problem since the piled remains of dead comrades blocked each other's view.[95]

Macrinus, who had lost the respect of his men, knew that he had lost something else, a victory. Macrinus forgot that the forces of Artabanus were merely a militia, as Parthia had no standing army, and he could only hold

---

[95] Herodian 4.15.2-5.

onto his men for so long, because they were unaccustomed to sustained efforts. Having been in the field for some months now, the Parthians had grown weary and wished to return home. With a temporary armistice in place, Macrinus could rethink his plans.[96]

The Parthians carried off their dead and the Romans likely carried theirs off the battlefield as well. Once the battlefield had been cleared, it was just a matter of time before a renewal of combat was to ensue. Macrinus was not going to let that happen, but it would not have mattered anyway because his men had lost faith in their newly crowned emperor. Macrinus offered friendship to Artabanus and explained that Caracalla was dead and that he, Macrinus, was the new emperor. To secure peace, Macrinus offered the Parthian king gifts and 200 million sesterces (fifty million denarii?). Artabanus thought it over carefully and agreed to peace, since the Romans had "suffered a suitable punishment." Besides, Artabanus' own army was terribly wounded. Afterward, Artabanus returned to Parthia while Macrinus hurried to Antioch.[97]

Even though Macrinus lost the battle, the entire affair was presented as if he won. The Roman Senate offered Macrinus the title of "Parthicus," but he refused it, and rightfully so. But regardless of his feelings, coins were still minted bearing the legend *Victoria Parthica*. Even though Rome held him as the victor, the fact of the matter

---

[96] Dio 78.27.1; Sheldon, 175.
[97] Herodian 4.15.7-9; Dio 78.27.1; Sheldon, 175.

is, he shamefully lost, costing Rome much money, but more importantly, prestige.[98]

FALL

Not long after the defeat at Nisibis, Macrinus himself would be challenged for the throne. On May 18, 218 CE, Elagabalus was proclaimed emperor by the III Gallica legion at Raphana. Afterwards, he marched on Antioch where Macrinus was located. The forces protecting Macrinus abandoned him, except for a loyal few. However, he was able to escape and pretended to be a courier during his flight, but was captured near Chalcedon and later executed in Cappadocia. Before his execution, he sent his son Diadumenianus to find refuge among the Parthians, but he was caught at Zeugma and executed. While Rome changed emperors, Parthia faced another rebellion.[99]

Parthia never would recover from this Pyrrhic victory over Rome in 217 CE. Due to losses in 116, 164, and 198/99 CE, Parthia had lost much prestige. While it is true that Parthia kept Rome in check, and did not allow themselves to be destroyed by the Romans, like the Celts and Carthaginians, the Romans were still able to dictate

---

[98] Sheldon, 175.
[99] Sheldon, 175-176.

politically and penetrate Parthian territory militarily. Parthia's inability to fend off the Romans allowed others, like its own family and those who held a considerable amount of power within their own regions, make a bid for the throne. When there is regime uncertainty, expect political upheaval. Even though Artabanus V had defeated Rome, the war with his brother Vologases VI resumed.

Iran would never find stability while the Arsacids were in charge. It would take a person of non-Arsacid birth to stabilize and unite Iran, and his name was Ardashir I of Persia. Ardashir revolted in 220 CE with the aid of several other Parthian sub-kings. Vologases VI was defeated first, but escaped, only to be defeated again for the final time in 229 CE. Artabanus would be the real prize in this matter, and even with Kushan and Armenian support, Ardashir was able to fend off all enemies and defeat Artabanus in three battles ending with his death in 224 or 226 CE. Ardashir ended the remaining Parthian resistance in 230 CE and started a new dynasty known as the Sassanids, thus ending the Arsacid dynasty that had ruled for nearly 500 years.[100]

---

[100] Farrokh, 168-169.

From Hadrian to the Collapse of the Parthian Empire

Figure 44 Vologases IV.
http://en.wikipedia.org/wiki/Marcus_Aurelius#mediaviewer/File:Coin_of_Vologases_IV_of_Parthia.jpg CC0

Figure 45 Marcus Aurelius. Photographer: Pierre Selim
http://commons.wikimedia.org/wiki/File:L%27Image_et_le_Pouvoir_-_Buste_cuirass%C3%A9_de_Marc_Aur%C3%A8le_ag%C3%A9_-_3.jpg
CC BY-SA 3.0

From Hadrian to the Collapse of the Parthian Empire

Figure 46 Marble portrait of the co-emperor Lucius Verus. Photographer: Pierre Selim. http://commons.wikimedia.org/wiki/File:Lucius_Verus_-_MET_-_L.2007.26.jpg
CC0

Figure 47 Marcus Aurelius receiving the homage of the Parthians. Image from John Haaren. Famous men of Rome (University Co. 1904), pp.249.

Figure 48 Bust of Septimius Severus (reign 193–211 CE) http://commons.wikimedia.org/wiki/File:Septimius_Severus_Glyptothek_Munich_357.jpg

Figure 49 Vologases V

Classical Numismatic Group.
http://commons.wikimedia.org/wiki/File:VologasesV.jpg (CC BY-SA 3.0)

From Hadrian to the Collapse of the Parthian Empire

Figure 50 Caracalla

From the Baths of Caracalla.
http://commons.wikimedia.org/wiki/File:Caracalla_MAN_Napoli_Inv6033_n01.jpg (CC BY 2.5)

Figure 51 Artabanus V

Classical Numismatic Group.
http://en.wikipedia.org/wiki/Artabanus_V_of_Parthia#mediaviewer/File:Artabanusiv.jpg CC BY-SA 3.0

CONCLUSION

What started as a peaceful meeting in 92 BCE between two cultures curious about one another ended violently in 217 CE. When one reads about the wars between Rome and Parthia, do it carefully It was not *Rome* that went to war with Parthia. Rather, certain Roman *personalities* went to war with Parthia, starting with Crassus and ending with Caracalla. Not every Roman leader desired to go to war with Parthia. Only when the west was secured did emperors desire to expand eastward to seek glory and riches. To rid the world of equals who were unwilling to become subservient was tantalizing, to say the least. War is the engine of the state and can be quite profitable.

Those who attempted to conquer Parthia underestimated the enemy multiple times, all in hopes that they could imitate their hero Alexander the Great, only to gain incremental victories and nothing more. The various generals and emperors sought glory and riches but remained ignorant of the people they sought to subjugate. So what was Rome's overall grand strategy when dealing with Parthia? The answer is, there was none.

There was no strategy in how to subjugate them, and if there was, those emperors who led campaigns had not the means nor the ability to implement their goals fully, as far as totally subjugating Parthia. Another way to look at it is that the Romans had a grand strategy when it came to conquest, but had none for governing after conquest, at least with Parthia. This does not mean that emperors failed in everything they set out to accomplish.

Rome had no tangential border with Parthia. They had many client states to help buffer them from Parthian invasions for some time, but the Romans had no grand strategy, a border, a scientific frontier that truly fixed their position. The idea is an illusion, for the emperor could do as he pleased, but even he was limited. While some emperors were successful in dealing with Parthia militarily, it was not borders that expanded, but their ability to invade deeper into Parthian territory that was at one time inaccessible. Trajan was the first to conquer Mesopotamia, but Rome's possession of the region was lost after his death when Hadrian became emperor. But it's the fact that he conquered the region temporarily that allowed future emperors to conduct similar campaigns with little fear of their adversaries.

However, even this became problematic for the emperors. While they had the ability to trample Mesopotamia under, they could not go further than their ability allowed. Unrest in the newly conquered region is one of many reasons why Rome could not hold the region effectively, plague was another, not to mention that overstretched legions and insufficient resources, along with the cost of war limited their ability to penetrate Parthia farther. Roman emperors were smart enough to know that they could not afford to use their legions on a grand scale, for they could not afford to lose them. In this sense, from the campaigns discussed in this book, the

Conclusion

Romans, while not as limited as the Parthians, were in many ways just as limited when it came to military campaigning like the Parthians. The only difference is that Rome could go on a bit longer.

If the emperors were successful in anything, they were successful in looting the Parthian treasure at Ctesiphon, as you have read. The emperors soon realized that it was best to loot them to keep them in check, rather than conquer them, but even this led to blowback, especially when Caracalla died in 217 CE.

The costs of maintaining security across Mesopotamia, never mind the dream of controlling the Iranian Plateau and the rich trade routes that flowed through the territory, was just too much and unrealistic for the Romans. It was easier to loot the Parthian treasury when the money back in Rome was running low or became lower in value due to debasing the coinage, thus replenishing their coffers with fresh money of higher value.

The same goes for the Parthian kings. Even though the Euphrates represented the border between the two powers in theory, it was just an illusion. Parthian kings, especially during the 50-30's BCE, took advantage of this and expanded their influence to the south in Judea and to the west into Anatolia before retreating into their dominion. They, unlike Rome, were not centralized and had no standing army.

The Parthian grand strategy was defensive. Unlike Rome, where the best defense is an offense, Parthia had no such ability, at least over the long term. As mentioned, Parthia had no standing army, but a militia, and relied primarily on the satraps to raise forces when in need. Parthia, unlike Rome, was not a centralized state, and if they committed the bulk of their forces to the west, they ran the risk of rebellions rising within Parthia or foreign invasion. Furthermore, they did not have the means to supply the men day in and day out. The militia had homes and families to attend. Therefore, military service was temporary and protracted military campaigns were out of the question.

Last, it should be made clear that even though Rome was aggressive, so was Parthia. It takes two to tangle. While Rome fired the first shots by marching into Parthian territory, Parthia retaliated, which is expected, but also brought the war into Roman-held territory from 50-30's BCE. Both sides, at times, played a game of proxy war as well. Thus, both sides were guilty of perpetuating further and future wars to come when there was no need what-so-ever. Peace and trade would have been far easier and less costly.

In the end, with Parthia gone, Rome's war in the east continued. A new power would emerge due to the vacuum Rome created. This power, unlike Parthia, was a centralized, leviathanic reflection of Rome. They were the Sassanids.

BIBLIOGRAPHY

Anderson, J.G.C. "The Eastern Frontier Under Augustus." In *The Cambridge Ancient History vol. X*, by F.E. Adock and M.P. Charlesworth S.A.Cook, 239-283. Cambridge: Cambridge University Press, 1934.

Appian. *Appian's Roman History, trans. Horace White, 4 vols.* Cambridge, MA: Harvard University Press, 1958.

Arrian. *Parthica, original Greek and English translation in F.A. Lepper, Trajan's Parthian War.* London: Oxford University Press, 1948.

Ashley, James R. *Macedonian Empire: The Era of Warfare Under Philip II and Alexander the Great, 359-323 B.C.* Jefferson, N.C.: Mcfarland & Company, 2004.

Ball, Warwick. *Rome in the East: The Transformation of an Empire.* London: Routledge, 2007.

Baumer, Christoph. *The History of Central Asia: The Age of the Steppe Warriors*. London: I.B. Tauris, 2012.

Beck, Roger. *Beck on Mithraism: Collected Works with New Essays*. Aldershot, Hants, England: Ashgate Pub, 2004.

Bennett, Julian. *Trajan Optimus Princeps.* London: Routledge, 2001.

Bernstein, William J. *A Splendid Exchange: How Trade Shaped the World*. New York: Grove Press, 2008.

Birley, Anthony Richard. *Hadrian: The Restless Emperor.* London: Routledge, 2003.

—. *Marcus Aurelius: A Biography.* Abingdon: Routledge, 2006.

--- "The Political History of Iran under the Arsacids." In *The Cambridge History of Iran, 2, ed.*, by Ilya Gershevitch, 98-99. Cambridge: Cambridge University Press, 1983.

Boak, Arthur. *A History of Rome to 565 A.D. 4th ed.* New York: Macmillan, 1955.

Bohec, Yann Le. *The Imperial Roman Army.* London: Routledge, 2001.

Bosworth, A. B. "Arrian and the Alani." *Harvard Studies in Classical Philology. 81*, 1977: 217-255.

Boyajian, Zabelle C. *An Anthology of Legends and Poems of Armenia* . London: J.M. Dent & Sons, Ltd, 1916.

Braund, David. *Rome and the Friendly King: The Character of the Client Kingship.* London: Croom Helm, 1984.

Brosius, Maria. *The Persians: An Introduction.* London: Routledge, 2006.

Butcher, Kevin. *Roman Syria and the Near East* . Los Angeles: J. Paul Getty Museum, 2003.

Caesar, Julius. *Commentarii de Bello Gallico.* New York: Harper & brothers, 1869.

—. *The Civil Wars, trans. A.G. Peskett.* Cambridge, MA: Harvard University Press, 1911.

Campbell, B. "War and Diplomacy: Rome and Parthia, 31 BC – AD 235." In *War and Society in the Roman World* , by J Rich and G. Shipley, 234-235. New York and London: Routledge, 1993.

Bibliography

Cary, Max and Howard Hayes Scullard. *A History of Rome Down to the Reign of Constantine* . London: Macmillan, 1995.

Chaumont, Marie Louise. "Cinnamus." *Encyclopædia Iranica, Volume V, CARPETS – COFFEE.* December 15, 1992. http://www.iranicaonline.org/articles/cinnamus-gk (accessed December 12, 2013)

Christensen, Peter. *The Decline of Iranshahr: Irrigation and Environments in the History of the Middle East, 500 B.C. to A.D. 1500.* Copenhagen: Museum Tusculanum Press, 1993.

Cicero, Marcus Tullius. *Epistulae ad Atticum, trans. E.O. Windstedt, 3 vols.* Cambridge, MA: Harvard University Press, 1956.

—. *Letters to His Friends (Epistulae ad Familiares), trans. W. Glynn Williams.* Cambridge, MA: Harvard University Press, 1958.

—. *The Orations of Marcus Tullius Cicero, trans. Charles Duke Yonge.* London: G. Bell & Sons, 1891.

Coene, Frederik. *The Caucasus: An Introduction* . London: Routledge, 2010.

Colledge, Malcolm A. R. *The Parthians.* New York: Praeger, 1967.

Dando-Collins, Stephen. *Legions of Rome: The Definitive History of Every Imperial Roman Legion* . New York: Thomas Dunne Books, 2010.

Daryaee, Touraj. *The Oxford Handbook of Iranian History* . Oxford : Oxford University Press, 2012.

Debevoise, Neilson Carel. *A Political History of Parthia.* Chicago, Ill: University of Chicago Press, 1938.

Dio Cocceianus, Cassius. *Dio's Roman History, trans. E Cary, Loeb Classical Library, 9 vols.* Cambridge, MA: Harvard University Press, 1954.

Euripides. *The Bacchae, trans. Ian Johnston.* Arlington, VA: Richer Resources Publications, 2008.

Farrokh, Kaveh. *Shadows in the Desert: Ancient Persia at War.* Oxford: Osprey Publishing, 2007.

Freeman, Charles. *Egypt, Greece, and Rome: Civilizations of the Ancient Mediterranean.* Oxford: Oxford University Press, 1996.

Frontinus, Sextus Julius. *The Stratagems, trans. Charles E. Bennett.* Cambridge, MA: Harvard University Press, 1925.

Fronto, Marcus Cornelius, Antoninus Pius, Lucius Aurelius Verus, and Marcus Aurelius. *The Correspondence of Marcus Cornelius Fronto with Marcus Aurelius Antoninus, Lucius Verus, Antoninus Pius, and Various Friends, trans. Charles Reginald Haines.* London: Heinemann, 1919.

Frye, Richard N. *The History of Ancient Iran.* München: C.H. Beck, 1984.

Goldsworthy, Adrian. *In the Name of Rome: The Men Who Won the Roman Empire* . London: Phoenix, 2004.

Gregoratti, L. "The Palmyrenes and the Arsacid Policy." *In Voprosy Epigrafiki: Sbornik statei (Problems of*

Bibliography

Epigraphy: Collected Articles). Avdeev, G., 2010: 4: 21-37.

Griffin, Miriam T. *Nero: The End of a Dynasty.* New Haven: Yale University Press, 1985.

Gruen, Erich S. *The Last Generation of the Roman Republic.* Berkeley: University of California Press, 1974.

Grunewald, Thomas. *Bandits in the Roman Empire: Myth and Reality* . London: Routledge, 2004.

——, and Baija Natha, and Etemadi, G.F. Puri. *History of Civilizations of Central Asia Vol. II.* Paris: UNESCO Publishing, 1994.

Haskell, H.J. *The New Deal in Old Rome: How Government in the Ancient World Tried to Deal with Modern Problems* . Auburn, Alabama: The Ludwig von Mises Institute, 2009.

Healy, Mark, and Angus McBride. *The Ancient Assyrians.* Oxford: Osprey Publishing, 2000.

Herodian. *Herodian, History of the Roman Empire since the Death of Marcus Aurelius, trans. Edward C. Echols.* Berkeley and Los Angeles: University of California Press, 1961.

Hildinger, Erik. *Warriors of the Steppe: A Military History of Central Asia 500 B.C. to 1700 A.D.* New York and Washington D.C.: Da Capo Press, 2001.

Hill, John E. *Through the Jade Gate to Rome: A Study of the Silk Routes During the Later Han Dynasty 1st to 2nd Centuries CE: An Annotated Translation of the Chronicle on the 'Western Regions' in the Hou Hanshu*

. Charleston, South Carolina: BookSurge Publishing, 2009.

Horace. *Horace. Odes, Epodes, and the Secular Song, Newly Translated into Verse by C. S. Mathews, Etc.* London: Longmans & Co, 1867.

Hornblower, Simon., Spawforth, Antony., and Eidinow, Esther. *The Oxford Classical Dictionary.* Oxford: Oxford University Press, 2012.

Hovannisian, Richard G. *The Armenian People from Ancient to Modern Times: From Antiquity to the Fourteenth Century Vol. 1.* New York: St. Martin's Press, 1997.

Hoyos, B. D. *A Companion to Roman Imperialism.* Boston: Brill, 2013.

Hurley, Vic. *Arrows against Steel: The History of the Bow and How It Forever Changed Warfare.* Salem, Oregon: Cerberus Books, 2011.

James, Ferguson, R. "Rome and Parthia: Power politics and diplomacy across cultural frontiers." *CEWCES Research Papers.* December 2005. http://epublications.bond.edu.au/cewces_papers/10 (accessed March 2014).

Josephus, Flavius. *The Complete Works of Josephus, trans. William Whiston.* Grand Rapids, MI: Kregel Publications, 1990.

Justinus, Marcus Janianus. *Epitome of the Philippic History of Pompeius Trogus, Trans. John Selby Watson.* London: Henry G. Bohn, York Street, Convent Garden, 1853.

Karasulas, Antony. *Mounted Archers of the Steepe 600 BC-AD 1300.* Oxford: Osprey Publishing, 2004.

Bibliography

King James Bible.

Knecht, Heidi. *Projectile Technology (Interdisciplinary Contributions to Archaeology)*. New York: Springer, 1997.

Kurkjian, Vahan M. *A History of Armenia*. New York: Armenian General Benevolent Union, 1958.

Lee, A. D. *Information and Frontiers: Roman Foreign Relations in Late Antiquity*. Cambridge: Cambridge University Press, 1993.

Lepper, F. A. *Trajan's Parthian War*. London: Oxford University Press, 1948.

Lewis, Naphtali and Meyer Reinhold. *Roman Civilization Vol 2: The Empire Selected Readings*. New York: Columbia University Press, 1990.

Lightfoot, C. S. "Trajan's Parthian War and the Fourth-Century Perspective." *JSTOR*. 1990. http://www.jstor.org/stable/300283.

Lindley, John and Thomas Moore. *The Treasury of Botany; A Popular Dictionary of the Vegetable Kingdom*. London: Longmans, Green, 1876.

Litvinsky, B. A. "'HELMET i. In Pre-Islamic Iran," Encyclopædia Iranica, Vol. XII, Fasc. 2, pp. 176-180." *Encyclopædia Iranica*. December 15, 2013. http://www.iranicaonline.org/articles/helmet-i (accessed June 21, 2013).

Lucian. *Lucian, Volume 1, trans. A.M.Harmon*. Cambridge, Mass: Harvard University Press, 2006.

Luttwak, Edward N. *The Grand Strategy of the Roman Empire: From the First Century A.D. to the Third*.

Baltimore and London: The John Hopkins University Press, 1979.

Mackay, Christopher S. *Ancient Rome: 1200 Years of Political and Military History* . New York: Cambridge University Press, 2004.

Mahal Singh, Bhupinder. *Punjab: The Nomads and The Mavericks*. New Delhi: Sunbun Publishers, 2000.

Marcellinus, Ammianus. *Roman History, Volume II, Books 20-26, trans, J. C. Rolfe*. Cambridge, MA: Harvard University Press, 1940.

Mayor, Adrienne. *Greek Fire, Poison Arrows & Scorpion Bombs: Biological and Chemical Warfare in the Ancient World*. Woodstock, NY: Overlook & Duckworth Press, 2003.

McGing, B. C. *The Foreign Policy of Mithridates VI Eupator, King of Pontus*. Leiden: E.J. Brill, 1986.

Millar, Fergus. *The Roman Near East 31 BC-AD 337*. London, England: Harvard University Press, 1993.

Minns, Ellis H. *Scythians and Greeks*. New York: Biblo and Tannen, 1971.

Mitchell, Stephen and James A. Arvites. *Armies and Frontiers in Roman and Byzantine Anatolia: Proceedings of a Colloquium Held at University College, Swansea, in April 1981* . Oxford, England: B.A.R., 1983.

Moffett, Samuel H. *A History of Christianity in Asia. 1, 1*. Maryknoll, N. Y: Orbis Books, 2009.

Neusner, Jacob. *A History of the Jews in Babylonia: The Parthian Period*. Chico, California : Schlors Press, 1984.

Bibliography

Nicolaus. *Nicolaus of Damascus' life of Augustus, trans.* Clayton M. Hall. Northampton, Mass: Johns Hopkins University, 1923.

Olbrycht, Marek Jan. "Subjects and Allies: the Black Sea Empire of Mithradates VI Eupator (120-63 BC) Reconsidered." In , by Ewdoksia Papuci-Władyka, 275-276. Oxford: Archaeopress, 2011.

Orosius, Paulus. *Historiae adversus paganos.* Hildesheim: Olms, 1967.

Ovid. *Fasti (Roman Holidays), trans. Betty Rose Nagle.* Bloomington, IN: University of Indiana Press, 1995.

Paterculus, Velleius. *The Roman History, trans.* Frederick W. Shipley. Cambridge, MA: Harvard University Press, 1961.

Pliny, H. Rackham, W. H. S. Jones, and D.E. Eichholz. *The Natural History.* London: Folio Society, 2011.

Plutarch. *Plutarch Lives, II: Themistocles and Camillus. Aristides and Cato Major. Cimon and Lucullus Vol. II* . Cambridge: Harvard University Press, 1997.

—. *Plutarch's Lives vol VI, trans. Bernadotte Perrin.* Cambridge, Mass: Harvard University Press, 1982.

—. *The Fall of the Roman Republic: Six Lives.* London: Penguin Classics, 1984.

Potter, D. S. "The Inscriptions on the Bronze Herakles from Mesene: Vologeses IV's War with Rome and the Date of Tacitus' "Annales"." *Zeitschrift Fur Papyrologie Und Epigraphik. 88*, 1991: 277-290.

Potts, Daniel T. *Araby the Blest: Studies in Arabian Archaeology* . Copenhagen: Carsten Niebuhr Institute of Ancient Near Eastern Studies, 1988.

Raymond, Joseph. *Herodian Messiah: Case for Jesus As Grandson of Herod* . St. Louis, MO: Tower Grove, Publishing, 2010.

Retso, Jan. *The Arabs in Antiquity: Their History from the Assyrians to the Umayyads.* London: RoutledgeCurzon, 2005.

Richardson, John. *Augustan Rome 44 BC to AD 14: The Restoration of the Republic and the Establishment of the Empire.* Edinburgh: Edinburgh University Press, 2012.

Richardson, Peter. *Herod: King of the Jews and Friend of the Romans* . Columbia, S.C.: University of South Carolina Press, 1996.

Rostovtzeff, M. *The Social and Economic History of the Roman Empire, 2 vols.* . Oxford: Oxford University Press, 1998.

Rothbard, Murray N. *What Has Government Done to Our Money?* Auburn, Alabama: Ludwig von Mises Institute, 2005.

Sampson, Gareth C. *The Defeat of Rome in the East: Crassus, The Parthians, and the Disastrous Battle of Carrhae, 53 BC.* Philadelphia: Casemate, 2008.

Bibliography

Sarkhosh Curtis, Vesta and Sarah Stewart. *The Age of the Parthians The Idea of Iran Volume II.* London: I.B.Tauris & Co Ltd, 2007.

Sayles, Wayne G. *Ancient Coin Collecting VI: Non-Classical Cultures.* Iola, WI: Krause Publications, 1999.

Scheidel, Walter. *The Cambridge Companion to the Roman Economy.* Cambridge: Cambridge University Press, 2012.

Schlude, Jason M. *Herod the Great: Friend of the Romans and Parthians?* March 29, 2013. http://www.biblicalarchaeology.org/daily/people-cultures-in-the-bible/people-in-the-bible/herod-the-great-friend-of-the-romans-and-parthians/. (accessed October 20, 2013).

Scott, Beth F. James C. Rainey, and Andrew W. Hunt. *The Logistics of War.* Maxwell AFB, Gunter Annex, Ala: AF Logistics Management Agency, 2000.

Scriptores Historiae Augustae (The Augustan History), trans. David Magie, 3 vols. Cambridge, MA: Cambridge University Press, 1958-60.

Scullard, H. H. *From the Gracchi to Nero: A History of Rome 133 BC to AD 68.* London: Routledge, 2010.

Seaver, James E. "Publius Ventidius. Neglected Roman Military Hero." *The Classical Journal, Vol. 47, No. 7*, Apr.,1952: 275-280.

Segal, Judah Benzion. *Edessa: The Blessed City.* Piscataway, N.J: Gorgias Press, 2005.

Sermarini, Joe. "Silver Content of Parthian Drachms." *Forum Ancient Coins.* September 20, 2012.

https://www.forumancientcoins.com/numiswiki/view.asp?key=Silver%20Content%20of%20Parthian%20Drachms (accessed March 13, 2014).

Sheldon, Rose Mary. *Rome's Wars in Parthia: Blood in the Sand*. London: Vallentine Mitchell, 2010.

Sherk, Robert K. "A Chronology of the Governors of Galatia: A.D. 112-285." *JSTOR*. Spring 1979. http://www.jstor.org/discover/10.2307/294236?uid=3739664&uid=2&uid=4&uid=3739256&sid=21104328529623.

Southern, Pat. *The Roman Army: A Social and Institutional History*. Santa Barbara, Calif: Oxford University Press, 2007.

Stark, Freya. *Rome on the Euphrates: The Study of a Frontier*. New York: Harcourt, Brace & World, INC., 1967.

Strabo. *Geography, trans. by W. Falconer*. London: George Bell & Sons, 1903.

Suetonius. *Lives of the Caesars, trans. J.C. Rolfe*. Cambridge: Loeb Classical Library, 1960, 2 vols.

Tacitus. *The Annals, trans. J. Jackson, 3 vols*. Cambridge, MA: Harvard University Press, 1958-60.

Temporini, Hildegard and Wolfgang Haase. *Aufstieg und Niedergang der romischen Welt: Geschichte und Kultur Roms im Spiegel der neueren Forschung*. Berlin: Walter de Gruyter, 1976.

The Encyclopaedia Britannica, 11th ed. Cambridge: Cambridge University Press, 1911.

Bibliography

Thorley, John. "The Development of Trade Between the Roman Empire and the East under Augustus." *Greece and Rome (Second Series)*, 1969: 209-223.

Thorley, John. "The Roman Empire and the Kushans." *Greece & Rome, Second Series, Vol. 26, No. 2. Published by: Cambridge University Press on behalf of The Classical Association*, Oct., 1979: 181-190.

Thorley, John. "The Silk Trade between China and the Roman Empire at Its Height, 'Circa' A. D. 90-130 ." *Greece & Rome, Second Series, Vol. 18, No. 1. Published by: Cambridge University Press on behalf of The Classical Association*, 1971: 71-80.

University, Tulane. "Roman Currency of the Principate." *http://tulane.edu/*.
http://www.tulane.edu/~august/handouts/601cprin.htm#_ftnref1 (accessed March 13, 2014).

Vagi, David L. *Coinage and History of the Roman Empire, C. 82 B.C.--A.D. 480.* . Chicago: Fitzroy Dearborn Publishers, 2000.

Van Creveld, Martin L. *Supplying War: Logistics from Wallenstein to Patton.* Cambridge: Cambridge Univ. Press, 2009.

Webster, Graham. *The Roman Imperial Army of the First and Second Centuries A.D.* . Norman: University of Oklahoma Press, 1998.

Wheeler, Everett L. *The Army and the Limes in the East. A Companion to the Roman Army, edited by Paul Erdkamp.* Malden, MA: Blackwell, 2007.

Wroth, Warwick. *Catalogue of the Coins of Parthia.* London: Printed by the Order of Trustees, 1903.

Yarshater, Ehsan. *The Cambridge History of Iran Volume 3.1.* Cambridge: Cambridge University Press, 1983.

INDEX

A

Abdus, 242, 243
Abgarus IX of Osrhoene, 367, 369, 381, 382
Abgarus VII of Osrhoene, 323, 324, 332, 340
Abgarus VII of Osrhoene, 323
Adenystrae (modern day Ebril), 335
Adiabene, 267, 273, 274, 299, 331, 332, 334, 335, 336, 367, 368, 370, 371, 375
Aegeae, 373
Aegean, 152, 323
Afranius, 25, 274
Ahenobarbus, Domitius, 188
Alabanda, 152
Alani, 250, 308, 309, 310, 350, 351
Albani, 330
Albania, 16, 177, 286, 311, 350
Albanians, 37, 246, 247, 248, 249
Albinus, Clodius, 370
Alchaudonius, 133
Aleppo, 325
Alexander Helios, 206, 208
Alexander Jannaeus, 229
Alexander of Antioch, 196, 199
Alexander the Great, 28, 46, 242, 253, 335, 338, 339, 379, 382, 401
Alexander the Oracle, 354
Alexander the Palmyrene, 218
Alexander, Julius, 340
Alexander, Tiberius, 304
Alexandria, 141, 143, 204, 208, 209
Amanus, 112, 113, 115, 157, 158
Amyntas of Pisidia, 175

Andromachus, 84, 85
Anilaeus, 237, 239, 240
Anthemusia, 324, 331, 359
Antigonus II Mattathias, 229, 231
Antioch, 108, 113, 116, 118, 122, 145, 176, 196, 220, 226, 259, 323, 333, 342, 357, 383, 390, 391
Antiochus I, 38, 39, 40
Antiochus the Philosopher, 382
Antipater, son of Herod, 229
Antoninus Pius, Emperor, 352, 353, 354, 379
Antony, Mark, 3, 137, 139, 140, 141, 142, 143, 144, 150, 151, 153, 154, 163, 164, 165, 175, 176, 177, 178, 179, 180, 181, 182, 183, 184, 185, 186, 187, 188, 189, 190, 191, 192, 194, 195, 196, 197, 198, 199, 200, 201, 202, 203, 204, 205, 206, 207, 208, 209, 210, 211, 225, 226, 342

Anullinus, 370
Apollonius, 48
Appius, 18
Apsilae, 330
Arabia Felix, 318
Arbela, 14, 25, 335, 385
Ardashir, 392
Ariamnes, 58, 59, 60, 61, 62, 63, 64
Ariarathes IX, 9, 12
Ariarathes VI, 8
Ariarathes VII, 8, 9
Ariobarzanes I, 7, 8, 10, 12, 13, 104
Armenia, 2, 3, 10, 11, 13, 15, 17, 18, 19, 20, 21, 22, 23, 25, 37, 40, 41, 53, 55, 60, 61, 84, 90, 91, 92, 103, 104, 108, 175, 176, 179, 183, 189, 198, 201, 202, 203, 204, 207, 208, 210, 213, 217, 218, 222, 223, 224, 231, 234, 235, 236, 237, 241, 242, 244, 245, 249, 259, 269, 270, 271, 272, 274, 275, 276, 278, 280, 281, 282, 287, 288, 289, 290, 291, 292, 293, 294, 295, 296, 297,

298, 299, 300, 301, 302,
304, 306, 307, 309, 310,
319, 322, 323, 324, 325,
328, 329, 330, 332, 333,
341, 350, 352, 353, 354,
355, 358, 359, 360, 365,
367, 371, 374, 381, 382
Arrian, 336
Arrianus, Flavius, 350
Arsamosata, 297, 326
Artabanus III, 234, 235,
236, 237, 238, 239, 240,
241, 242, 243, 244, 245,
246, 249, 250, 251, 252,
253, 254, 255, 256, 257,
258, 259, 267, 268, 273
Artabanus V, 381, 382,
383, 384, 385, 386, 387,
388, 389, 390, 392
Artavades II, 183
Artavasdes I of Media,
179
Artavasdes II, 53, 55, 60,
61, 91, 92, 108, 176, 179,
180, 183, 184, 203, 204,
206, 207, 208, 222, 224
Artavasdes III, 235

Artaxata, 21, 206, 236,
245, 271, 285, 286, 287,
306, 326, 331, 358
Artaxes, son of
Artavasdes II, 208, 210,
217
Asia, 2, 13, 15, 17, 105,
136, 139, 145, 151, 153,
154, 155, 175, 177, 210,
211, 275, 323, 356, 373
Asia Minor, 13, 17, 105,
136, 145, 151, 153, 154,
177, 210, 275, 373
Asinaeus, 237, 240
Assyria, 336
Ateius, 46
Athambelus, 338
Athens, 105, 164, 206, 322,
323, 356
Atropa Belladonna, 195
Augustus, 89, 212, 217,
219, 221, 222, 223, 232,
233, 234, 235, 241, 272,
310
Axidares, nephew of
Osroes I, 319, 323, 327,
328

B

Babylon, 42, 49, 150, 228, 231, 259, 269, 336, 339, 375
Babylonia, 103, 237, 238, 337, 361, 375
Bactria, 45, 349, 363
Bactrians, 352, 363
Bakur (Pacorus), 353
Barzapharnes, 146, 147, 148
Bassus, Caecilius, 131, 132, 133, 134, 321
Batnae, 331
Battle of Carrhae Carrhae, 1, 3
Battle of Magnesia, 93
Beroea, 325
Berytus, 204
Bibulus, Marcus Calpurnius, 107, 108, 117, 121, 123
Bithynia, 8, 9
Black Sea, 11, 70, 246
Bolanus, Marcus Vettius, 291, 292
Brundisium, 47, 103, 144, 153, 322, 356, 373
Brutus, 137, 138, 139, 144, 153

C

Caelius Rufus, Marcus, 116, 118, 119
Caesar, Gaius, 223, 224
Caesar, Gaius Julius, 3, 44, 45, 46, 49, 101, 102, 118, 119, 121, 127, 128, 129, 131, 132, 133, 134, 135, 136, 137, 154, 165
Candidus, Claudius, 370
Capito, Insteius, 284, 285
Cappadocia, 7, 8, 9, 12, 13, 39, 104, 108, 109, 112, 113, 159, 270, 275, 276, 277, 293, 294, 298, 300, 321, 322, 325, 326, 350, 354, 365, 391
Caracalla, Emperor, 4, 379, 380, 381, 382, 383, 384, 385, 386, 390, 399, 401, 403
Caspian Gates, 198, 329
Caspian Sea, 198, 246, 371
Cassius Dio, 1, 19, 22, 25, 42, 48, 59, 73, 88, 90, 109, 113, 122, 128, 129,

130, 135, 152, 183, 320, 335, 343, 374
Cassius Longinus, Gaius, 52, 58, 61, 64, 83, 84, 85, 101, 102, 107, 108, 111, 113, 114, 115, 116, 117, 119, 137, 138, 139, 140, 144, 153
Cassius, Avidius, 3, 356, 357, 359, 360, 361, 362, 363, 364, 365, 366
cataphract, 66, 67, 68, 74, 75, 76, 78, 79, 80, 93, 156, 158, 161, 190, 387, 388
Caucasian Albanians, 246
Caucasus, 16, 244, 246, 249, 281, 308, 309, 330
Channaeus (Pharnaeus), 159, 160
Charax, 223, 269, 338, 339
China, 218, 363
Cicero, 17, 39, 40, 43, 103, 104, 105, 106, 107, 108, 109, 110, 111, 112, 113, 115, 116, 117, 118, 119, 120, 121, 122, 129
Cilicia, 7, 12, 101, 103, 104, 105, 106, 107, 108, 109, 112, 113, 115, 117, 118, 120, 133, 140, 145, 146, 151, 156, 157, 175, 176, 225, 236, 242, 276, 308, 310, 342
Cinnamus, 267
Cizre, 335
Clarus, Erucius, 340
Claudius, Emperor, 272
Cleopatra, 140, 142, 143, 150, 176, 178, 179, 203, 204, 208, 209
Cleopatra, daughter of Mithridates VI, 11
Commodus, Emperor, 365
Coponius, 82
Corbulo, Gnaeus Domitius, 275, 276, 277, 278, 279, 280, 281, 282, 283, 284, 285, 286, 287, 288, 289, 291, 292, 293, 294, 295, 296, 297, 298, 299, 300, 301, 303, 304, 305, 307, 308, 331
Corduene, 24
Corinth, 322, 356
Cornelianus, L. Attidius, 354, 355

Crassus, Marcus Licinius, 3, 44, 45, 46, 47, 48, 49, 50, 51, 52, 53, 54, 55, 56, 57, 58, 59, 60, 61, 62, 63, 64, 65, 69, 73, 74, 78, 79, 80, 81, 82, 83, 84, 85, 86, 87, 88, 89, 90, 91, 92, 93, 94, 95, 102, 129, 130, 135, 136, 165, 178, 179, 188, 190, 197, 200, 211, 342, 401

Crassus, Publius Canidius, 176

Crassus, Publius Licinius, 49, 64, 65, 73, 74, 75, 76, 77, 78, 79, 94

Ctesiphon, 4, 37, 41, 42, 227, 235, 254, 267, 269, 336, 337, 338, 339, 341, 351, 361, 362, 375, 376, 377, 378, 384, 403

Cyrrhestica, 109, 118, 120, 160

Cyrrhus, 323

Cyrus, 242

D

Dahae, 234, 256, 273

Dariel Pass, 329

Dausara, 359

Deiotarus, 112, 116, 119

Dellius, Quintus, 206

Diadumenianus, 391

Domitian, Emperor, 311, 317

Dura Europos, 332, 335

Dura Europus, 344, 365

Dyrrachium, 356

E

Ecbatana, 15, 305, 368

Ecdippa (Az-Zeeb), 148

Edessa, 339, 355, 359, 360, 369, 385

Elagabalus, Emperor, 391

Elazig Pass, 326

Eleazar, 50, 259

Elegeia, 326, 328, 329, 331, 354

Elizabeth, 228

Epiphanea, 115

Erato, Queen, 222, 223, 224

Eriza, 326

Erzerum, 278

Euphrates River, 2, 7, 12, 14, 23, 24, 26, 39, 43, 47, 54, 56, 57, 58, 59, 88,

Index

107, 108, 110, 117, 118, 120, 121, 137, 141, 143, 160, 164, 178, 179, 180, 219, 223, 233, 236, 237, 243, 250, 251, 252, 253, 257, 258, 259, 278, 291, 296, 297, 298, 301, 305, 308, 311, 325, 326, 330, 331, 335, 336, 337, 343, 344, 350, 355, 358, 359, 360, 369, 370, 374, 375, 377, 403

F

Flaccus, Cornelius, 89, 284, 285
Fronto, M. Claudius, 359
Fronto, Marcus Cornelius, 363

G

Gabinius, 23, 42, 43, 44
Galatia, 8, 47, 112, 275, 276, 294
Gallus, Flavius, 190, 191
Gallus, Gaius Cestius, 303
Germanicus, 218, 219, 235, 236

Geta, 379
Gordius, 12
Gordyean Mountains, 334
Gordyene, 20, 23, 25, 41, 332
Gotarzes I, 14, 15
Gotarzes II, 268

H

Hadrian, Emperor, 3, 320, 341, 342, 343, 349, 350, 351, 352, 402
Hatra, 341, 369, 377, 378
Herod, 147, 148, 149, 150, 158, 175, 225, 226, 227, 229, 230, 231, 235, 258, 289
Hiero, 254, 255
Hieronymus, 77
Homullus, Marcus Julius, 321, 326
House of Suren, 55
Hyracanians, 352
Hyrcanian, 288
Hyrcanians, 290, 363
Hyrcanus, 146, 147, 148, 149, 150, 226, 227

I

Iamblichus, 110
Iberia, 16, 176, 244, 246, 272, 280, 308, 311, 350
Ichnae, 48, 77
Ignatius, 82
Indus River, 364
Iotape, daughter of King Artavasdes I of Media Atropatene, 208
Isidore of Charax, 223
Izates bar Monobaz, 267, 273

J

Jason of Tralles, 91
Jerusalem, 50, 147, 149, 158, 225, 226, 227, 229, 230, 322
Jesus, 227, 228, 229, 230, 231, 414
Joseph, 220, 221, 225, 226, 227, 228, 229, 233, 235, 239, 249, 250, 259, 268
Josephus, 38, 39, 229, 237, 238, 248, 267
Judea, 50, 103, 145, 146, 151, 158, 175, 177, 224, 225, 226, 227, 231, 258, 322, 403
Julius Caesar, 44, 94, 95, 107, 128, 132, 135, 154, 209
Justin, 1, 11, 40, 41, 67

K

Khorasan, 371
Khosrov I, 374, 375, 382
Kingdom of Armenia, 10
Kinopolis, 365

L

Labienus, Quintus, 137, 138, 142, 143, 145, 146, 151, 152, 153, 155, 156, 157
Laetus, Julius, 370
Laodice, 8, 38, 40
Laodicea, 105, 118, 120, 323, 357
Lateranus, T. Sextius, 370
Legerda, 288
Lesser Armenia, 136, 205, 274, 308, 310
Luca
    Lucca, 44
Lucian, 16, 354, 364

Index

Lucius Verus, Emperor, 3, 7, 25, 143, 151, 245, 274, 294, 303, 353, 355, 356, 357, 358, 359, 362, 363, 364, 366, 369
Lucullus, 17, 18, 19, 38, 45, 52, 57, 68, 101, 303
Lycia, 323

M

Macrinus, Emperor, 386, 387, 389, 390, 391
Magi, 227, 228, 229, 230, 231
Manesos, 344
Manisarus, king of Gordyene, 332
Mannus, king of the Scenite Arabs, 324, 331, 332, 359, 360
Marcellinus, Ammianus, 336
Marcus Aurelius, Emperor, 3, 353, 355, 358, 360, 365, 379
Marcus Titius, 220
Mardi, 198, 329, 331
Margiana, 66, 89
Margianian steel, 66

Marissa
 Marisa, 149
Martialis, Julius, 386
Mary, XIV, 2, 93, 227, 228
Mebarsapes of Adiabene, 331, 332
Media, 15, 38, 40, 41, 42, 201, 206, 210, 224, 286, 363, 364, 368, 385
Media Atropatene, 179, 180, 181, 183, 210, 234, 268, 286, 288, 309, 350
Mediterranean Sea, 323
Merv, 89, 269
Mesene, 218, 219, 338, 343, 352
Mesopotamia, 3, 14, 23, 42, 51, 53, 59, 62, 83, 103, 111, 218, 237, 253, 257, 318, 320, 330, 331, 332, 333, 334, 339, 341, 343, 344, 351, 360, 365, 366, 370, 371, 375, 383, 385, 386, 387, 402, 403
Metsheta, 308
Misenum, 364
Mithridates II, 10, 11, 12, 14, 15, 17, 25, 41

Mithridates III, 37, 38, 40, 41, 42, 43, 44, 45
Mithridates IV, 351, 352
Mithridates of Iberia, 308
Mithridates VI of Pontus, 8, 9, 10, 11, 12, 13, 16, 17, 18, 19, 20, 22, 26, 27
Mithridates, son of Pacorus II, 352
Moneses, 291, 292, 293
Monobaz II, 267, 290, 299, 305
Mopsuhestia, 115
Moschi, 281
Moschian Mountains, 281
Mount Carmel, 146
Mount Massius (Tur 'Abdin), 334
Musa, 219, 221, 232
Mylasa, 152

N

Nabataean kingdom, 317
Naharmalcha (Royal River), 337
Narses, 371
Neapolis, 306
Neharda, 237, 239
Nero, Emperor, 272, 273, 274, 275, 276, 282, 291, 293, 294, 295, 296, 299, 300, 301, 302, 303, 305, 306, 307, 308, 309, 311, 328
Nerva, Emperor, 317, 321, 322
Nicephorium, 48, 253, 359
Nicomachus, 77
Nicomedes III, 8, 9, 10
Nicomedia, 382
Niger, Pescennius, 367, 368, 369, 370, 374, 378
Ninus (Nineveh), 14, 335
Nisibis, 1, 19, 292, 331, 332, 334, 339, 341, 360, 365, 368, 369, 370, 375, 387, 391

O

Octavian, 137, 143, 144, 151, 153, 178, 203, 205, 207, 208, 209, 211, 212, 226
Octavius, 81, 85, 87, 88
Ophellius, 148
Orfitus, Paccius, 279, 280
Ornodapates, 121

Orobazes, Parthian envoy, 12, 13
Orobazus, 7
Orodes I, 14, 15
Orodes II, 37, 38, 40, 41, 43, 44, 48, 50, 51, 53, 54, 55, 60, 81, 88, 89, 91, 92, 94, 95, 108, 110, 120, 121, 122, 129, 130, 131, 133, 137, 138, 142, 157, 164, 226
Orodes III, 232, 233
Orontes River, 364
Osaces, 109, 115, 117, 122
Osrhoene, 23, 24, 59, 323, 331, 332, 350, 359, 367, 368, 369, 381
Osrhoes, 360
Osrhoes (Chosroes), 354
Osroes I, 319, 322, 323, 324, 330, 332, 337, 339, 340, 344, 350, 351
Osroes II, 367
Ozogardana, 336

P

Paccianus, 90
Pacorus II, 318, 319, 324
Pacorus of Media Atropatene, 305, 309
Paetus, Lucius Caesennius, 294, 295, 296, 297, 298, 299, 300, 302, 304, 307, 308
Palmyra, 141
Parthamasiris, 323, 325, 326, 327, 328, 339
Parthamaspates, 340, 349
Pazyryk, Russia, 70
Pelignus, Julius, 270
Petronius, 87, 88
Phaedimus, M. Ulpius, 342
Pharasmanes I of Iberia, 244, 245, 246, 247, 248, 249, 280, 350, 351
Phasaelus, 147, 148, 149, 150
Phraates III, 17, 18, 19, 20, 21, 23, 24, 25, 26, 27, 28, 37, 38, 41
Phraates IV, 164, 165, 177, 178, 179, 180, 182, 187, 203, 205, 208, 209, 210, 211, 212, 213, 219, 220, 221, 226, 233, 243, 244, 251, 252, 254, 272

Phraates V (Phraataces), 219, 220, 221, 222, 223, 224, 231, 232, 241

Phraates, youngest son of Phraates IV, 243, 244

Pliny the Elder, 47, 89

Plutarch, 1, 7, 8, 25, 41, 42, 47, 49, 55, 58, 61, 62, 65, 66, 67, 74, 80, 89, 90, 104, 127, 135, 183, 194, 199

Polemon, Median ambassador, 205

Pomaxathres, 88

Pompey, 20, 21, 23, 24, 25, 26, 27, 37, 38, 41, 43, 44, 45, 46, 47, 49, 52, 57, 59, 68, 101, 102, 109, 110, 118, 119, 121, 127, 128, 129, 130, 131, 134, 135, 303

Pontus, 9, 11, 13, 17, 19, 22, 23, 175, 182, 184, 235, 236, 294, 295, 296, 303, 310

Praaspa, 180, 182, 186, 188, 203

Praesens, C. Bruttius, 329

Prince Pacorus, 109, 110, 115, 118, 120, 121, 122, 143, 145, 146, 147, 148, 149, 150, 151, 155, 157, 158, 159, 160, 161, 162, 163, 164

Priscus, Statius, 270, 271, 356, 358, 359, 360

Probus, 370

Ptolemy XII, 43

Pulcher, Appius Claudius, 103, 104, 105, 115

Pülümür Pass, 326

Puteoli, 306

Q

Quadratus, Ummidius, 270, 276, 277, 289

Quietus, Lusius, 329, 331, 334, 339

R

Raphana, 322, 391

Rhadamistus, 270, 271, 272

Rhandeia, 297, 304

S

Sacauracian Scyths, 16
Samosata, 24, 38, 39, 163, 308, 322, 325, 354, 364
Sanatruces I, 16, 17
Sanatruces II, 339
Santra, Appius Maximus, 339
Saramallas, 226
Sarmatian, 247, 248, 250
Sarmatians, 246, 248, 249
Sassanids, 392, 404
Satala, 322, 325, 326
Saxa, Lucius Decidius, 141, 145
Scythians
  listing
    Scythian, 70, 71
Seleucia, 24, 42, 49, 51, 58, 63, 90, 212, 234, 253, 256, 269, 337, 340, 360, 361, 362, 375, 383
Seleucia Pieria, 323, 342
Selinus, 342
Sentius, 335
Septimius Severus, Emperor, 4, 343, 366, 367, 368, 369, 370, 371, 372, 373, 374, 375, 376, 377, 378, 379
Severianus, M. Sedatius, 354
Severus, G. Julius, 291, 328, 356, 369
Severus, Verulanus, 289, 291, 292
Sextilius, 18
Sidon, 145, 204
Sillaces, 48, 51, 91
Sinnaca, 84, 85
Sinnaces, 242, 243, 252
Sippar (Abu Abba), 336
Sistan
  Sakastan, 55
Sohaemus, 358, 359
Sophene, 274
Sosius, Gaius, 225
Spasinus, 338
Sporaces, ruler of Anthemusia, 324, 331, 332
Statianus, Oppius, 181, 182, 183, 184, 207, 208
Strabo, 70
Sulla, 7, 8, 12, 13
Sura, 359

Surena, 42, 51, 53, 54, 55, 63, 65, 66, 68, 73, 75, 78, 80, 83, 84, 86, 87, 89, 90, 92, 93, 94, 95, 230, 254

Syria, 14, 15, 26, 42, 43, 44, 45, 47, 48, 49, 59, 84, 85, 95, 101, 102, 107, 108, 109, 110, 111, 112, 113, 115, 116, 118, 120, 121, 122, 123, 130, 131, 132, 133, 134, 136, 141, 142, 143, 144, 145, 146, 148, 157, 158, 159, 160, 163, 176, 204, 211, 212, 218, 220, 223, 225, 235, 236, 242, 244, 245, 251, 253, 258, 270, 275, 289, 291, 292, 296, 300, 303, 308, 322, 323, 325, 352, 354, 355, 357, 359, 360, 365, 367, 370, 373, 378

T

Tacitus, 246, 248, 292

Tarcondimotus, 109, 110

Tarsus, 113, 120, 140

Taurus, 109, 113, 155, 159, 297, 331

The Antonine Plague 165-180 CE, 361, 364

Tiberius, Emperor, 213, 217, 218, 222, 235, 241, 242, 243, 244, 252, 258, 310

Tigranes I, 10

Tigranes II, 10, 11, 12, 13, 14, 16, 17, 18, 20, 21, 22, 24, 26, 27, 37, 40, 41

Tigranes III, 217, 222

Tigranes IV, 222, 224, 235

Tigranes the younger, 20, 21, 23

Tigranes VI, 289, 290, 291, 302, 304

Tigranocerta, 19, 93, 271, 286, 287, 288, 292

Tigris River, 23, 42, 257, 330, 331, 332, 334, 335, 336, 337, 338, 341, 360, 363, 375, 377, 385

Tiridates I of Armenia, 272, 279, 280, 281, 282, 283, 284, 285, 286, 288, 289, 290, 291, 299, 302, 303, 304, 305, 306, 307, 309, 328

Index

Tiridates II, 210, 211, 212, 220
Tiridates III, 244, 245, 251, 252, 253, 254, 255, 256, 257, 258
Tiridates, prince of Armenia, 382
Titus, Emperor, 191, 311
Traiana, 322
Traianus, Marcus Ulpius, 309, 321
Trajan, Emperor, 3, 311, 317, 318, 319, 320, 321, 322, 323, 324, 325, 326, 327, 328, 329, 330, 331, 332, 333, 334, 335, 336, 337, 338, 339, 340, 341, 342, 343, 349, 351, 354, 355, 361, 364, 366, 375, 377, 378, 402
Trapezus, 283
Tyre, 131, 132, 145

V

Vagises, 51
Vardanes I, 268
Vardanes II, 274, 277
Velleius Paterculus, 181, 223, 224
Ventidius, Publius, 153, 154, 155, 156, 157, 158, 159, 160, 161, 162, 163, 164, 165, 225
Verus, Martius, 3, 353, 356, 360, 363, 365
Vespasian, Emperor, 308, 309, 310, 311
Vetus, Gaius Antistius, 133
Via Appia, 322
Via Egnatia, 321, 356
Via Traiana, 322
Vibius Fronto, 237
Vitellius, Lucius, 245, 249, 250, 251, 252, 253, 258, 259
Volandum, 284, 285
Vologases I, 268, 269, 271, 272, 273, 274, 276, 277, 279, 280, 281, 290, 291, 292, 293, 294, 295, 296, 297, 298, 299, 300, 301, 302, 303, 304, 305, 307, 308, 309, 318
Vologases II, 318
Vologases III, 330, 349, 350, 351, 352

Vologases IV, 352, 353, 354, 355, 358, 361, 365, 366, 367

Vologases V, 366, 367, 368, 369, 370, 371, 373, 374, 375, 376, 378, 381

Vologases VI, 381, 382, 383, 392

Vologesia, 344

Vologesocerta, 269

Vonones I, 233, 234, 235, 236, 237, 241

Vonones II, 268

W

Wael, son of Sahru, 355

White Village, 204

X

Xiphilinu, John, 335

Y

York, 378

Z

Zab, Greater, 371

Zagros Mountains, 337

Zamaris, Babylonian Jew, 220, 221

Zeno, son of Polemon of Pontus, 235, 236

Zeno-Artaxias III, 236, 237, 241

Zenodotia, 48

Zeugma, 24, 39, 56, 82, 160, 179, 322, 325, 391

Index

Made in the USA
Middletown, DE
31 October 2014